Invented Cities

Invented Cities The Creation of Landsca

Yale University Press   New Haven and London

Mona Domosh

in Nineteenth-Century New York & Boston

Designed by Deborah L. Dutton.

Printed in the United States of America

Library of Congress Cataloging-in-Publication Data

Domosh, Mona, 1957–
    Invented cities : the creation of landscape in nineteenth-century
New York and Boston / Mona Domosh.
        p.   cm.
    Includes bibliographical references and index.
    ISBN 0-300-07491-3 (pbk. :alk.paper)
    1. City planning—New York (N.Y.)—History—19th century. 2. City
planning—Massachusetts—Boston—History—19th century.
    3. Landscape—New York (N.Y.)—History—19th century.   4. Landscape—
Massachusetts—Boston—History—19th century.   I. Title.
HT168.N5D66 1995
307.1′216′09747109034—dc2   95-6740
                                                                                     CIP

A catalogue record for this book is available from the British Library.

The paper in this book meets the guidelines for permanence and durability of the Committee on Production Guidelines for Book Longevity of the Council on Library Resources.

10 9 8 7 6 5 4 3 2

To my grandmother, Irene Zagoren Domosh,
and to the memory of Norman Domosh,
Bertha Miller Frankel, and Israel Frankel

Contents

Acknowledgments ix

Introduction 1

1. New York and Boston in the First Half of the Nineteenth Century 7

2. Creating New York's Retail District 35

3. Constructing New York's Skyline 65

4. Developing Boston's Back Bay 99

5. Preserving Boston's Common and Planning Its Park System 127

Conclusion 155

Notes 159 / Sources for Illustrations 177 / Index 179

Acknowledgments

This book has evolved out of research and analyses conducted over a ten-year period, and I am indebted to all those who have provided me with moral and material sustenance and who have listened and responded imaginatively to my ideas. Many of those ideas originated with Martyn J. Bowden, who initially sparked my interest in New York and Boston, and whom I thank for challenging me to think creatively about past geographies. Walter Delaney, Michael Steinitz, and Joseph Wood read and commented on various drafts of this text, and I am extremely grateful for their gracious and thoughtful suggestions. A special thanks to Barbara Hutchings for tracking down some elusive facts. At Yale University Press, I thank Noreen O'Connor for her careful reading and editing of the text and Judy Metro for ushering this project through the publication process.

I am fortunate to have a network of friends who continue to provide me with the assurances I need to take intellectual risks, particularly Janette Benson, Liz Bondi, Denis

Cosgrove, Stephen Daniels, Susan Ford, JoBeth Mertens, Peggy Mevs, Joni Seager, and Michael Steinitz. So, too, I am grateful to my family, in particular my father, who taught me through example how to bring to life the character of past places, and my mother, for ensuring I had the skills necessary for such a task. After several years of academic nomadism, I am fortunate to have a found a home at Florida Atlantic University, and I appreciate my colleagues, in particular those in the College of Liberal Arts and the Women's Studies program, for creating a community of scholars and friends. I thank Walter Delaney for his curiosity, wit, and love, and for the friendship that has sustained me through the final stages of this project.

Part of the research for this book was carried out with funds from the Geography and Regional Science program of the National Science Foundation, award number SBR-8808743. The conclusions drawn from this research are not those of the NSF. Portions of earlier versions of the introduction and chapter 1 were first published in the *Annals of the Association of American Geographers*, and parts of earlier versions of chapters 1 and 4 appeared in the *Journal of Historical Geography*. Sections of an earlier version of chapter 3 were first published in "The Symbolism of the Skyscraper: Case Studies of New York's First Tall Buildings," *Journal of Urban History* 14, no. 3 (1988): 320–345, reprinted by permission of Sage Publications, Inc.

Introduction

The built forms of late nineteenth-century New York City and Boston differed dramatically. New York's landscape exemplified the ultimate material expression of a capitalist city. Its commercial and residential districts were experiencing unlimited expansion, both horizontal and vertical, and its mercantile and financial elite class continued a never-ending search for outlets for conspicuous consumption, using their residences and commercial buildings as the most evident forms of display. New York was in many ways what Christine Boyer calls the "quintessential bourgeois society."[1] In contrast, Boston's bourgeois classes fashioned their city and its landscape into a cultural capital and a center of intellectual society. The expansion of commercial districts was limited by certain civic values that were translated into a ban on skyscraper construction and regulations that prevented development of the Boston Common. The city's elite class maintained its residential stake near the central business district, and conspicuous

consumption was moderated by standards of good taste. If New York was the quintessential bourgeois society, then the social scene in Boston in the late nineteenth century was characterized by its urban gentry.

However, this divergence between New York and Boston was not always so
apparent. Throughout the eighteenth century, New York and Boston were economic
rivals and followed similar patterns of development in their built form. In the first half
of the nineteenth century, when the social and economic structure of each city began
to take on distinct characteristics, the middle and upper classes of each city began to
use those distinctive characteristics to define themselves, and part of that process was
the shaping of the urban landscape. Faced with the massive upheavals characteristic
of the Victorian era—industrialization, immigration, and spatial expansion—the middle and upper classes of each city attempted to secure for themselves a stable social
position and physical location in the city on which they could imprint their own values
and aspirations. The cultural landscape of the city became a form of self-representation.

This book will describe how the middle and upper classes of Boston and New
York inscribed their visions of social order and social life on the landscapes of their
cities in the latter half of the nineteenth century. It tells how people create the worlds
they live in and, in so doing, produce visible representations of their individual and
group beliefs, values, tensions, and fears. This study also shows how landscape, like
other forms of representation, is created within specific economic and social contexts
that give it shape and meaning. So, as New York and Boston began to diverge in the
nineteenth century, so did their two-dimensional locational patterns and three-dimensional architectural forms. This is not to say that this divergence indicates some essential difference in the functioning of the two cities. Upper-class life in New York and
Boston was characterized by a commitment to both commerce and culture. New
York's vision of itself as a city of commerce did not preclude cultural maneuverings.
Its skyscrapers were more than economic vessels for capital investment—most were
commissioned by entrepreneurs and carefully designed by architects to represent
wealth, prestige, and status. Conversely, Boston's cultural ambitions as expressed in the
formal design of the Back Bay were used to insure investments and make speculative
fortunes. Yet Boston's Back Bay and New York's skyscrapers indicate quite different
visions of urban life and culture. These landscape forms of self-representation were not
just artificial creations used for publicity, but were also integral to the social, economic, and spatial structuring of the city. The social behavior determined by the layout of
the department store and the architectural style of residences were as much forms of
self-representation as were paintings of those houses and stores. In other words, the
built environment was used by the controlling classes as forms of personal, group, and
civic representations. This book is an attempt to examine the material construction of

each city's landscape as it developed in the mid- to late nineteenth century, and to see those landscapes as forms of representation, as "constructions" of each city's middle and upper class's sense of identity.

Urban landscapes are created as much out of local social structures and ongoing social and cultural processes as they are out of macroeconomic forces. The symbolic landscapes of nineteenth-century New York and Boston are rooted in and, in turn, represent the complex economic, social, and cultural reality that characterized New York and Boston in the latter half of the nineteenth century. This comparative study shows that, contrary to many of the assumptions in urban geography, city builders and city buildings in the nineteenth century did not always follow similar paths of development.[2] By comparing the visions and ideologies that guided city builders in New York and Boston, I argue that two urban development trajectories, although similar in their broad contours, differed considerably given their distinctive cultural contexts.

This project has at its base two conceptual frameworks: an understanding of the interplay between socioeconomic structures and individual actions and intentions; and a critical understanding of the processes that produce built form, including the influence of architects, planners, political systems, and the general aesthetic and cultural environment. My analysis, therefore, will require extensive forays into social, economic, and political history, architecture and architectural history, historical geography, and urban planning. To understand the cultural contexts in which the landscapes of New York and Boston were embedded, I used the tools of economic and social historians, examining and interpreting archival material and secondary sources that help explain social structure in general and the intentions and meanings of particular individuals. I followed the cross-sectional approach of urban historical geography, a method that provides consecutive pictures of a landscape at regular time intervals, to clarify data derived from historical atlases and city directories concerning the changing locations of key elements of the landscape.

The most challenging methodological issue concerned the interpretation of the relationship between landscape patterns and the contexts from which those patterns derive their meaning. My general method, based loosely on techniques borrowed from art history, is what Denis Cosgrove and Stephen Daniels refer to as iconography.[3] A variation of this method, which I have discussed elsewhere, involves interpreting the landscape at several levels, from the individuals directly responsible for its development, to the particular social world in which that individual operates, to the general cultural and economic situation that shapes that world.[4] If the city can be thought of as a work of art, as Donald Olsen has suggested, then it can also be read as both a product, a creation of individuals living in a particular time period and place, and as a commentary on that time and place.[5] I will be treating the landscapes of New York and

Boston as both cultural products and cultural commentary, looking to cultural context to understand and explain landscape, and interpreting the landscape to understand and explain cultural context. Robert Darnton, in his collection of essays entitled *The Great Cat Massacre*, makes sense of documents within the cultural framework of eighteenth-century France by being able to "tease meaning from documents by relating them to the surrounding world of significance, passing from text to context and back again."[6] The relationship between landscape and the people who inhabit or create that landscape is also one of context and text. A particular type of social structure will provide the contextual clue to understanding, for example, the displays of architecture in Boston's Back Bay, which is itself the context for understanding Boston's upper class. Landscape will be treated as both text and context; as both the center of meaningful activity and the framework in which such activity occurs.

The latter half of the nineteenth century, a time of considerable turmoil in urban America, was, according to one of the most original interpreters of the era, a time when "all that is solid melts into air."[7] Yet only in retrospect do the massive upheavals of the time come into focus; for most people living through those years, the concerns of the immediate future blurred a recognition of long-range trends. Thus, I will focus my discussion on the forces of major disruption—immigration, industrialization, and spatial dislocation—only as they pertained to and impinged upon people's everyday life and decisions.

This study differs from traditional historical geographies in several ways. First, whenever possible, I will focus on case studies in order to fully explicate the relationship between individuals and the landscapes they create. I make no claims to the representativeness of these individual studies—it is impossible to argue that one story can characterize all others. These close analyses illuminate the processes of production of landscape, revealing a contextual knowledge more specific than one based on generalizations. By centering my analysis on the cultural meaning of landscape, instead of its functional or technological underpinnings, my explanations are site and time specific and therefore not readily applied to other matters. Second, rather than comparing the cities point by point, I will be following the general concerns outlined above in my discussions of both cities, focusing on different themes: the most illuminating aspects of landscape representation in nineteenth-century New York pertain to its displays of wealth in its commercial landscape (retail and financial buildings), whereas Boston's wealth was most evidently displayed in its domestic landscape (parks and residential architecture). Landscapes that were considered the best forms of self-promotion by contemporary observers were the most fertile territory to explore; for example, no contemporary account of New York in the 1880s was complete without extolling the wonders of the city's skyscrapers, just as Boston's chroniclers were sure to dwell on the beauty of the Back Bay. These four landscape representations (New York's retail district and commercial skyscrapers, the Boston Common and the Back Bay) frame a comparison of how urban visions were translated into urban forms in the latter half of the nineteenth century in New York City and Boston.

Third, I make no claims that this study will cover all classes of society. My focus is on the middle and upper classes in each city, which were, in general, empowered to shape the urban landscape. This is not to deny that other classes in society had a role in creating their worlds—through the efforts of such organizations as labor unions and women's community associations, factory workers and clerical workers often shaped their own environments. But I focus on the powerful middle and upper classes precisely because the expressions of wealth and power in the landscape constitute the focal point of this study. Certainly the working classes provided the labor necessary to the wealth accumulation of the upper class, and in this sense they appear in these stories as important yet secondary players in the social and economic context. In addition, although women and gender ideology were certainly involved in the creation of nine-teenth-century landscapes, I have only emphasized their role in my analysis of the cre-ation of New York's retail district, since in this case gender ideology was integral to my interpretation of the origins of modern consumer districts. Because nineteenth-century gender ideology was used to legitimize consumption, women and the qualities they were thought to embody played significant roles in shaping the retail landscape. My explanation of the differences in the retail districts in New York and Boston requires an understanding of how nineteenth-century gender ideology was articulated and deployed within those differing socioeconomic structures. Because the intent of this book is not to examine women in the city, but to explore how particular social structures and ide-ologies shape the urban landscape, gender ideology was considered only when it was an important factor in guiding development of two such different built environments.

Numerous studies have suggested that work on the built environment must incorporate an understanding of the individuals who shape that environment and the socioeconomic context in which those individual decisions are made.[8] This type of work has been referred to as "new" cultural geography because it adds to the tradi-tional landscape theme a concern for social, economic, and cultural context and theo-ry.[9] However, relatively few empirical studies attempt such an interpretation of land-scape.[10] Within the American context, studies of the relationship among economy, society, and urban form have been limited to the contemporary landscape, or to a single building type. Few scholars have attempted detailed studies of the history of American urban form in its relationship to societal structure. Much of the work that relates the built form of nineteenth-century American cities to a broader context has focused on the material expressions of major economic transformations.[11] These studies provide a good base for understanding the general form of Boston and New

York in the late nineteenth century, as cities changing from a mercantile structure to an industrial one, but these explanations do not address specific historical contexts and, therefore, cannot account for specific differences in built form.

This work also builds on the work of historical geographers who documented the evolution of central business districts but examined only the two-dimensional manifestations of those districts, not the architectural form, and left unanswered the question of the relationship of those locational patterns to their socioeconomic context.[12] Similarly, studies of the evolution of urban residential patterns have tended to focus on the two-dimensional pattern to the exclusion of building form and cultural context.[13]

Many aspects of the development of New York and Boston in the late nineteenth century are well documented. Works that examine the context, however, generally do not link that examination to built form. Studies of the emerging nineteenth-century urban system established the various linkages that contributed to New York's dominance as an economic center, but did not discuss urban form.[14] Historian Frederick Cople Jaher's in-depth analyses of the structure of the elite classes in Boston and New York provide a substantial background, but they leave the control and shaping of urban form unexplored, as do many other works that examine the social, economic, and cultural context of late nineteenth-century New York and Boston.[15]

Most of the work on the history of building forms in Boston and New York has been conducted by architectural historians. Their studies are of two types: surveys of buildings that are of architectural merit in each city, and thematic analyses of particular buildings, types of regions, or time periods.[16] The surveys, useful sources of data, do not provide a comprehensive picture of a city because they only focus on the parts of the built form that are of architectural interest. The thematic works offer a better picture of portions of the architectural fabric of the city, but they fail to link their specific focus to the other parts of the building pattern. In addition, few of these studies successfully relate architecture to its broad socioeconomic context. I will build on much of this work by historians, geographers, and architectural historians to "tease" meaning from and give meaning to the urban landscapes of late nineteenth-century New York and Boston.

1 New York and Boston in the First Half of the Nineteenth Century

I see that the word of my city is that word from of old,

Because I see that word nested in nests of water-bays, superb

Rich, hemm'd thick all around with sailships and steamships,

    an island sixteen miles long, solid-founded.

Numberless crowded streets, high growth of iron, slender,

    strong, light, splendidly uprising toward clear

    skies,...

City of hurried and sparkling waters! city of spires and masts!

City nested in bays! my city!

—Walt Whitman, *Leaves of Grass* (1855)

Like Whitman's poetry, nineteenth-century New York was a city of extremes and excess. It represented all that was wonderful and terrible in the new and modern city—its wealth and poverty, ambition and hopelessness, and human intellect and spiritual impoverishment. Historian Edward Spann says of mid-nineteenth-century New York: "In its slums, dirt, materialism, violence, congestion, rush, politics and municipal mismanagement, it could depress, degrade and offend the human spirit. In its wealth, intelligence, power, opportunities, freedom, and in the seemingly endless wonders of its streets, it could exalt, exhilarate and, occasionally, even charm strangers and citizens alike."[1]

The excesses of New York's life were most forcefully expressed in the city's landscape. For Whitman, New York was a city of "spires and masts" of "numberless crowded streets" and "high growth of iron." With these words, Whitman identified characteristics of New York's landscape that were to become the symbols of the modern city—

the sheer mass of urban growth, vertical as well as horizontal, and the new building materials that made such growth possible. Already by mid-century, New York's Wall Street, Broadway, and Fifth Avenue were beginning to take on the characteristics that would make them symbols of the modern capitalist city.

By mid-century, Boston, too, was being shaped into a physical form that would identify the city as modern. The enormous wealth generated from the textile factories in the towns surrounding Boston was drawn into the metropolis and expended on public and private institutions, on luxurious residential communities, and on the maintenance of parks and tree-lined avenues. The city's seaport activities continued to contribute to the city's economy, but the port's significance as a symbol of the city was being usurped by the State House sitting atop Beacon Hill, and the Common that lay at the foot of the hill.

Unlike New York, Boston did not seem to generate extremes of emotion. If anything, it was praised for its attempts to create a gentle and moral society; the city contained its share of hopelessness and poverty, but also more than its share of public institutions that were meant to ameliorate those conditions. In his *American Notes*, Dickens described life in Boston, portraying the city's public institutions "as nearly perfect as the most considerate wisdom, benevolence, and humanity can make them. I never in my life was more affected."[2] Boston was becoming known as a city of culture, and its landscape echoed and reinforced that identification.

The impulses that led to the creation of New York's and Boston's distinctive landscapes were derived from each city's particular economic, social, and cultural factors in the early nineteenth century. Although both cities' population grew and urban forms expanded spatially, albeit at relatively different scales, the specifics of each city's history made these experiences distinctive. The events that catapulted New York into a position of economic primacy in the United States paralleled the development of a social structure that placed a high value on commerce. Boston's claim to cultural supremacy was supported by a social structure that provided financial support to both cultural activities and the building of cultural institutions, and whose ideology held that commercial pursuits were moral only if they contributed to cultural pursuits. This intimate relationship among economic history, social structure, and cultural enterprise provides the essential context in which to examine the development of landscape in New York and Boston.

Boston's Socioeconomic Context

Although much of Boston's mid-century wealth was derived from investments in the textile industry, the members of the industrial ruling class retained close ties to their pre-Revolutionary era forebears, particularly those involved in mercantile activities.

The early eighteenth-century concentrations of wealth in Boston were based on long-distance trading, particularly to the Far East, an enterprise characterized by risking large sums of capital.[3] Those monies were often secured through personal ties, which eventually were made concrete through marriage. As a result, even in the early part of the nineteenth century, most of the wealth of the city was concentrated in the hands of a relatively few interrelated families, unlike other cities on the eastern seaboard, where a diversified economy and constant new waves of migrants diluted this family-based structure.

After the Revolution, the economic position of the trading merchant was disrupted. Without the protection afforded by the jurisdiction of the British Empire and the British fleet, trading was difficult and investments in commerce risky. In addition to these new elements of uncertainty, the social status of the new merchant class was under attack. A significant portion of Boston's prominent families, including many of its merchants, had fled to England during the war, leaving gaps at the top of the social hierarchy and, therefore, no recognizable, established elite class. Ideas of deference and the criteria for what constituted a ruling class needed to be renegotiated after the Revolution. Colonial notions of natural allegiance to the crown were countered by republican values of public service to a community of citizens.[4] Under the traditional British system, power was bestowed by virtue of one's birth. Under the new republic, however, no "natural" authority existed. The new criteria would have to be based on a person's actions, and a ruling class would be granted deference on the basis of its deeds. Boston's emerging elite, therefore, faced a world in which the avenues to social and cultural power—to legitimacy as a ruling elite—were through politics, public service, and philanthropy. The rather uncertain future of commercial enterprise could not guarantee the sustained wealth necessary for successful entree into these worlds. After 1800, however, the opportunity to invest in large-scale industrial operations that would generate certain and ongoing income seemed the ideal solution. Merchants like Francis Lowell, who had visited industrial communities in England and Scotland, were intrigued by the possibilities of creating such enterprises in America, and began to plan and construct the first large-scale industrial system in America. Their efforts led to quick and dramatic economic success.

By mid-century, a group of about eighty Boston merchants known as the Boston Associates controlled almost all of the firms that comprised the Lowell and Waltham textile manufacturing system. The industrial output of the firms constituted one-fifth of American manufacturing capacity.[5] However, the Associates did not envision themselves as industrialists—they abhorred the consequences of industrialization in Britain and attempted to create a system less vulnerable to the disruptions of labor unrest.

To achieve this end, they carefully instituted at Lowell a corporate structure that ensured the continual payment of dividends to themselves as stockholders, and that embodied a more paternalistic and less divisive social structure. The decision by Francis Lowell to employ female workers in the mills kept wages low and prevented the establishment of a permanent working class of men.[6] Women were meant to work in the mills for a limited time, usually until marriage, and then return to their domestic duties on the farm.[7] This system challenged neither the basic agrarian nature of America nor its republican values.[8] The female mill workers were kept under strict supervision while working in the factories, at all times "cared" for by the mill owners. This so-called benevolent economic system served the Associates well—it generated long-term and fairly effortless wealth, while promoting the image of a civic-minded and socially legitimate elite class. These men saw themselves not as industrialists but as benign public servants—they were, in the words of Unitarian reformer Theodore Parker, "men to whom the public owes a debt which no money could pay, for it is a debt of life."[9]

Such public service was considered integral to the city's self-identity. Boston's elite espoused an ideology of commitment to the community and to the welfare of its citizens. Exactly how that ideology developed and the complexities of how it translated into political agendas can only be understood by analyzing the structure of Boston's elite class. Boston's elite wielded power across a range of spheres (economic, cultural, and political) and shared a common set of values. It exhibited a high degree of class solidarity and was not open to new members. Boston's mercantile elite, like that of many other North American port cities, was characterized by a family-based business structure, where several prominent extended families controlled a large proportion of the economy. Yet, unlike most other cities, the type of social structure also characterized Boston in its early industrial phase.[10] The Boston Associates controlled more than the city's industrial output—they controlled most of the important economic sectors of the city. Seventeen of the Associates were directors of Boston banks and commanded more than forty percent of the city's capital; twenty of them controlled seven insurance companies responsible for forty-one percent of marine insurance and seventy-seven percent of fire insurance; and eleven members served on the boards of the five railroads operating in New England.[11] Unlike New York, where the constant infusion of new blood quickly diluted the dominance of family companies, Boston maintained this concentrated and family-oriented business structure well into the early twentieth century.[12]

As signs of solidarity, the Boston elite belonged to the same formal clubs and informal social groups, were linked by marriage, and adhered to a common value system. As such, the Boston elite has often been referred to as the Brahmins, connoting a type of caste system.[13] The value system of the Brahmins became more clearly defined after mid-century, when the relative economic power of Boston declined. Having lost their chance at dominance in the national economic and political spheres, members of the Boston elite turned their energies to their own city and to cultural endeavors.[14] Borrowing ideas from such authorities on the relation of culture and society as Carlyle, Coleridge, and Ruskin, the Boston elite developed an ideology that commercial pursuits were moral only if they contributed to cultural pursuits. As Martin Green notes, "Boston merchants, and to some extent the bankers and industrialists who succeeded them, had the idea that commerce should go hand in hand with philanthropy, and even culture; and should give way to them as soon as the individual had secured himself an adequate sum."[15] Cultural pursuits legitimated the elite's accumulated wealth and their powerful positions in the city. As public servants and sponsors of the arts, members of the Boston elite created an image of themselves as the city's natural leaders.

Although at the national level the Boston economic elite was losing influence, it increasingly gained control over local political and cultural spheres.[16] As Jaher and others have shown, the old Boston mercantile elites joined ranks with the new textile magnates and together controlled the political life of Boston and the state up through the mid-nineteenth century.[17] The Massachusetts Whig Party, dominated by this elite class, became the platform for control and effectively shaped public policy in the early to mid-nineteenth century.[18] Boston's upper class also controlled the city's cultural endeavors, from the fine arts to the educational system, as well as Boston's built environment (see chapters 4 and 5).

Because Boston's economy in the first half of the nineteenth century was growing at a slower rate than that of New York, its leading families stabilized themselves over several generations, and became conservative in their economic outlook.[19] Given its family-structured economy, much of Boston's capital was tied up in trust funds, and those inheritances were invested in established enterprises rather than more profitable but risky business ventures. For example, Boston's merchants could have competed with New York as the national retailing center if they had capitalized on their relative proximity to the textile manufacturing in the Merrimack River Valley, for until approximately 1850, Boston was the center for sales of these manufactured goods. Yet after that date it appears that representatives of the textile companies moved their headquarters to New York to utilize an established network of middlemen. This network reduced the risks to the textile manufacturers by ensuring immediate sales, but also reduced their profits. Despite warnings from members of Boston's business community concerning the dangers of losing the textile trade, New York continued to gain control of the sales of domestic manufactured goods.[20] With their fortunes already made and their class position solidified, Boston's elite was willing to forgo excess profit in exchange for economic security.[21] As a result, Boston's retailing sector expanded as a response to an increase in local consumption, but was never able to compete with that of New York.[22] This strategy characterized most of the sectors of Boston's economy. As economic historian Robert Dalzell and others have pointed out, the ideology was particularly effective in preventing any serious economic crises, but at the cost of limiting commercial growth. The economic policy that the elite followed effectively blocked the commercial efforts of others, thereby ensuring their own economic jurisdiction: "Moreover . . . by 1845 the Associates had settled on a policy of using their resources to block, insofar as they could, the further development of New England's economy; that having themselves contributed in major ways to the work of change, they wished to call a halt."[23]

After the Civil War, Boston's economy never regained its earlier vigor, while New York's economy continued its rise to supremacy.

New York's Socioeconomic Context

Robert Albion pinpoints 1815 as the turning point in the history of New York's port. In that year, the British chose New York as the site to unload the surplus manufactured goods that had been accumulating since the embargo of the War of 1812.[24] New York merchants were able to capitalize on that advantage, and in the following decade New York City surpassed Philadelphia and Boston to become the largest city and seaport in the United States.[25] The completion of the Erie Canal in 1825 provided a major tie to the hinterland, and the introduction of the first regularly scheduled freight shipping lines to Europe consolidated New York's initial advantage as a well-sited and protected harbor.

Because of these initiatives, New York began to function more as a national economic center than a regional one.[26] For example, New York succeeded in capturing a large share of the prime export market of the United States prior to the Civil War—the southern staple, cotton. Although New Orleans was a strong competitor, New York merchants purchased the greatest share of imported goods in exchange for cotton, and those goods passed into the United States through New York's harbor. In 1830, thirty-six percent of the import-export trade of the United States passed through the port of New York and, by 1850, the proportion almost doubled to seventy-one percent.[27] That rate of increase in trade through New York's port was, in large measure, due to the city's successful recovery from the economic panic of 1837. Spurred on by the European demand for agricultural products that followed the crop failures in Ireland and the Continent, New Yorkers became very active investors in railroad construction in order to link the Western agricultural regions with the city. In 1851, the Erie Railroad reached Lake Erie and the Hudson River Railroad was completed, thereby connecting the upstate railroad network to the port of New York.[28] These efforts countered Boston's early attempts to capture trade from the west and established New York as the major terminus for America's emerging railroad network.

While railroad construction consolidated New York's supremacy in trade from the interior, the investment by New York merchants in the construction of new steamships galvanized the city's international trading dominance. In the mid-1840s, New York merchants established a system of international steamship trade that far surpassed sailships in terms of speed and efficiency. Because New York merchants now traded more goods on a regular schedule than could the merchants of any other Atlantic seaport, the city became a magnet for shipping companies. Symbolic of New York's unquestionable mercantile dominance over Boston was the Cunard Line's decision to shift most of its business to New York, despite the fact that the line had originally chosen Boston as its Atlantic port.[29]

Thus, by 1850, New York was responsible for exporting most American raw materials, drawing on the vast resources of agricultural regions in upstate New York and the emerging middle western regions, and taking over as the major shipping port for the large amounts of cotton from the lowland South. The port also served as the main importer for European goods and the distributor of those goods on railway networks to the other parts of America.

Because of this mercantile supremacy, New York merchants developed strong ties with the British investors, the largest source of capital at the time, and the city became a magnet for American capital, as investors sought out the city's well-developed financial networks. In addition, New York's function as the major port city necessitated the establishment of a sophisticated marketing structure to collect and distribute goods. This commercial infrastructure, combined with a large capital supply, gave New York City the competitive edge in most commercial and financial activities of the time. For example, New York's banks supplied the capital for the greatest source of wealth in the second half of the nineteenth century—the great railroad expansion in America. Between 1849 and 1860, railroad mileage grew from approximately 7,000 to 30,000 miles, financed by Wall Street. The business historian Alfred D. Chandler concludes his discussion of railroad finance: "Thus in the 1850s, Wall Street and the mortgage bond played the same role in transportation finance that Boston and common stock had played in the 1840s and that Philadelphia and the sterling bond had played in the 1830s. But because the railroad growth of the 1860s was so much more extensive than the railroad and canal building of the two earlier decades, Wall Street by 1860 was indisputably the nation's primary market for railroad securities."[30]

The economic primacy of New York was both the result of and a major influence on the peculiar nature of its economic elite. New York's ever-expanding business class was far from conservative. Historian Frederick Cople Jaher has summarized the differences between the nature of the economic elite classes in New York and Boston: "New York merchants were more innovative than their Boston counterparts, their businesses had shorter lives, and they were considered greater credit risks." Their innovative behavior may have resulted from the diverse geographic origins of the population of New York, the constant infusion of new blood into the business community, and the resultant inability to maintain long-term family control over businesses.[31] This open-ended situation fostered an ambitious and highly competitive merchant and business class.

From its inception as an integral part of the Dutch trading empire, New York City had maintained a strictly commercial raison d'être. Unlike some of the other Atlantic seaports, particularly Boston, New York's original settlement process had no religious overtones. People arrived in the port of New York to better their economic situation, not to establish utopian civic or religious communities. This individualistic outlook precluded many attempts to organize cultural or civic institutions at the same time that it encouraged competitive commercial enterprises. In addition, the increasing diversity of population made it difficult to identify common goals that could form the basis of a long-term consolidated ruling class. Certainly many of the successful Dutch families developed into what could be called a ruling class, but they were constantly being outranked by newer groups who were succeeding in the city—first, the English and the Scots, then the Germans and the Irish. According to Edward Spann, by 1850, 45.7 percent of the 515,000 New Yorkers were foreign-born, and by 1885 the figure was 50 percent.[32] This dynamic and diversified population brought to the city much-needed skills and labor for a growing commercial economy, yet the newcomers' economic successes contributed to the instability and permeability of the city's ruling classes. As a result, New York's economic elite was never able to control the city's political or cultural spheres. Their power was not concentrated, members did not share a common value system, and the group itself was neither cohesive nor stable.[33]

In the 1840s, New York's mercantile elite had become a fairly consolidated group. Members of this group were often interrelated, they sent their children to the same schools, attended the fashionable churches (Trinity Church or Grace Church), belonged to the same clubs, and maintained similar business interests.[34] In contrast, the men who controlled New York's financial, industrial, and real estate wealth had some family connections, and at times shared the same economic goals, but they were a fairly diverse group, with new members constantly being added. With the decline of mercantile control in the mid-nineteenth century, the city's economic elite became further diversified to include investment and commercial bankers, insurance and utility company executives, lawyers and other professional specialists, railroad magnates, landowners, and speculative investors. As the city's role as the national economic center expanded, specialized and often conflicting elite interests prevailed. And as David Hammack points out, the "increasingly large and diverse economic elites found it impossible to develop and support a single economic program."[35] Membership in clubs devoted to wealth like the Union Club and Metropolitan Club did not significantly overlap with those devoted to culture, nor with those devoted to what Hammack calls ancestry-worship, like the Knickerbocker and the St. Nicholas. In sharp contrast to Boston, no single set of norms prevailed among the elite. As Hammack states: "One set nourished a reclusive clannishness; another provided the setting for conspicuous consumption of a public-be-damned variety; a third supported what a visiting English Liberal approvingly called 'the very earnest, philanthropic, public-spirited class.'"[36]

Mayoral politics during the middle of the nineteenth century was highly factionalized and constantly shifting. There were at least five major political organizations that routinely set forward candidates for mayor, some identifying themselves as reform candidates and others as professional politicians. New York's Swallowtail Democrats, representing the economic elite, were increasingly challenged for power by the noneconomic elite, and by middle-income and organized labor groups, in the late nineteenth century. Mayoral politics in the second half of the century was characterized by consensus, not by absolute rule from the top. Thus, New York's economic elite were forced to deal with other interest groups far earlier and to a much greater extent than did the elite of Boston.[37]

New York's elite were also a far more permeable group than was Boston's upper class. The emergence of wealthy ethnic groups (the German Jews, for example) and the increasingly diversified economic structure of the city, made it difficult for any one group to remain in power without accommodating others. As Jaher has shown, only one-fifth of New York's millionaires in 1892 were members of the antebellum mercantile elite, compared to one-third of Boston millionaires.[38] The result of such diversity, lack of solidarity, and high degree of permeability was a city without one single ruling class. In contrast to Boston, this particular social structure accelerated rather than restrained the forces of the urban land market. Access to New York's economic and cultural heights was wide open, limited only by a merchant's ambition and capacity for hard work.

New York's Spatial Context

New York's landscape in the 1850s was undergoing tremendous change as the city experienced another economic boom. Its economy was fully recovered from the panic of 1837, and its port was beginning to feel the effects of the California gold rush. Both domestic and foreign trade increased, as easterners and foreigners boarded New York-based steamships bound for California via the isthmus of Panama. California's growing population became one of New York's most lucrative export markets, and much of the discovered gold made its way back to the city.[39] The 1850s were also a period of growth for New York's dry goods and clothing industry. New York had captured most of the retail trade from Boston and was the major port of entry for European textiles and luxury items.

Such massive economic growth required more space in the city for commercial uses. In particular, the expanding dry goods industry needed more warehouse space to store its increasingly diversified stock and more retail space in which to sell it. And the emerging financial firms required countinghouses, larger offices, and more banks and lawyer's offices. The expansion of these facilities contributed to two spatial processes that were already under way in Manhattan—the segregation of economic activities, and the expansion of those activities north up Manhattan Island. Districts devoted almost exclusively to one type of economic activity had been part of New York's urban fabric almost from its inception. Mercantile activities were located along the riverfronts, particularly along the East River, but also increasingly along the Hudson: an emerging financial district was centered on Wall Street as early as 1805, but the area came to be completely devoted to finance only in the late 1820s.[40] Warehouses were located along Pearl Street and retail shops on Broadway (fig. 1). Residential areas were generally interspersed, although a concentration of houses of the wealthy could be found along the Battery and to the west of Broadway. Yet until mid-century, the lines separating these districts were not distinct, nor were districts exclusively given over to one type of function. Shops were often found on one floor of a building otherwise devoted to warehousing, and often small clusters of residences would be set amid an otherwise commercial district. This situation would change in the second half of the century.

The economic and spatial expansion of the late 1840s and 1850s began to create a locational pattern that geographer James Vance argues has its basis in the capitalist economic system—a pattern based on land values and access to economic resources.[41] For New York, much of what constituted its built environment up to this point became devoted to mercantile, commercial, and financial activities. Those who could afford to move their residences went north, fleeing the noise and congestion and seeking the most fashionable residential enclave. The streets to the west of Broadway near Trinity Church, an area that at one time had constituted a fairly wealthy residential area, was gradually taken over by commercial activities. The buildings changed uses from residential to commercial, or the structures were torn down to make way for large warehouses and shops to house New York's expanding dry goods and clothing trade. Broadway was becoming congested with pedestrian and commuter traffic (horsecars and omnibuses), as well as commercial traffic for deliveries to the shops that bordered both sides of the street and the smaller cross streets (fig. 2). Packed into the buildings on Wall Street were the offices of insurance companies, bankers, lawyers, and stockbrokers.

1. Bird's-eye view of New York from the southwest, 1850. Broadway is the wide boulevard that extends from the right foreground, north up the island, until it disappears from view just past City Hall. Mercantile activities are indicated by the numerous docks along the East River (*right*), and the Hudson River (*left*). The steeple halfway up Broadway on the west side is that of Trinity Church, and Wall Street, where the emerging financial district was located, runs just opposite to it and extends to the East River. (Courtesy of the Museum of the City of New York, Gift of Miss Anna M. Bogart)

2. Broadway and Duane Street, 1870s, looking south toward the spire of Trinity Church. The major thoroughfare in the city, Broadway was often congested with public stagecoaches and pedestrian traffic. (Collection of the New-York Historical Society)

3. Union Square, looking north from 14th Street, 1849. Union Square is depicted as an ornamental park area, surrounded by the residences of mid-century New York's fashionable classes, who had moved north away from the city's expanding commercial districts. (Collection of the New-York Historical Society)

The fashionable addresses were above 14th Street, focusing on the streets surrounding Union Square (fig. 3), and, in the 1860s, around Madison Square at 23rd Street
between Fifth and Madison avenues. By 1860, 344,000 people, nearly forty percent of
New York's population, lived north of 14th Street. It was, of course, predominantly the
middle and upper classes who could afford this move; the lower classes, many of whom
were recent immigrants, lived in tenement-style housing on the edges of the commercial districts. The institutions associated with the upper classes also moved north, following their clientele. Grace Church relocated to Broadway between 8th Street and
Union Square in 1846, and First Presbyterian Church moved from Wall Street to Fifth
Avenue and 12th Street in 1844. The stylish Union Club, the first successful men's club
in New York, built a costly and conspicuous clubhouse on Fifth Avenue and 21st Street
in 1855, and Columbia College, where many of the elite sent their sons, moved to 49th
Street and Madison.[42]

By 1850, then, segregation of land uses within the city was clearly apparent—
commercial, financial, and emerging retail districts south of 14th Street, those who
could not afford to move north remaining in tenement-style housing, and the middle
and upper classes moving progressively northward up Broadway and onto Fifth
Avenue. A view from the top of one of the city's five- or six-story buildings would
have revealed a fairly clear pattern of clustered economic activities. The clustering was
relatively easy to identify visually because each economic district was identified by
particular building materials, styles, heights, street patterns, and activities. In combination, these features created a distinctive three-dimensional landscape.

After the fire of 1835, which had done severe damage to lower Manhattan, most
of the area's commercial buildings were rebuilt in the Greek Revival style, characterized by a simplicity of form and ornament and attention to the monumentality of the
street front. The style was meant to remind viewers of the classical proportions and
harmony of the Greek temples. Exterior decoration was limited to a small portico with
columns supporting a simple lintel, or a series of columns built into the façade and
extending the entire width of the building, or, on a very expensive building, perhaps a
small freestanding colonnade. Many of the lintels above the doorways and windows
and the brickwork on the corners of the buildings were designed to look like marble,
a sign of prestige given its expense and its allusion to Greek temples. This Greek
Revival style was a popular design for the newer buildings that housed financial activities and for the small shops with warehouse facilities that were being constructed on
Pearl Street and Broadway. Coexisting with these new buildings were the older commercial structures that predated the fire—many of them built during the early years of
the century in the Georgian style. In areas that previously had been residential, such
as Broadway and Wall Street, single family homes were altered to fit the needs of com-

mercial tenants, or, as on Broadway, shops would be fitted into the first stories, while people continued to live on upper floors.

The view from the Battery at the southern tip of the island up Broadway would most certainly halt at the monumental City Hall Building at the northern edge of the park that had once served as the city's common space (fig. 4). Its white marble façade must have surely stood out in a city built almost exclusively of wood or brick. Its location at the intersection of Broadway and Park Row was considered so far uptown in 1811 when it was completed that it was assumed few would ever view the building from the north—thereby allowing the frugal city managers to save money and finish the back side of the building in brownstone. The structure, stylistically a combination of French Renaissance and Georgian, was an incredibly ornate building for New York of 1850, and stood out not only because of its marble façade, but also because it was sited just to the north of a park, thereby allowing the full display of its grandeur.[43] In the 1840s, the park area became the focus for the city's newspaper industry, and lining Park Row to the south of the Park were four- and five-story Federal and Greek Revival structures that housed the offices of the city's daily newspapers (fig. 5). Being across from City Hall—the source of much of the news—and fairly close to Wall Street, Park Row was well suited for the newspaper industry. And west of the park along Broadway was the most elegant hotel at the time in New York, the Astor House. Constructed in 1836, it too was fronted in marble and was considered one of the marvels of the city, as it contained such extravagances as "gas lights, running water, seventeen

4. City Hall Park as it appeared in 1869, a small urban park. City Hall Park had served the colonial city as its common grazing area for livestock. New York's marble-fronted City Hall had at one time been the northern boundary of the city, but by 1850 the city had grown considerably, up to Union Square.

5. Park Row, south toward the New York Times Building, 1860. At the southern end of City Hall Park, Park Row served as the center of the city's newspaper offices. The Italianate style of the 1858 Times Building stood out among the surrounding Federal Revival style buildings, foreshadowing the architectural and height competitions that would characterize the newspaper industry headquarters in the last decades of the nineteenth century.

bathrooms, and two showers."[44] And just to the north of the park, the newest addition to this display of marble was Stewart's department store (fig. 6). Completed in 1846, with additions several years later, the store was the first of its kind in the city. The building, known as the Marble Palace, was considered an architectural wonder and was unique in the city in cloaking a commercial building in the latest architectural style. Stewart's store, designed in what was called the palazzo style—a style based loosely on the Italianate—provided an architectural model for commercial buildings in the city and set the trend for other retail establishments that soon followed it north up Broadway.

North on Broadway from City Hall there were still some fashionable dwellings, but increasingly during the 1850s these were being supplanted by dry goods stores as they pushed north from lower Broadway. Upper-class residential enclaves could now be found encircling Washington Square, Union Square, and Gramercy Park, and, increasingly, lining Fifth Avenue between Washington Square and Central Park (fig. 7). These sumptuous new homes were often fronted in marble, an obvious indicator of wealth, and were designed according to the latest architectural fads (fig. 8). According to historian Kenneth Scherzer, these upper-class enclaves constituted the first homogeneous neighborhoods in the city, as Protestant, native-born, wealthy New Yorkers sought to flee what was increasingly a commercialized downtown inhabited by recent immigrants.[45] The ostentatious residential architecture was characteristic of a city where social standing needed to be constantly reconfirmed by displays of wealth, one of the most direct forms being housing.

6. *(opposite)* A. T. Stewart's department store after being rebuilt in 1850. Lithograph by Henry Hoff. Stewart's marble-fronted department store, located at Chambers Street and Broadway, and bordering City Hall Park, was considered an architectural marvel. In combination with the City Hall, the Astor House, and the newspaper buildings on Park Row, the Marble Palace, as it was called, confirmed the image of the park area as the architectural showpiece of the city. (Collection of the New-York Historical Society)

7. A view of the city looking south along Fifth Avenue from 37th Street, 1859. The brownstones along Fifth Avenue indicate the characteristic house type, although several large single-family residences on the west side of the avenue reveal the emerging upper-class associations. (*Harper's Weekly*, 23 April 1859)

By the late fifties, Central Park, although far from complete, became the major display area for private carriages, also symbols of social standing. As one guidebook describes the area: "On pleasant afternoons, the Park presents a brilliant appearance, and reveals not only the worth and wealth, but the pretension and parvenuism of this aristocratic-democratic city. One could hardly believe he was in a republican country to see the escutcheoned panels of the carriages, the liveried coachmen, and the supercilious air of the occupants of the vehicles, as they go pompously and flaringly by."[46] Central Park served as a parade ground for the wealthy, although many of the areas surrounding the Park were occupied by shanty settlements or farmland.

Farther down Broadway, around 18th Street, the emerging retail district was housed in Italianate palazzos, often framed in cast iron, that were increasingly replacing residential areas. City Hall Park was a civic focus, but also a center of architectural display. Broadway south of the park was lined with Greek Revival commercial buildings, and along the narrow Wall Street, five-story buildings housed offices of banks, insurance companies, and stock brokerage houses.

Frequently interspersed in this commercial area, particularly east of Broadway, were dense residential districts, home to many of the city's newest immigrants. By 1855, seventy percent of the Lower East Side was foreign born. Here, often in houses that had once been occupied by wealthy families, several large families would be

8. Fifth Avenue north of 27th Street, c. 1865. The upper-class residential enclave along Fifth Avenue is marked by trees, wide sidewalks, and ornate lamps, fences, and stair rails. The fashionable classes of the city were already beginning to flee the areas around Union and Madison squares. (Collection of the New-York Historical Society)

crowded in unpleasant and unsanitary conditions. According to Edward Spann, the area's density, estimated in 1850 at 45,000 people in one-quarter square mile, only worsened as the business district expanded and reduced the number of residential buildings.[47] These areas stood in stark contrast to the northern upper-class enclaves and were an important catalyst to the upper-class retreat up the island.

Boston's Spatial Context

In 1840, a Bostonian looking out over the city from the top of Beacon Hill would have seen a thriving commercial port city, albeit one that was outgrowing its borders (fig. 9; see fig. 12). The relatively small and congested land mass was overlaid with a seemingly random street plan and circumscribed by an irregular coastline. Yet within that seemingly chaotic area one could discern a clustering of activities not that dissimilar to the landscape of New York City. Commercial entities were readily identifiable near the docks. Long Wharf, and its extension onto State Street, long the focus of shipping activities, was still the central axis for commercial activities (fig. 10). Spreading north and south of that axis were three- and four-story buildings that housed the city's emerging warehousing, retail, and financial activities. The architectural centerpiece of this thriving district was Quincy Market, a two-story granite market house, five hundred and fifty feet long and fifty feet wide, that was constructed in 1825 and opened in 1826, in conjunction with two other granite warehouses on each side (fig. 11).[48] Named in honor of Josiah Quincy, the mayor who initiated the construction efforts, Quincy Market and the accompanying buildings were highly regularized in their form and aligned along central axes that ran perpendicular to the water. In addition, the buildings were designed by a single architect, Alexander Parris, who used the fashionable Greek Revival style for the main market and the two flanking buildings. The overall effect was quite magnificent, as the buildings provided an ornamental and functional passageway between Faneuil Hall, the city's market since its construction in 1742 and at times the location for town meetings, and the wharves and docks along the water.

This complex stood in stark contrast to the intricate and irregular street pattern of the surrounding commercial area, which was lined with buildings of different ages and architectural styles, built to accommodate the needs of small entrepreneurs and business owners. The banks and insurance companies, clustered along State Street, were generally in buildings no more than four stories in height, some originally dwellings, many retaining some residential characteristics since often one or more stories would be rented out as housing. A retail focus had developed along

9. *(below)* Aerial view of Boston, 1850. Lithograph by John Bachman. This view of the city from the southwest highlights in the foreground the Public Garden and the Common, which seem to occupy a disproportionate amount of the city's land mass. The importance of mercantile activities is marked by the large number of docks and warehouses, particularly the cluster surrounding Long Wharf (*midground*). The State House overlooking the Common marks the upper-class enclave of Beacon Hill. The marshes of the Back Bay, in the immediate foreground, are crossed by Beacon Street (referred to as the Neck), which connects the city with its surrounding rural and suburban areas. (Courtesy of the Bostonian Society/Old State House)

10. *(top, opposite)* State Street, looking west toward the Old State House, 1870. By mid-century, the city's financial activities had clustered around the Greek Revival and Federal Revival buildings of State Street. (Courtesy of the Bostonian Society/Old State House)

11. Quincy Market flanked by the South and North Market buildings, 1828. Considered the architectural showpieces of the city's commercial district, the granite market and warehouses are testimony to Mayor Josiah Quincy, who initiated the effort and for whom the market was named, and to the importance of mercantile activities for Boston's early nineteenth-century economy. (Courtesy of the Boston Athenaeum)

12. Boynton map of Boston, 1844. The commercial areas of the city are located inland from the many wharves, while fashionable residential areas have moved farther away from the docks, in particular to Beacon Hill, located just to the right of the Common. State Street runs from Long Wharf to the Old State House, and the Quincy Market complex is to the right of State Street along Commercial Street. (Courtesy of the Boston Athenaeum)

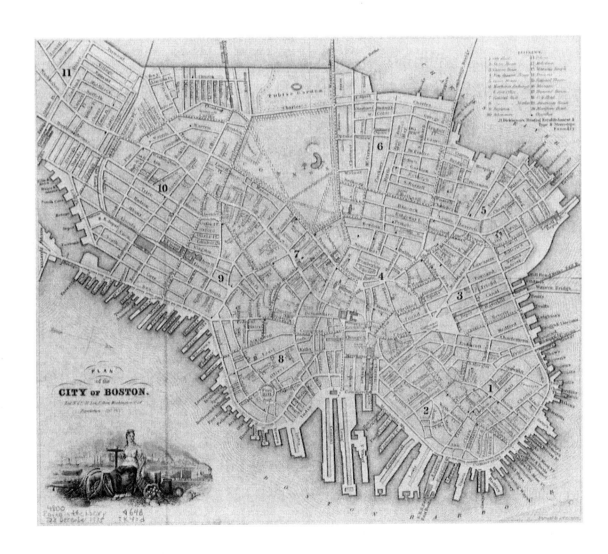

13. The State House, designed by Charles Bulfinch and completed in 1798, overlooked the Common. The Neoclassical building was a hallmark for the city, and it made the area surrounding it a fashionable district.

Washington and Summer streets, where one could find the decorative store fronts of Boston's leading dry goods emporiums.

Inland from the commercial focus of the city were streets filled more with residential buildings, particularly as one approached Boston Common. Spared from development by many years of legislative maneuverings, the Common was an open expanse of land, surrounded on three sides by residential quarters, and on its southern end by the waters of the city's Back Bay (fig. 12). At one time the city's public grazing land, the Common was, by 1830, off-limits to livestock. It then served as a parade ground, with tree-lined malls built along Park and Beacon streets in 1815. Facing the Common at the top of Beacon Hill stood the monumental State House, designed by Charles Bulfinch in the Neoclassical style and completed in 1798 (fig. 13). According to architectural historian Douglass Shand-Tucci, the building was clearly derivative of William Chambers's Somerset House in London, which Bulfinch greatly admired, although Bulfinch's distinctive touch made the State House a more "delicate" building.[49]

Behind this stately brick structure were streets lined with the homes of Boston's wealthy. Many of the elite of the city had moved from their original enclave on Fort Hill, close to the docks, to areas further removed from the hustle and bustle of the commercial district. Some moved further south, into the area referred to as the "new" South End where, along Franklin Street, Bulfinch designed and had built in 1794 an architecturally innovative housing scheme called the Tontine Crescent. Inspired by the Georgian crescent at Bath, England, Bulfinch designed a row of sixteen brick houses painted gray with white pilasters, spread out on both sides of a central archway. The crescent curved around a central tree-lined park and, at one end of the park, Bulfinch designed Boston's first theater (fig. 14).[50] Other members of the city's turn-of-the-century elite moved to Tremont Street—in particular to Colonnade Row (fig. 15), a fashionable row of homes also designed by Bulfinch—to Park Street, and Beacon Street, and to behind the State House on Beacon Hill.

It was on Beacon Hill that Harrison Gray Otis, arguably the most prominent of Boston's citizens at the time, had three houses constructed, each grander than the other, setting the tone for emulation, and all designed by Bulfinch. Otis, one of the original and most committed of the Mount Vernon Proprietors (a group of men who owned and developed land on Beacon Hill), lent his early support to the area by commissioning Bulfinch to construct his first dwelling on Mount Vernon Street in 1801.[51] Other prominent Boston citizens had been enticed away from the South End to Beacon Hill, making it, by mid-century, a prestigious enclave (fig. 16). Most of the homes were designed in the Federal and Georgian styles, often with elegant private gardens behind iron fences. Louisburg Square, based on the London model of town houses surrounding an open square, provided both an architectural centerpiece for the district and effective protection from commercial incursion from the north slope of the hill (fig. 17).[52] The upper-class residential area continued down Park Street past the residence of Abbott Lawrence, one of the richest men in Boston, and along the southern edge of the Common on Tremont Street.

The area to the southwest of the Common, the new South End, was under construction throughout much of the mid- and late nineteenth century. The narrow land bridge referred to as the Neck was widened, and street blocks were laid out in relation to Washington Street, the only through street on the original neck. Whitehill's description of the area as it developed in the 1850s provides an accurate and interesting view of the upper-class neighborhood: "a region of symmetrical blocks of high-shouldered, comfortable red brick or brownstone houses, bow-fronted and high-stooped, with mansard roofs, ranged along spacious avenues, intersected by cross streets that occasionally widened into tree-shaded squares and parks, whose central gardens were enclosed by neat cast iron fences."[53]

The South End, however, did not maintain this air of propriety for long, as it quickly became home to tenements, and middle- to lower-income residents. The elite residential focus was turning toward the Back Bay region in the 1860s and 1870s, and this placed the South End on the periphery of the central elite and too close to the commercial areas of the city.

By the 1840s, the North End, Boston's Revolutionary-era elite residential district, had become home to the new immigrants to the city, many of whom were Irish.

14. The first Boston theater. The completion in 1794 of Tontine Crescent (*left*) with the theater designed by Bulfinch helped establish the South End as a district of upper-class residences. Inspired by the Georgian Crescent in Bath, England, the Tontine Crescent reflected the Boston elite's desire to emulate English architecture.

15. Colonnade Row, Tremont Street near West Street, c. 1852. Another fashionable residential development designed by Charles Bulfinch, Colonnade Row was completed in 1812 and indicates the movement of the upper class to the areas around the Common. (Courtesy of the Bostonian Society/Old State House)

16. Chestnut Street, looking toward Walnut Street, c. 1869. One of the thoroughfares laid out in the original scheme for Beacon Hill, Chestnut Street has been lined with upper-class Federal period residences since the nineteenth century. (Courtesy of the Bostonian Society/Old State House)

17. Louisburg Square, from Pinckney Street, c. 1895. Based on the model of town houses surrounding an open park area that characterized much of the early development of London's West End, Louisburg Square was a home to Boston's elite by mid-century. (Courtesy of the Bostonian Society/Old State House)

Historian Oscar Handlin estimates that by 1850, about 35,000 Irish lived in Boston, and five years later, there were more than 50,000.[54] Most of the Irish immigrants lived either in the North End or in the Fort Hill region. The Irish lived in crowded tenements, three- and four-story structures, many of which had previously served a commercial function. The crowded conditions in the North End worried many proper Bostonians, particularly as the Irish population grew throughout the 1840s and 1850s and expanded south and west, heading dangerously close to the commercial core of the city, and even to some upper-class districts.

Partly in response to this perceived threat, the Boston elite began to turn their attention inland, away from the waterfront and the commercial heart of the city. As Tamara Plakins Thornton has shown, many members of Boston's mid-century elite began to envision themselves as country gentry, as they took up residence in estates in the farmland surrounding Boston.[55] From the 1820s onward, most of the newly generated wealth of the elite was derived from industrial enterprises located in small towns outside of Boston. The city itself was seen not as a site of revenue producing—although that idea was never absent—but as a domestic space, a place to live and play, to attend the theater and stroll through parks and gardens, and to make social calls, with some business meetings at offices along State Street. With commercial enterprise no longer of paramount importance, Boston's long stretches of docks and wharves were increasingly of little economic or even symbolic significance. What was important was financial and other business-related offices downtown, cultural institutions, domestic enclaves, and civic spaces. The Common served as a focus, given its potential as a civic space—the State House stood on the northwest side, and Beacon Hill, an elite enclave since the late eighteenth century, sat just behind it.

To the west of the Common stood the Mill Pond, a body of water separated from the tides of the Charles River by the long, thin Mill Dam (constructed for the Boston and Roxbury Mill Corporation in 1821), and, beyond that, the surrounding countryside of Roxbury. Boston's mid-century elite found this area enticing. Both Beacon Hill and Fort Hill were, to differing degrees, being encroached upon by commercial and lower-class areas. The opportunity to create a domestic space that represented their identity was an important one for the Boston Associates. It was here, to the west of the Common, that a new elite enclave was constructed, from the 1860s and through the 1880s. This Back Bay development was an enormous project, requiring the consolidation of land holdings and the delivery of huge amounts of fill to sites in the city by rail. By the time of its completion, Back Bay had taken over from the South End as the new upper-class enclave and formed an extension of upper-class interests in the city, from Beacon Hill to the Common and Public Garden, and then west along the major axis of Back Bay, Commonwealth Avenue.

By mid-century, both New York and Boston were experiencing industrialization and immigration, and with those forces, the expansion of commercial districts, the creation of districts where immigrants lived in tenements, the movement of upper- and middle-class residential areas out of the downtown, the development of parks and other open areas for display and recreational activities, and the spatial separation of retail, finance, and wholesale activities. Yet Boston and New York had already begun to diverge in the overall pattern of their built forms and in the specifics of that form's design. In New York, commercial expansion north up Broadway, including the development of a distinct retailing area, proceeded at a rapid pace, whereas in Boston, the commercial district's expansion was quite limited, with retailers not significantly altering their locations. New York's immigrant population was simply larger than Boston's, and, therefore, the extent of overcrowding and poor living conditions was far greater. As a result, New York's upper classes fled up the island at a great pace, reaching Central Park by the late 1850s. In Boston, the elite moved west at a much slower pace and temporarily halted their movement with the completion of the Back Bay in the 1870s and 1880s. Boston Common, kept free from commercial encroachment, served as a symbolic center to the city, while New York's common, City Hall Park, served as an architectural display focus and was eroded on all sides by widened streets and commercial development. It was only with the creation of Central Park that New York could boast of a large civic space, yet that space was used primarily as a display ground for the city's elite. In essence, Boston maintained much of what has been called a preindustrial form—the elite continued residing in the city, commercial districts expanded slowly, and areas close to the central business district were kept free from commercial development. New York's built form experienced the full consequences of industrialization—massive spatial expansion of commercial districts, movement of middle- and upper-class residents out of the downtown, and little, if any, undeveloped space close to the central business district. The growth of New York's retail district, including its effects on residential areas, provides the first case study for examining how and why this expansion occurred.

2 Creating New York's Retail District

The admiration excited by the imposing exterior of this vast block of building—the largest in this continent, we believe, devoted to the business of a single mercantile firm—is greatly intensified by an examination of its interior....The whole building, indeed, is thoroughly and unmistakably characteristic of Mr. Stewart. Constructed of iron and plenty of glass—fire-proof, with abundant light and ventilation—perfectly adapted to all its purposes, and securing the comfort of all within—it betrays the thoughtfulness of a merchant intent upon business, but not so intent as to be unmindful of the physical necessities of those in his employ.

—"Stewart's Store," *Appleton's Journal of Popular Literature, Science, and Art* (1870)

The reactions to Stewart's department store on Broadway between 9th and 10th streets that had opened in 1862 were indeed filled with admiration, not only at its size—an entire block—but at its construction and design. Alexander T. Stewart spared no expense in building his new cast-iron palace, using the latest construction materials (glass and iron) and the most fashionable architectural design. That this was thought characteristic of Stewart is not surprising—the building that had previously housed his store was in its time as innovative in design and in location as his new store. In his life as well as his business practices, Stewart characterized the bourgeois spirit of New York until his death in 1876 and the subsequent foundering of his store in the 1880s. He came to epitomize the dry goods "princes" of mid-century New York—men who expanded their stores and decorated them with the latest architectural styles, and who, though probably unconsciously and indirectly, were responsible for reshaping New York's commercial district.

With the overwhelming primacy of the port of New York as an import-export center by 1830, the dry goods sector of New York's economy was set for explosive growth. As warehousing activities expanded away from the docks and wharves, the city's retailers began a spatial movement as well. Throughout the last half of the nineteenth century, New York's retailers continued to locate their stores further up Broadway, not far behind the northward movement of their best customers, the upper and middle classes. In addition, the buildings they had constructed, particularly the department stores, became larger and more ornate and began to incorporate aspects of what has been called the domestic sphere—lounges, art galleries, restaurants, and meeting spots for women. In essence, this new retailing area was a different type of urban environment, one that brought style and leisure to the downtown. As historian Gunther Barth suggests: "The department store brought into the bustle of downtown the civility that most men had reserved for those aspects of city life they considered properly the social sphere....Much of that new charm stemmed from the substitution of a shopping district for a wholesale or business district as the core of the city. Magnificent buildings and attractive sidewalks introduced into the downtown section the same sense of spatial order that the department store had brought to large-scale retailing."[1]

This new shopping district represented a radical reworking of the downtown, in a two-dimensional sense as it expanded north and changed residential areas into commercial, and in a three-dimensional sense as it created an ornamental and domestic environment. Christine Boyer has documented the various elements that together comprised this district, the Ladies' Mile, which extended along Broadway from 14th Street to 23rd Street: "This procedural space juxtaposed the centers for hotels, theaters, artists' galleries, private clubs, and political assemblies in complex relationship to the city's major focus of entertainment: consuming."[2] This entertainment district included more than just retail shops; other forums for consumption were located in structures as ornate and fashionable as department stores. But it was the demands of commerce that spearheaded this new landscape, creating the social and aesthetic climate that attracted the theaters and galleries. The march of retail shops up Broadway displaced residential areas, making way for the fashionable entertainments to follow.

This displacement of residential districts by retailers resulted from several interrelated factors. On the one hand, New York's retailers, like retailers in all cities, sought to be close to their best customers, the upper middle class. Therefore, as that class began to move slightly north of the commercial core of Manhattan in the early eighteenth century, retailers were keen to follow. In addition, the success of a retailer often depended not only on proximity to the appropriate people, but also on a store's association with the fashionable classes. Yet as shops took over residential real estate further north, the upper middle class, desirous of the most fashionable location, reacted by fleeing the invading commercialism. The ideology of bourgeois life dictated a homogenous residential environment, free from commercial incursions. This residential spatial movement, of course, often led to the process beginning all over again. In nineteenth-century New York, as in many other cities, residential displacement and retail expansion occurred almost simultaneously, the one movement feeding the other. Yet in New York, with its massive economic growth and resultant unstable and permeable social classes, this process occurred with astounding ferocity, remaking portions of the city almost overnight and shaping vast new districts. These continuous changes in both spatial location and architectural form represented what Boyer has called "the rituals of power that commerce commanded."[3] An important component in the creation of these rituals was the incredible growth of an ambitious and upwardly mobile middle class.[4] Even though this class did not "command" commerce, it provided the masses of consumers necessary to support the department stores and other forums for what historian William Taylor has called commercial culture.[5]

This chapter will explore how this relatively new middle class participated in establishing the ornamental district of Ladies' Mile by examining the world of New York's nineteenth-century department stores, considered by many the archetypal symbols of American middle-class life.[6] Understanding the department store and the new landscape forms and districts it helped to create requires analyzing the shifting values of middle-class life in the nineteenth century, the construction of a culture of consumption, and the relationship of both factors to women and the societal view of the feminine. A general history and geography of retailing in New York, highlighting the development of the department store, and with it the idea of shopping and its relationship to the role of women, provides the context for an examination of the actual locational pattern and three-dimensional forms. This two-step approach shows how New York's economic elite classes, with their acute need to maintain the values of production—self-denial, hard work, utilitarianism—in the face of massive consumption, created a retail district whose form and function helped fill that need and symbolized those often conflicting demands.

Shopping, Women, and the World of Consumption

By mid-century, New York's retail district was focused on lower Broadway, with shops located along Catherine Street and Maiden Lane.[7] Most of these dry goods shops were quite small and were located on the ground floor, with wholesale areas and office space on the second and third stories (see fig. 2). Purchasing an item in these small retail spaces was quite different from shopping in later years in the large department stores.

Because there were few standardized prices or goods, a purchase involved a personal encounter with the owner of the shop and discussion of the quality of the item and the price. In addition, goods were not usually displayed in the shop; given the limited space, most items were stored in back rooms or on different floors and were brought out only when requested by a customer. Generally, a customer asked to see a particular item, haggled over the cost, and, if satisfied, bought the item. The shop, therefore, was little more than a backdrop for the drama of the personal encounter and act of purchase. For mid-century New Yorkers, buying an item at a dry goods store was no different from any other personal business transaction. But that process was soon to change.

Mid-nineteenth-century industrialization, particularly in textiles and in boots and shoes, led to the standardization of goods and the concurrent standardization of prices. For example, a yard of calico fabric manufactured at the Lowell textile mills would be sold at one price to wholesalers, who would then offer it to retailers. If retailers purchased large amounts of that cloth, they would pay a lower price per yard. With such savings, the retailer could make more profit by selling that item at the standard price, or pass on the savings to the customer, assuming that selling large amounts of the cloth would lead to additional profits. Either way, standardization of goods and prices meant that dealing in bulk became profitable for retailers, who needed more room to store and sell these items. In this way, industrialization and standardization directly led to the development of the department store. In addition, industrialization made affordable a larger array of goods. Mass production lowered the cost of many dry goods, making it possible for the middle classes to own a vast array of personal and household material possessions.[8] To be competitive, then, retailers needed more space to house the new variety and quantity of offerings.

Yet it was not just the size of stores that needed adjustment, but also the design. First, the large variety of goods made it increasingly difficult for customers to be familiar with the range of wares available. The goods needed to be displayed so that customers could assess the offerings and decide what to buy. Retail stores needed space to display those wares and had to create an environment where customers were encouraged to view the goods. Second, standardization of goods and prices had eliminated the need for direct dealings with an owner. Indeed, with larger stores and more variety of goods, it was no longer even possible for customers to speak with the owner. Instead, customers were helped by a salesclerk—an employee whose job did not involve price-setting but, instead, helped to display goods and assisted customers in their comparative shopping.

The act of purchasing, therefore, had become inconsequential. But in these large emporiums, the act of purchasing was more than compensated for by the activity of shopping. In these new palaces of consumption, shopping became an event in and of itself. Since standardization and mass production meant that goods were, at least in theory, equally accessible to the middle and upper classes, status was accorded not only by the possession of particular commodities, but by the means through which "the commodities become accessible and are acquired." As the goods themselves were increasingly standardized, and as the act of consumption became more impersonal, it was almost as if "the stage on which it took place became correspondingly more important."[9] Thus, the need for retailers to display a large variety of goods and encourage people to buy them, combined with the way the activity of shopping indicated and maintained social status, led to large, ornate, stylish, and leisured spaces for shopping—to what Rosalind Williams calls dream worlds of mass consumption.[10]

Women were intricately involved in the department store, not only in their role as customers, but also as store employees. Although department stores originally hired men to be the salesclerks, increasingly throughout the latter half of the nineteenth century women entered those jobs. And women also provided much of the labor in the textile and garment industries, industries that were reliant on the department store and vice versa. Because women constituted the major class of consumers, the retail environment was designed for them, embodying the bourgeois notions of respectability considered necessary for the middle- and upper-class woman. New York's consumer spaces were feminized—they were meant to appeal to late nineteenth-century bourgeois women—and therefore they had to integrate culture with commerce, the domestic with the public, the feminine with the masculine.

From the beginning, women were targeted as the major class of consumers. As early as 1846, accounts of the opening of Stewart's department store mentioned women as an established consumer class. The *New York Herald* stated that, inside the store, "we found the ladies, as usual, busy pricing goods and feasting their eyes on the profusion of gorgeous articles for sale."[11] The opening of the store prompted another commentator to suggest that at least half of women's time was spent shopping: "Half the time of the fashionable ladies of New York, at the lowest calculation, is spent in the dry goods store, in laying out plans for personal decoration. Dress forms a subject of the most grave and serious contemplation. It may be said to be the first thing they think of in the morning, and the last at night—nay, it is not the subject of the dream."[12]

According to Elaine Abelson, shopping became almost a daily ritual for middle-class women, taking up an overwhelming share of their time and becoming a major form of women's work. Throughout the nineteenth century, a new ideology of middle-class life dictated that home production was no longer acceptable.[13] America's industrial powers needed new markets and new products to keep their ever-expanding factories running profitably, and commodification of the home provided seemingly endless possibilities. The Civil War fueled increasing industrial production in the north, and, when the war ended, those

industries sought new outlets to keep their factories running at capacity.[14] By the end of
the nineteenth century, food, shelter, clothing, and home furnishings had all become commodities, and women's work shifted from domestic production to public consumption.

The development of the ready-to-wear clothing industry, and with it the introduction
of fashionableness to the middle class, had a sweeping impact on industrial growth and
the retailing trade. Although fully finished clothing was not available until the 1870s,
merchants had spent years paving the way for women to believe that factory-produced
clothing was better, cheaper, and simply more modern than homemade clothing.
Advertisements and household advice dispensed through ladies' magazines appealed to a
woman's sense of duty to provide the best up-to-date care for her family and reminded
her of status that was associated with the most stylish clothing. Yet this fundamental
change in how people led their lives, a change that convinced most middle-class women
that ready-to-wear clothes were better than those made at home, was not sufficient to
maintain the continual increase in sales demanded by dry goods manufacturers and merchants. Sales were kept high by creating a situation of open-ended demand, in other
words, by introducing fashion to middle-class life. The dictates of fashion—characterized
by perpetual changes in style and therefore built-in obsolescence—were conveyed in a
rhetoric stating that women needed, at a minimum, a new wardrobe each season, and, to
be truly fashionable, the wardrobe had to include an outfit appropriate for every distinctive occasion. By the late 1870s, a woman could find advertisements in such magazines as
Harper's Weekly and *Harper's Bazar* for clothing appropriate for every occasion: for
going for promenades (fig. 18), carriage rides, and walks; for staying in the house, receiv-
ing guests, and having dinner; for going out in the evening; for riding, skating (fig. 19), visiting the seaside; and for traveling and getting married. And, for children, each age group
had appropriate garb. To give some sense of what sort of production this demand fueled,
it is estimated that one elegant evening dress in the 1860s required approximately 1,100
yards of fabric.[15] An 1872 guide to New York estimated that it was not unusual for fashionable women to have wardrobes worth more than $20,000.[16] A description of the dress
worn by a society woman to a charity ball should set the scene:

> There was a rich blue satin skirt, en train. Over this there was looped up a
> magnificent brocade silk, white, with bouquets of flowers woven in all the nat-
> ural colors. This overskirt was deeply flounced with costly white lace, caught
> up with bunches of feathers of bright colors. About her shoulders was thrown
> a 1500 dollar shawl. She had a head-dress of white ostrich feathers, white lace,
> gold pendants, and purple velvet. Add to this a fan, a bouquet of rare flowers,
> a lace handkerchief, and jewelry almost beyond estimate, and you see [her] as
> she appears when full blown.[17]

18. Promenade costume, 1876. For strolling along Broadway and Fifth Avenue in the late afternoon, fashionable women wore elegant outfits, complete with parasol and hat. (Cover of *Harper's Weekly*)

19. Women's and children's skating suits, 1876. The truly stylish woman required a separate outfit for each activity, particularly if on public display, as when ice skating. (*Harper's Weekly*)

These extreme examples from the very wealthy of New York set the tone and style for the middle-class woman to emulate. She might not be able to afford gold jewelry or an overskirt of lace, but a middle-class woman could have touches of lace on her dress, and at least a small piece of appropriate jewelry. The point was to maintain vigilance and be aware of all fashion changes. Constant consumption, therefore, was required of the middle-class woman, not only because her appearance and that of her family were important indicators of social status, but also because correct consumption reflected on her role as mother and wife. Shopping had become such an onerous occupation for some women that New Yorker Clara Pardee wrote in her diary in 1893:"I am so sick of the stores and clothes…would rather the clothes grew on like feathers!"[18]

Department stores' needs for high volume sales reinforced the new consumerism associated with the fashion industry—perpetual changes in style required constant consumption. Department stores became active participants in the fashion world as they fueled demand by displaying fashion alternatives in a setting that imbued those commodities with social meaning. At the same time, department stores, because they sold mass-produced and therefore less expensive items, made available to more women the possibility of being fashionable. This further stimulated production, which led to new demands for consumptions and vice versa.

In New York, where social status was, for most people, always subject to negotiation, the culture of consumerism was of critical interest. And for women, fashion was of particular interest, because fashion allowed one to display status independent of occupation or position. A man's status could be conveyed by his job, or membership in a club, or his relative position in a particular segment of society. A woman's status was dependent on a man's, as his wife or child or mother. Fashion, however, was a status indicator that was specific to the woman. Her choice of styles, fabrics, and colors were her own decisions and therefore indicative of her "good" taste, and hence of her social status. But in what ways did associating shopping with women serve the emerging bourgeois society?

Feminist historians, among others, have shown the importance of the separation of spheres to the reigning ideology of late nineteenth-century middle-class life.[19] In addition to the male-female, culture-commerce divide, production and consumption were ideologically kept separated. In reality, of course, these two different aspects of industrialization were completely interrelated: production was completely reliant on consumption, and vice versa. The values of production—self-denial, hard work, utilitarianism—were distinct from those of consumption, because successful consumption required self-indulgence, leisure time, and playfulness. How, then, could these two value systems be maintained and encouraged without undermining each other? How could hard work be encouraged at the same time as self-indulgence? The values of production could be maintained in the face of a growing need for consumption by aligning production with the world of men, and consumption with the world of women. Women could be self-indulgent, while men worked hard to support them. In addition, since women were thought to represent "naturally" moral characteristics, they could consume without fear of overindulgence. Women's moral character would keep their materialism in check, thereby protecting the family's moral status.

In her analysis of Victorian Britain, Sally Shuttleworth argues that the distinction between consumption and production was symbolically played out in a variety of cultural discourses. In particular, she suggests that discussions of diseases concerning men's and women's bodies in contemporary medical literature reveal cultural anxieties concerning the separate economic and social spheres. Many "women's" diseases of the era were thought to be caused by women inhibiting their natural bodily flows, while for men, the problems were thought to be caused by not controlling their bodies. Thus, cultural anxiety focused around the issues of desire and self-control; women were meant to give in to their natural desires, men to resist them. This anxiety, Shuttleworth argues, was a result of the uncertainties the new bourgeois class was facing—an economic system that required constant and continual consumption to fuel its productive sector, and a social system where conspicuous displays of wealth could not assure social legitimacy.[20]

Relegating the sphere of consumption to women eased some of those tensions. Women could be consumers and visible symbols of material wealth without undermining their social standing because, it was thought, women's virtue would keep their materialism from contaminating the family's moral character. As long as women's acquisitiveness did not get out of control, their role as consumers served the needs of bourgeois society and economy. In fact, contemporary commentators attributed the success of the department store to women's consumer desires. The opening of Stewart's 1846 "marble palace" elicited the following remark in the *New York Herald*: "As long as the ladies continue to constitute an important feature in the community, the dry goods business must be in a flourishing condition....In fact, dry goods are a passion with the ladies, and whilst they continue to remain so the business must flourish; for woe to the luckless husband who refuses his wife money for shopping."[21]

Women's passion for fashion was good for business and did not threaten the established values of productivity. E. L. Godkin's analysis of the success of the dry goods trade led him to the needs of American women: "The pre-eminence and attractiveness of the dry-goods trade in this country is due mainly to the great purchasing power and varied requirements of American women....The consequence is that the dry-goods man has a sphere of activity opened to him such as is presented to no other trader—women are his principal customers, and their wants are innumerable, whether for use or ornament, and their fancy is a harp of a thousand strings, on which a skillful salesman may play an endless variety of tunes."[22] Thus the gender hierarchy helped maintain the distinction between consumption and production, a distinction necessary in a system that required indulging one's desires through consumption and, at the same time, controlling desire through self-discipline in order to increase production. Thus, with women as the major class of consumers, the new culture of consumption was not disruptive. Department stores incorporated women and the feminine into their landscape: the domestic was brought into the public arena.

Housing the Retailers

As department stores moved north into residential areas, they created new landscapes, districts that spatially and socially were associated with the domestic enclaves they were striving to be near. This movement also disassociated them from the financial, wholesale, and office districts to the south, that is, from the male-defined workplaces of the city. When Alexander Stewart opened his department store on Broadway at Chambers Street, just north of City Hall, in 1846, it was heralded by some as foolhardy (fig. 20). It was considered uptown and on the wrong side of the street—the west side was considered more fashionable, as it was more removed from the docks along the East River, closer to the elite residential area, and supposedly more sunny. Yet Stewart's emporium was a huge economic success, making him a millionaire and allowing him to expand his store within several years of its opening. The store was the first retail establishment to move out of the more generalized wholesaling area further south and east, and its success brought many followers. By the early 1850s, Lord and Taylor had moved from Catherine Street to the corner of Grand and Chrystie streets, and Arnold and Hearn on Canal Street had split into two companies, with Hearn Brothers moving to 425 Broadway and Arnold Constable to Canal Street. Seamon and Muir was on Worth Street, with the store of Strong and Adriance next door.[23]

By 1862, however, Stewart needed more space for his growing business and moved the retailing portion of his store uptown following his customers (the upper middle class of New York was now living as far north as Union and Washington squares), to Broadway between 9th and 10th streets, leaving his downtown store to serve as a warehouse (fig. 21). And, as was the case after Stewart's bold move several years earlier, other stores followed. James McCutcheon and Company opened its store just to the south of Stewart's, at 748 Broadway, B. Altman moved to Third Avenue, two blocks west, and R. H. Macy's moved to Sixth Avenue, several blocks east and north.[24]

Throughout the 1870s and 1880s, department stores continued to move north up Broadway, and, particularly in the 1890s, onto Sixth Avenue.[25] In 1875, the retailing focus was on Broadway between 10th and 23rd streets. A commentator in 1872 noted

20. Stewart's dry goods store, Broadway at Chambers Street, 1860. Stewart's marble-fronted palace bordered City Hall Park, and when it opened in 1846, it marked a new stage for the emerging retail industry in New York, in terms of both its operating procedures and its location and architectural form.

21. A. T. Stewart's retail store. Stewart's move to Broadway at 10th Street was considered foolhardy by many, but his new palace was an immediate success, and other retailers soon copied its uptown location and cast-iron construction.

its prominence: "The fashionable retail stores of New York lie chiefly along Broadway, between the St. Nicholas Hotel [at Mercer Street] and Thirty-fourth street. A few are to be found in the cross streets leading from the great thoroughfare, and some are in the Sixth avenue, but Broadway almost monopolizes the fashionable retail trade of the city."[26] Within the next fifteen years, however, Sixth Avenue began to form another major shopping artery. By 1875 it was already a secondary focus, with Macy's, O'Neill's, Stern Brothers nearby (figs. 22, 23). O'Neill's department store was noteworthy for its yellow color. The *Real Estate Record* seemed to think this advertising strategy was also good aesthetics: "Instead of the ordinary red, he has given his store a coating of yellow with black lines and brown trimmings, which is certainly very attractive and striking."[27]

By the mid-1880s an entire district—from 10th Street up to 23rd Street, and from Sixth Avenue east to Broadway—was dedicated to retail and entertainment. Previously this area had been residential, but, with the encroachment of commercial activities, the middle and upper classes of New York continued their flight northward, moving up Fifth Avenue toward Central Park. As Christine Boyer has documented, New York's elite residential district moved northward throughout the nineteenth century, moving first out of lower Broadway to the area around Union Square and then even further north to 23rd Street and Madison Square in the 1850s.[28] Philip Hone reported in his diary the rapid transformation of Broadway into a commercial street that precipitated residential movement north: "The mania for converting Broadway into a street of shops is greater than ever. There is scarcely a block in the whole extent of this fine street of which some part is not in a state of transmutation. Three or four good brick houses on the corner of Broadway and Spring Street have been leveled. I know not for what purpose, shops no doubt. The houses, fine costly edifices to me, are to make way for a grand concert establishment."[29]

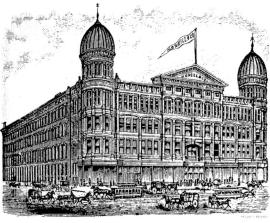

22. Stern Brothers' department store, 1878. The new focus of retailing near Sixth Avenue is evident in the ornate façade. (*Frank Leslie's Illustrated Weekly*)

23. O'Neill's department store. The highly ornate store, with its cast-iron façade, stood out because of its curved end towers topped with domes. (*Harper's Weekly*)

Throughout the last half of the nineteenth century, New York's upper and middle classes moved more than forty blocks north. And following behind them was the emergent retail district, as it expanded north (map 1). Instead of gradually expanding block by block, the district passed over intervening blocks and relocated in a totally new area, reflecting both rapid and intense spatial expansion.

Retail coalesced around Sixth Avenue in this leapfrog manner.[30] A commentator writing in 1921, looking back on that development, says the area "grew by leaps and bounds and it soon became the great shopping district for the retail dry goods trade...the transformation was rapid after Macy's made the break at the corner of Sixth Avenue."[31] These new department stores were unmistakably decorative. With Stewart's cast-iron store in place on Broadway, other magnificent stores were built on Broadway, Sixth Avenue, and 23rd Street. John Kellum, one of New York's popular architects of cast iron, designed James McCreery's store on Broadway across from Stewart's (fig. 24), and another cast-iron building for Tiffany's on Broadway at 15th Street. The Tiffany store was built on the site of Renwick's Church of the Puritans, which had been torn down to make way for the store—one of the many casualties of the retail district's northward expansion. Arnold Constable and Company moved north to the southwest corner of Broadway and 19th Street into a marble-fronted building that was soon enlarged with the addition of a mansard roof, and, several years later, a new cast-iron façade on Broadway. The building was described as the "last word in elegance, one could drive a horse and carriage through the wide aisles." The store's atmosphere was "so restful that one can shop in leisure and comfort, and incidentally, buy far more, than one intended."[32]

Lord and Taylor moved to the corner of 20th Street and Broadway, into a building designed by James Giles that was identifiable by its towerlike corner pavilion that rose above the rest of the structure (fig. 25). As the company explained, a move north was unavoidable: "The Lord and Taylor stores on Grand Street were in flourishing condition, but no merchant can afford to ignore the trend of population. In 1867 the firm had added 106 Chrystie Street to the buildings at 251–271 Grand Street, but this was soon found to be inadequate. A move uptown was inevitable."[33] Lord and Taylor now had the chance to compete on the new architectural frontier, and so created a building that was not only distinctive in design, but also in materials and mechanical devices. An 1872 commentator described the building as "magnificent....It is one of the finest and most picturesque edifices in the city, and is filled with a stock of goods equal in costliness and superior in taste to anything that can be bought at Stewart's."[34] The building was the first in New York with an iron frame, and the first store with a steam-driven public elevator. The store's promotional pamphlet depicts a trip on that

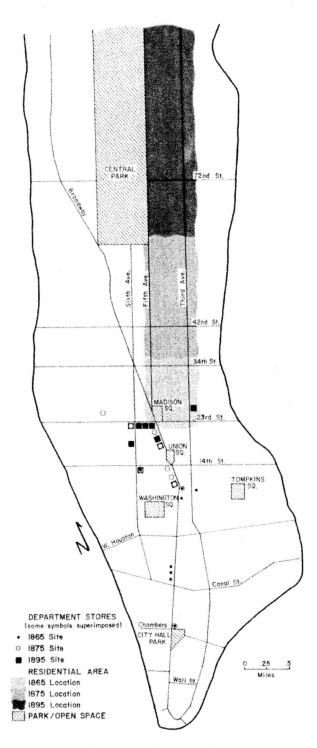

Map 1. Major Department Stores and Elite Residential Areas in Manhattan, 1895

24. McCreery's department store, 1869. One of the first emulators of Stewart's, McCreery's store moved across from Stewart's at 801 Broadway into a cast-iron building designed by the same architect, John Kellum. (*Harper's Weekly*)

25. Lord and Taylor's store. Lord and Taylor moved from Grand Street to the corner of Broadway and 20th Street in 1869, into a mansard-roofed building distinguished by its corner tower and its iron frame, apparently the first such building in the city. The use of plate-glass windows allowed shopping to move beyond the interior of department stores onto the paved sidewalks and streets.

elevator during the store's opening-day festivities in 1869 (fig. 26). The women are dressed in their fashionable best, and from their relaxed and settled poses, they seem to be enjoying their elevator ride. These novel features helped Lord and Taylor continue its commercial success, and throughout the nineteenth century the store expanded from its original location, eventually absorbing the entire block and reaching west to Fifth Avenue in 1906.[35]

By the turn of the century, the new retailing focus for New York City was a district centered on Fifth Avenue between Union and Madison squares, extending east to Sixth Avenue and west to Broadway. It was an area of ornamental architecture and grand boulevards, of restaurants and bars, and of small boutiques and large department stores. It was, above all, an urban landscape designed specifically for consumption. Urban dwellers had certainly purchased goods before, but in areas not devoted strictly to consumption. This new retailing district differed from its predecessors in that it

26. Customers riding in the novel steam-driven elevator of the Lord and Taylor store on opening day.

catered solely to consumers. Its three-dimensional form also differed dramatically from its predecessors. While the new department stores were dramatically larger than earlier dry goods stores, they also broke new ground in the degree of ornamentation, the attention to decorative detail and display of goods, the concern with internal organization of departments, and the catering to the personal needs of the shoppers, who, in most cases, were women.

Stewart's Palaces

The story of the most influential retailer in nineteenth-century New York—Alexander T. Stewart—and the two department stores he had constructed illustrates this process. One of New York's most successful merchant princes, Stewart was an innovator in retailing and a keen observer of and active participant in the New York real estate market. Stewart himself characterized New York's commercial spirit in many ways. He came to New York from Ireland in 1820, and in 1876 he died the second richest man in New York, much of his fortune made in real estate speculation.[36] Little interested in local political or social issues, except when they had a direct effect on his businesses, Stewart came to dominate the commercial scene of New York. Both of the commercial palaces he had built to house his stores spearheaded the northward march of retailing in the middle part of the nineteenth century.

The marble palace he had constructed in 1846 on Broadway at Chambers Street represented a bold move for several reasons—it was the largest store meant solely for retail, it was located away from the generalized commercial areas of the city, and it was designed to be an ornamental structure for the display of wares. To appreciate the boldness of this move, one has only to compare the world of Stewart's new store with its predecessors. First, its location was ideal for shopping—it was removed from the narrow streets and noise and congestion of lower Manhattan. In contrast, the wide expanse of Broadway was perfect for carriages, and women could be dropped off at the door of the store without venturing into the narrow side streets. The particular block that Stewart chose was also significant. The portion of the block that bordered Reade Street had been the site of the Washington Hotel, once a famous meeting spot of the city, and considered a handsome building and worthy of note along that stretch of Broadway. But, more important, the location bordered City Hall Park, a central area of the city that witnessed large amounts of pedestrian activity, and from which a handsome building could be displayed without interference from other structures. Stewart's store had occupied three other locations on Broadway, but now, with a well-established and expanding business and plenty of money, he decided to build a structure meant strictly for his own store. Stewart had already made his first million, and such success called out for an appropriate statement. He found the ideal location—uptown, on the east side of Broadway instead of the more established west side, and next to the Park.[37]

That statement was made most forcefully in the design of the new structure. The building was meant for symbolic display; it was not functional in the sense of its smaller predecessors—it was meant to be an aesthetic object, to speak of the propriety of the goods it held within. Social historian Michael Miller's analysis of the architecture of the Bon Marché in Paris (one of the first and one of the grandest of France's department stores) is equally appropriate to Stewart's new store: "In its architecture it brought together the culture's commitment to functionalize its environment and the culture's irrepressible need to secure solidity and respectability for its works. In its values it flaunted the culture's identification with appearances and material possessions, reaffirmed the culture's dedication to productivity, personified the culture's pretensions to an egalitarian society."[38]

According to the business historian Harry Resseguie, the design of Stewart's new store was innovative in several ways. The five-story building was designed specifically for retailing merchandise, with an open rotunda in the center off of which the various retailing departments were found. It had plate-glass first-floor windows, and the entire façade was of white marble (fig. 27).[39] That it was a building designed specifically for retailing may not seem revolutionary today, but in the 1840s it represented a new trend in the dry goods business. Most earlier businesses were located in small, residential-looking buildings, and expansion simply meant adding on to one or both sides of the structure. Stewart clearly had a different idea in mind when he designed his new store—it was to be a building meant specifically for displaying and selling his wares, and it was to appear as such.[40]

The white marble exterior made quite a visual impact in a city constructed almost exclusively of brick and wood. Designed in the Italianate style, the building's exterior details were appropriate to a Renaissance palace. The ground story had Corinthian columns separating the large plate-glass windows, quoins on the corners, and cornicework above the windows. Such a grand structure—the largest retail store in New York at the time—was intended to impress the viewer, and its appearance elicited much comment. The *Evening Post* described "the looming front of a marble palace, five stories high, decorated in the most beautiful style of art...in front of which...an incessant current of carriages may be seen approaching and leaving and as upon Jacob's ladder an unbroken file of angels, ascending and descending its marble steps."[41] And Philip Hone wrote in his diary several weeks before the building opened: "Mr. Stewart's splendid edifice, erected on the site of Washington Hall...is nearly finished, and his stock of dry goods will be exhibited on the shelves in a few days. There is nothing in London or Paris to compare with this dry goods palace."[42]

27. Stewart's store, Broadway at Chambers Street. After the store was enlarged in 1850, the extent of Stewart's white marble façade and plate-glass windows constituted an even more daring architectural statement than its earlier 1846 form. It was one of the first buildings to be designed almost exclusively for retail display. (Collection of the New-York Historical Society)

The dome and the choice of Italianate style were not accidental. Stewart was the first New Yorker to understand that the department store could be seen as a public institution. Within the architectural vocabulary of the time, the dome with accompanying rotunda had traditionally been reserved for public structures. Stewart and his architects apparently were familiar with two examples of such uses—the City Hall located just to the south of his new structure and the Merchants' Exchange Building—and it is possible that the City Hall could have served as a model for Stewart, since it used marble on its façade.[43] That Stewart used an architectural device associated with public life to be the crowning element of his new commercial building should not be surprising. His store was meant to be a public institution in that it was to serve the masses by offering goods and services to a large populace. The building was not only a functionally designed merchandizing structure but also a cultural adornment to the city. A dome with its public associations would attract customers at the same time that it would add cultural legitimacy to the commercial impulse.

The use of Italianate architecture, which harked back to the Renaissance palaces of the Italian urban aristocracy, was also a clear statement of Stewart's cultural ambitions. The earlier Greek Revival style was not deemed appropriate for the new commercial class—it was relatively plain and austere, with little ornamentation, and was considered out of place and out of proportion by New York's mid-century business class. As Weisman points out, the palace style "mirrored the rise of a mercantile royalty who no longer were satisfied with shingles and homespun, but who yearned instead for the trappings of nobility."[44] The style associated with the Italian nobility of the Renaissance was far more appropriate to a new commercial enterprise than the previous Greek Revival style. What seemed to matter to most to men like Stewart was an aristocratic appearance, and Stewart's new store fulfilled that demand.

Thus, Stewart was intent on designing a building that would provide an appropriate setting for consumption. An appeal to civic and aristocratic notions would provide his store with some cultural legitimacy, at the same time as it would diminish its commercial impact, and therefore would not interfere with its suitability as a venue for women to spend their time. It was already clear in 1846 that women would be the store's major patrons, yet, under the reigning gender ideology of separate spheres, they could be allowed to do so only if they did not become too tainted with commercialism. In order not to disrupt established gender categories, the store had to build in the qualities associated with nineteenth-century femininity and the domestic sphere: symbols of civic and cultural aspirations, well-ordered and arranged displays, services and amenities designed for women, and an environment in which one was safe and protected.

The store's large interior was arranged to maximize the display of goods for comparative shopping, as well as to create an atmosphere in which women were shielded from the rigors of the workplace so that they could cultivate domestic virtues. Translated into the architectural vocabulary of the department store, it meant that the space was highly ornamental, incorporated civic and cultural associations, and included design features that provided for women's "leisure" activities, such as promenading and socializing. The interior of Stewart's store centered on a dome, which was eighty feet high and seventy feet in circumference, and the oblong-shaped rotunda under it. This central rotunda was decorated with wall and ceiling frescoes, an ornate chandelier that shed light on the entire grand hall, and at one end had large mirrors imported from Paris which made the room look much larger than its dimensions of one hundred feet by forty feet.[45] Just opposite the main entrance in the rotunda was a flight of stairs that led up to a gallery that ran around the rotunda "for the ladies to promenade upon."[46] The rich interior displays included mahogany countertops, marble shelves, and a ladies' parlor complete with large mirrors, apparently the first such convenience in a commercial structure.[47] It was clear to observers that these amenities were meant to appeal to women: "New York can now boast of the most splendid dry goods store in the world....Mr. Stewart has paid the ladies of this city a high compliment in giving them such a beautiful resort in which to while away their leisure hours of the morning."[48] As historian William Leach suggests, it was women who were identified with small, ornamental items, with "fancy goods," and these were the enticements of the department store. For a man to set foot in a department store for his own pleasure was seen as a symbolic act of emasculation.[49] The desire to while away leisure hours in such an ornamental setting was a decidedly feminine attribute.

Based on this appeal to women and other of Stewart's clever business practices, his store was a huge success.[50] The impact of the store on subsequent commercial construction in New York was significant, starting a vogue for this new style up and down Broadway. An 1854 editorial in *Harper's* conveys its influence:

> A few years ago when a man returned from Europe, his eye full of the lofty buildings of the Continent, our cities seemed insignificant and mean....He felt that the city had no character, but he could not see what was wanting. But the moment Stewart's fine building was erected, the difficulty appeared....[It] was a key-note, a model. There had been other high buildings, but none so stately and simple. And even now there is, in its way no finer street effect than the view of Stewart's buildings seen on a clear blue brilliant day, from a point low in Broadway....It rises out of the sea of green foliage in the park, a white marble cliff, sharply drawn against the sky.[51]

That the building was impressive when it opened in 1846 cannot be denied, and the "white marble cliff" did indeed become a "key-note" of New York's emerging landscape. It was a fine display of the best that New York could offer—plenty of merchandise for any who could afford it, presented in a dramatic manner. The description of opening day activities in the *New York Herald* points to the atmosphere of spectacle: "When we visited the store, about 12 o'clock, we found a line of carriages drawn up in front reaching from Chambers to Reade streets. Crowds of fashionable people were passing in and out, and all were warm in their expressions of gratification of all the beautiful and tasteful arrangements and architecture of this whole building....The sales at the store yesterday were very brisk and the clerks were kept busy throughout the day."[52]

Less than fourteen years after his Chambers Street store opened, Stewart decided his prospering business needed to move further uptown, in order to capitalize on the movement of the upper middle class. He bought what had been an old farm on Broadway between 9th and 10th streets, and had constructed on the site a grand architectural display that became known as Stewart's Cast-Iron Palace.[53] Although many contemporaries considered such a move uptown foolhardy because the area was not thought convenient to its upper-class clientele, Stewart's new store was a huge and immediate success.[54] Keenly aware of real estate trends, Stewart knew quite well that the elite were moving into the area near Washington and Union squares and that his customers would certainly be attracted to such opulent architecture.

Stewart used the very latest in construction techniques and spared no expense on decor—apparently the building cost $2,755,000.[55] The new department store, designed by John Kellum (a popular New York architect, who was also responsible for Stewart's home on Fifth Avenue), was considered an architectural marvel (fig. 28). Stewart surprised his contemporaries with his choice of building material for the façade, selecting cast iron instead of marble. Stewart himself had begun the vogue for marble façades with his earlier store on Broadway. But again Stewart set the trend, and, by choosing iron, Stewart allied himself with the latest in industrial technology, particularly as the Civil War brought to the public's awareness the increasing use of iron for new engineering and transportation projects.[56] The use of iron also allowed for greater window space and therefore permitted more natural light to enter the store on all stories. The six-story building, designed in the palazzo style and constructed of iron and glass, was not to be missed by visitors to the city. Like Stewart's marble palace, his new cast-iron palace became a landmark.

In this new location, Stewart was able to put into practice what he had learned during the years of business at his old store, and continued the idea of the department store as stage of consumption designed to fit the prevailing gender ideology. The interior space was designed to contrast with the chaos of the surrounding urban form. The highly structured and symmetrically arranged aisles and counters contributed to a sense of the orderliness of the store, of, as historian Gunther Barth describes it, "a

28. Stewart's cast-iron palace, 1869. Stewart's new uptown store set another architectural trend with its use of cast iron and its Italian palazzo style. (Collection of the New-York Historical Society)

29. Interior of Stewart's Astor Place store in the 1880s. The interior featured galleries that encircled a large rotunda, lighted by a large skylight. This design contributed to the atmosphere of spectacle in the store. (Collection of the New-York Historical Society)

utopian order that was a relief after the disorderly anarchy of modern city life that engulfed the building."[57] Stewart maintained the civic allusions of his earlier store, centering his new building around a large rotunda (eighty feet by forty-eight feet) and dome, at the same time magnifying the display aspects of the interior.[58] The entire store was dominated by a skylight that provided direct light to the large main floor. The five upper stories were arranged as encircling balconies, thus providing natural light to all floors and enabling shoppers to observe one another as they strolled through the enormous building (fig. 29). This design contributed to the atmosphere of spectacle in the store, with shoppers able to view all the activities at the main gallery, while seeing across and up and down to the various departments that surrounded them. This presented women customers with a fairly limitless visual experience, as they watched not only each other, but also the range of wares for consumption.

Creating the Feminine Landscape

Yet despite all this commercialism, the presence of women ensured that the forces of consumption would not disrupt the values of productivity. In other words, women as the main class of consumers allowed the new culture of consumption to flourish without seriously disturbing the economic order. In its appeal to women and its incorporation of aspects of the domestic, Stewart's store also made the consumption necessary to support industrialization ideologically more acceptable. Yet gender also helped mediate another set of tensions—that between the commercial and the cultural. Stewart's store was attacked by New York's culture critics because it was designed as a civic structure— with dome, rotunda, and Italianate style—yet was the quintessential commercial enterprise. By so doing, it risked blurring the distinction between commerce and culture—an ideological tenet that was important to New York's middle and upper classes.

Stewart's first store met with much approval, due as much to its novelty as its actual design, but his second store sounded the warning signs for contemporary critics. Many found cast-iron architecture to be cheap and not worthy of much attention. P. B. Wight's comments on Stewart's store show the degree of disdain:

It bears all over it an evidence of cheapness, especially when we observe it is of iron…a cheapness which comes from the desire to save pattern-making. In all probability, not more than six patterns were required to cast the several thousand tons which are put in this great iron wall. There is nothing inside of this store except iron columns, all cast from one pattern and no end of plaster-corniced girders, save the great cast-iron well-hole over the glove counter with its bull's eye skylight above. This is a perfect mine of wasted iron, which, if properly used, would construct several respectable buildings. It is safe to say that this building has done more to retard architectural progress in New York than any other dozen buildings of the worst possible designs. It overawes the thoughtless by its sheer size and seizes the sympathy of the sentimental by the purity of its white paint,—when it is fresh.[59]

That the commercial style of architecture was becoming unacceptable to the arbiters of good taste is not surprising; distinctions in class were often based on taste, and here we see the put-down both of Stewart himself—for mixing commerce with culture and producing cheap architecture—and of his customers who are taken in by the size and seized by "the sympathy of the sentimental." Epitomizing the bourgeois spirit, Stewart's department store is seen as a threat to that spirit in blurring the distinctions on which the bourgeois class is legitimizing itself, between the world of money and production and the world of culture and leisure. On the one hand, New York's middle and upper classes looked to the world of culture to provide a mantle of moral authority for their commercial successes. It was therefore incumbent upon them to maintain a cultural world untainted by the commercial impulse. Hence, the disdain over the "cheap" architecture of the new Stewart's store—a commercial enterprise could never hope to acquire any cultural propriety. On the other hand, the two worlds were in fact dependent on each other. By using an architectural style to associate the store with a known past, Stewart invoked the predominant logic of Victorian architecture.[60] Most of New York's prominent commercial buildings were designed with the idea of providing a known and legitimized history to these commercial enterprises (see chapter 3). This cloak of an idealized past was not meant to hide commerce, which did not need to be hidden; instead, it associated the commercial with the cultural. A marble store with a rotunda indicated in architectural language that the commercial prince who owned the store was indeed of the ruling class, and the customers who shopped there could acquire for themselves such legitimacy by buying the appropriate items.

An apparent contradiction begins to emerge, however. On the one hand, middle-class life needed to separate the cultural and the commercial so that this class could feel culturally legitimate and therefore superior to others, those without "taste." And yet the middle and upper classes also needed the economic support of those without taste, and so offered them a chance to acquire taste by shopping in appropriately ornamented stores and buying the correct items. This led to a mixing of the categories of culture and commerce. This contradiction was inherent to the functionings of a bourgeois class in a democratic political system—a class dependent on economic wealth, and yet seeking cultural legitimacy. To maintain that wealth, they had to sell their culture to those who increasingly could afford it. Yet to distinguish themselves from those same people, the elite needed to separate the cultural realm from the mere commercial.

One can understand why the design of the new Stewart building provoked strong reactions among the tastemakers of New York. As with the city's first skyscrapers, many commercial buildings were perceived by the city's cultural elite, a fairly small subset of the economic elite, as architectural aberrations. They appealed to the wrong type of people, those who had not acquired the "correct" taste and were being sold a cheap reproduction. This blurring of the commercial and the cultural that the store represented not only created "bad" architecture, it attracted people who were taken in by the sheer delight of the spectacle. The architecture did not fulfill the pure goals of art—the building could not be read for its historical and moral codes because these styles were considered mere disguises of unbridled commercialism. This threatened those concerned with maintaining aesthetic standards.

The use of cast iron as a significant ornamental element in New York's retail structures also called into question the distinction between craftsmanship and mechanics. Cast iron was prefabricated into patterns at the foundry, and these patterns were simply affixed to steel or masonry framing. The use of cast iron, therefore, precluded the need for bricklayers or stonemasons; in fact, no traditional craft-related work was required. Cast-iron architecture, then, presaged the use of the steel frame and the rise of modernist architecture. Yet in its time it was disdained by cultural authorities for its cheapness and lack of aesthetic qualities. Many commentators wondered why cast iron continued to be used even after the fires in Boston and Chicago in the 1870s had shown the material's susceptibility to fire. Architect Leopold Eidlitz indirectly responded to that question in his attack on the use of cast iron: "Iron never can, and never will be, a suitable material for forming the main walls of architectural monuments. The only material for that purpose always has been, and now is, stone.... A building bedizened with cast-iron ornamentation would give to the question, for what purpose the building is erected, would be plain to me as though it was written upon it with large cast-iron letters: 'FOR SHOW MORE THAN FOR ANY OTHER PURPOSE.'"[61] Eidlitz was, of course, correct—cast iron was indeed for show, since it was the most stylish and up-to-date building material of the time, and it allowed much larger windows for display, exactly what commercial entrepreneurs wanted in the design of their new buildings. Stewart's cast-iron palace set the tone for New York's commercial enterprises, and much of the architecture of what has come to be known as the Ladies' Mile is of this cast-iron palace style, loosely based on the Italianate style. The arbiters of good taste could do little except complain.

Yet for most middle-class New Yorkers, the department store seemed not a threat at all, but rather a mediation between commerce and culture. One could now shop in the most ornamented of locations, surrounded by beautiful architecture, and often the sounds of the symphony (fig. 30). With the main shoppers being women, that "timid, non-commercial class," how could the department store be seen as threatening?[62] Historian William Leach has shown how religion was figured into the equation of women and fashion, thereby making less threatening these palaces of consumption. The association of religion with fashion had already become familiar to most Americans by mid-century—as a commentator noted in 1856, "real ladies and gentlemen are those who belong both to the Church and to fashion."[63] Department store owners built on this association, calling their stores cathedrals, and their goods objects of devotion. A commentator compared Stewart's new store with Grace Church, and spoke of the store as dedicated to the worship of dry goods: "In walking up Broadway on the west side of that most magnificent of thoroughfares, a person must naturally find two striking objects to contemplate at that point where the street makes a bend. One is the graceful, slender, gray spire of Grace Church, piercing the blue atmosphere; the other is the gigantic mass of iron, painted of a white color, erected by Alexander T. Stewart to the worship of dry-goods, covering two acres of ground, and Theban in its Old World massiveness."[64]

Department stores learned to schedule the openings of their collections at Christmas and Easter, thus further aligning religion and fashion, and institutionalizing the commercialization of religious holidays. As William Leach suggests, "The department stores, and the fashion industry that underlay them, penetrated into and conta-

30. Lace room in Stewart's store. As the major class of consumers, women mediated between commerce and culture, shopping without danger of overconsuming because of their "naturally" moral characters. (*Frank Leslie's Illustrated Newspaper*, 1879. Collection of the New-York Historical Society)

minated the life of established religion, creating a paradoxical marriage between commodity capitalism and religious life that has persisted into our own time."[65] Department stores, then, were central to both the commercialization of religion and the association of religion with consumption. And, since religion formed an integral part of the women's sphere, the department store served to reinforce the alignment of the feminine with consumption. By turning shoppers into "worshipers" in "cathedrals" of commerce, the store owners hoped to portray consumption as a moral act, a kind of religious duty of women.

The department store solidified this association among women, femininity, and consumption. And because department stores were by far the most influential forces in the late nineteenth-century retail market, they were also the most powerful shapers of the urban environment. The use of glass in department stores was of particular importance in the display of the private world in the public spaces of the city. Plate-glass windows were originally adopted in department stores in order to bring in more natural light, but it did not take long for entrepreneurs to recognize their potential use for the display of goods. By the 1870s, plate-glass windows on the ground floor of most retail stores allowed women to shop without ever stepping off the sidewalk (see fig. 25). And behind those windows were displayed household items from bedroom sets to crystal, garments from corsets to evening gowns. The private world was put on public display in the heart of the city.

At the same time as public spaces were becoming arenas for private consumption, the private, domestic space was becoming commercialized. The domestic sphere of home and family was meant to be untainted by commercial concerns; the home was to be a haven from the economic world. But again, the very circumstances of bourgeois life undermined this separation. Style as well as keeping up with fashion for themselves and their family required bourgeois women to spend ever-increasing sums of money on their homes. Not only was the location and external appearance of the home important for status, but throughout the last half of the nineteenth century, home decoration and design became symbols of wealth and taste. By the end of the century, department stores had expanded into the home decoration business, supplying not only the commodities but also the experts who carefully designed rooms and even complete homes that could be viewed within department stores. These settings provided models of appropriate household fashions for women to emulate in their own homes. Home was not the refuge from the economic world that the ideology of separate spheres ordained; rather, the domestic sphere had become completely commercialized, with most of its furnishings bought at the department store to express the economic status of the occupant.

The department store, then, helped to turn the private domestic world into a realm of publicly purchased and appraised commodities; it was integral in the association of women with consumerism, thus making continuous consumption ideologically acceptable; and it was by and large responsible for feminizing the downtown. Department stores were privately owned and catered to people's private, domestic needs, yet they provided forums for public exchange and created new public spaces; they were the palaces of consumption par excellence, yet that consumption was fueled by mass production; and though owned and managed by men, they were staffed by women, and catered to women and women's "sphere." The department store, in both form and function, then, fulfilled many of the contradictory demands of America's economic system in the mid- to late nineteenth century, and it, and the downtown area that it helped to fashion, need to be understood in that light.

Outside the stores, wide sidewalks enabled women's fashionable dresses to stay clean, while paved, and increasingly gas and electrically illuminated streets added to the propriety of the area for women. Rapid transit networks enabled women to come downtown to shop in the morning, return to their middle-class enclaves further uptown for lunch, and return to shop that same afternoon. When the first elevated train opened on Sixth Avenue in 1878, crowds of women used it to flock to the new stores. New Yorker Clara Pardee wrote in her diary in May 1893 that she went downtown to shop in the morning and in the afternoon, returning home for lunch.[66] But the shopping experience was not limited to the interiors of the stores. Plate-glass windows allowed New York's public streets, Sixth Avenue and Broadway, to become arenas for the display of private goods. And as the public spaces became more and more dedicated to consumption and display, they became increasingly feminized— New Yorkers literally had created a Ladies' Mile. Although some scholars have argued that the participation of women in the creation of this new urban environment was somewhat emancipatory, it is difficult to suggest that this was its guiding principle.[67] Women's participation in the public life of the city was integral to maintaining the existing social and economic order. Nonetheless, as the largest class of consumers in the city, women, and the qualities ascribed to them by nineteenth-century society, played significant roles in the shaping of New York's landscape in the second half of the nineteenth century. The presence of women and the domestic sphere in department stores provided the cultural legitimacy sought after by the bourgeois owners, who were continually looking for ways of affirming and displaying their wealth and power in the city.

3 Constructing New York's Skyline

The general features of the new edifice had been clearly outlined by Mr. Pulitzer. The imposing dome, which distinguishes the building from every other in the metropolis, was originally and entirely Mr. Pulitzer's conception. The same may be said of the splendid three-storied entrance arch, an equally notable and effective feature. Mr. Pulitzer further insisted that, erected upon so commanding a site, the structure must be in every sense an architectural ornament to the metropolis; that it must be of the first order, embodying the very latest and best ideas in constructive wit, it must also be the best equipped newspaper edifice in existence.
—"The Pulitzer Building," *New York World*, 10 December 1890

Joseph Pulitzer's new home for his *New York World* newspaper was a focus of controversy for the city's culture critics and observers. Was the building really an "ornament" to the city, or was it an aberration? To what degree was the design attributable to the architect, George Post, or his patron, Joseph Pulitzer? How long would it remain the tallest building in the city? Certainly such controversy was more than welcome by Pulitzer, as it ensured that his building would be noticed and thereby be a symbol of his commercial and cultural aspirations. The story of the design, construction, and reaction to Pulitzer's new home for his newspaper not only reveals the specifics of Pulitzer's situation, but also suggests, in a more general sense, many of the issues at the heart of skyscraper development in New York.[1] Although the development of the skyscraper has often been explained as a response to rising land values, the story of the World Building points to factors that complicate that explanation.[2] Like most of the early skyscrapers in New York City, the World Building was not built in the area of the city that commanded the highest land rents, nor was it meant to generate income through office space rental.[3] Rather, the World Building expressed, in clear visual terms, Pulitzer's aspirations—his need to express his newly found power, his competitiveness with the other newspapers in the city, his concerns to legitimize his commercial impulse, and his attempts to participate in the civic realm of urban life.

Pulitzer was not alone in his use of a tall building to symbolize his status and that of his business—such edifices were being constructed along Broadway and around City Hall Park beginning in the late 1870s. And, within the next thirty years, the construction of more than three hundred skyscrapers in Manhattan transformed the city's iconography (figs. 31, 32). From a city that was readily identifiable by its four- and five-story brick commercial buildings, punctuated by several church spires, New York became a center of skyscraper development, and the skyline became the city's signature. This physical transformation both reflected and actively represented fundamental social and economic changes occurring in late nineteenth-century New York. Most apparent was the growing need for offices to house the increasing numbers of white-collar employees. Almost thirty-one percent of New York male workers in 1890 were classified as white collar, owing to the expanding service sector and the spatial separation of office from factory.[4] This is, in many respects, similar to the dry goods business, where the retailing portion was separated from wholesaling in the early to mid-nineteenth century. Just as the department store created a new and decorative space for selling goods that were made and often stored elsewhere, so too the skyscraper provided new spaces for managers and owners, bureaucrats and clerks to administer their increasingly complex businesses.

Yet, as is apparent from the epigraph, these new commercial buildings were meant as more than mere containers for businesses; they were also meant to be architectural ornaments for the city, symbols of culture as well as commerce. In the design of this first generation of New York skyscrapers, architects attempted to find an architectural vocabulary appropriate for cultural expressions of commerce. Daniel Bluestone's analysis of the aesthetic of skyscraper design in Chicago applies equally to New York: "Here, too, was an aesthetic that created a necessary connection between commerce and culture, denying their incompatibility and suggesting that refinement might emanate from tasteful workplaces." As in Chicago, New York's extremely competitive and aggressive business class was keenly aware of the potential of these "buildings for advertising their wealth, taste, and even their public spirit."[5] It was industries that were most competitive and that were, for specific reasons, looking for material expressions of cultural and civic legitimacy that had greatest interest in sky-

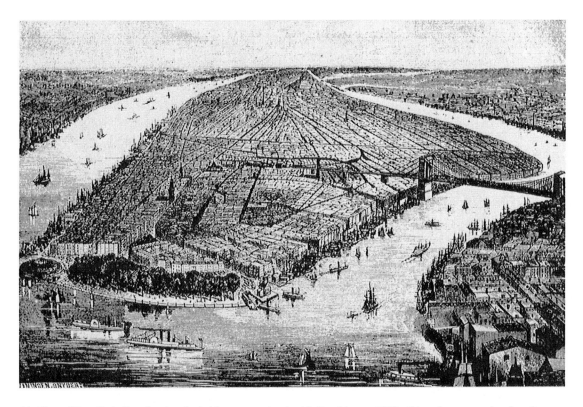

31. View of New York City, showing the bridge connecting it with Brooklyn, c. 1872. Although not completed until 1883, the Brooklyn Bridge carried such symbolic weight that its completed span was rendered in this view. Its towers are by far the city's tallest structures, with only the church steeples breaking the four- and five-story skyline.

32. Bird's-eye view of lower New York, 1911. The towers of the Brooklyn Bridge are hard to distinguish in this view, having lost their distinctiveness with the completion of other bridges across the East River and been overtaken on the skyline by more than a handful of skyscrapers. Little remains of the four- and five-story structures that had characterized the city until the 1870s.

scraper construction. New York's skyline was certainly the result of technological accomplishments, increasing land values, and the requirements of office space, but, equally important, it served as the symbolic expression of the power of New York's emerging merchant and entrepreneurial class. The social structure of nineteenth-century New York was fundamentally implicated in shaping the development of the skyscraper, one of the most significant aspects of its landscape, and, in turn, that landscape legitimized and represented the class of people who controlled the city's social and economic structure.

This analysis, then, differs from a traditional urban geography that explains patterns in the city as they relate to land values. The decisions by many members of New York's entrepreneurial class to construct tall buildings were based as much on a promotional impulse and notions of corporate imagery as an evaluation of real estate economics. The first generation of skyscrapers in New York reflected the energy of late nineteenth-century commercialism, including massive economic expansion and unbridled real estate speculation. The concomitant rise in land values made the skyscraper financially desirable; the competitiveness of the economy made it a promotional success. Skyscrapers, therefore, fulfilled symbolic as well as functional needs for New York's business class. The calculations for where to locate a skyscraper took into account visibility and display as well as accessibility to workers and other businesses.[6] An outline of the locational pattern of New York's first tall buildings leads into an analysis of the people and institutions responsible for that pattern. New York's skyscrapers were constructed first in the areas near City Hall Park and close to Wall Street in the 1870s. But soon after, their pattern expanded fairly rapidly northward, as the city's business classes looked for new areas in which to display their wealth and taste. The movement of the concentration of skyscrapers northward was part of the entire spatial expansion of New York in the mid- to late nineteenth century that was fueled by economic growth—residential areas moving north, followed by retailers, and then the new tall office structures.

The Locational Pattern

New York's emerging industrial and commercial classes were increasingly dissatisfied with mid-century architectural possibilities. The Greek Revival style was proving unwieldy for large commercial structures and unsatisfactory as a form of material display. The new palace style of architecture, popularized by Stewart's department store on Broadway, captured the imaginations of enterprising merchants looking for a competitive edge and a way of displaying their new status and material wealth. These new entrepreneurs located their structures on Broadway because it was the widest, longest, and most central street and, therefore, presented a succession of prominent sites in lower Manhattan. It would have made little sense for these merchants to locate their monuments to their wealth and position on narrow streets where they would not have been noticed or appreciated by the public.

In retrospect, these commercial palaces can be seen as prototypes of the first tall buildings, and their locations anticipate the pattern of tall building construction. Although the palace motif as an architectural style declined gradually after 1870, the motivation to build ornate commercial structures reached its climax with the early skyscrapers of the 1870s and 1880s.[7] The development of the passenger elevator, and subsequent improvements in the 1870s that made the tall building commercially viable, allowed merchants to house their enterprises in buildings that were towering as well as ornate. The possibility of exceeding the accepted five- or six-story height limit offered merchants and entrepreneurs a new way of expressing their rise to nobility.

The Development of Tall Buildings, 1875–1897

By the 1870s, New York City's commercial focus had expanded several miles north from its original core near the Battery and to the east along the East River (maps 2, 3, 4, 5). This horizontal expansion, however, was not accompanied by any remarkable vertical growth; none of New York's commercial structures rose higher than five or six stories. The only spikes on the profile of the city were churches; lower Manhattan could be easily distinguished by the steeples of Trinity Church, on Broadway at Wall Street, and Saint Paul's Church, on Broadway at Fulton Street (see fig. 31). Church spires still towered over the shops, warehouses, and offices of the fastest-growing city in the western world.

The first two buildings to challenge Trinity's steeple for dominance of the New York skyline were completed in 1875.[8] The Tribune Building and Western Union Telegraph Building were outstanding because of their height, but they were also lavish architectural structures. The Tribune Building, designed by Richard Morris Hunt in the Second Empire style, was located at the corner of Spruce and Nassau streets (fig. 33). It reached a height of 260 feet, only 26 feet short of the Trinity spire. George Post's 230-foot-tall Western Union Building, located at the corner of Broadway and Dey streets, was similar to the Tribune Building in design, with a mansard roof and elaborate central tower. These two buildings stood unchallenged on the commercial skyline for more than ten years because they were completed at the beginning of an economic depression that constrained building construction until 1880.[9]

By 1881, four other buildings, located close to the Tribune and Western Union buildings, near City Hall, could be distinguished on the Manhattan skyline.[10] These six

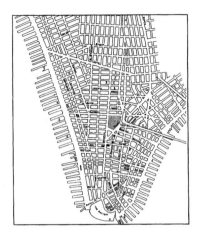

Map 2. Tall Buildings in Manhattan, 1881

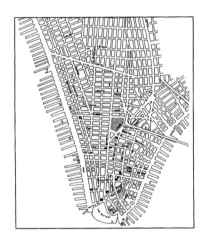

Map 3. Tall Buildings in Manhattan, 1885

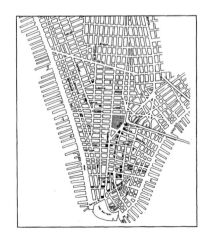

Map 4. Tall Buildings in Manhattan, 1891

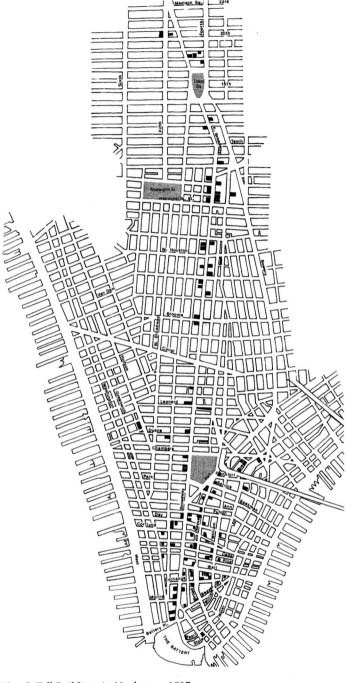

Map 5. Tall Buildings in Manhattan, 1897

33. Park Row, 1877. Although not considered tall by modern skyscraper standards, the Tribune Building stood out from the other newspaper buildings along Park Row, making it a landmark in the city. (Collection of the New-York Historical Society)

buildings constituted a readily visible cluster of tall structures and were the first examples of significant vertical expansion in New York. Contrary to what economic theory might lead one to expect, this development occurred at City Hall Park, not at the corner of Broad and Wall streets, the intersection that commanded the highest land rents.[11] City Hall Park is a triangular lot formed by Park Row meeting Broadway at a 45-degree angle, and the intersection of these two streets created the largest open space in lower Manhattan. The park was the center for much of the city's social activity, and the construction of the nearby Brooklyn Bridge in the 1870s added to its appeal as a focus of public attention.[12] After the area had been established as a center of social activity and, subsequently, of tall building construction, it became even more attractive for businesses concerned with creating architectural expressions of their wealth and power. From the park pedestrians could view the encircling buildings, and the open space of the park allowed the full height of the buildings to be appreciated. Spectators who came to watch the bridge construction were also treated to the spectacle of the first commercial buildings to push skyward.

By 1885, the focus of tall building construction had shifted south on Broadway, and Wall Street's first tall buildings appeared. The Wall Street cluster consisted of the Mills Building at the corner of Broad Street and Exchange Place, the Mechanics Bank Building, the U.S. National Bank Building, and the Mortimer Office Building (all on Wall Street), and the Liverpool, London, and Globe Insurance Building, two hundred yards away on William Street. All of these buildings were nine stories in height. At the same time, on lower Broadway, the Washington Building was located across from the Battery, and the Welles Building was on the eastern side of Broadway near the corner of Beaver Street. Another building added to the City Hall cluster was the Potter Building, on a prominent site at the corner of Park Row and Nassau Street. By 1885, fourteen buildings of nine to ten stories in height were located in three clusters on Manhattan.

During the period 1886–91 several new tall buildings were constructed within the established clusters at City Hall Park, Wall Street, and lower Broadway. The average height level remained ten stories, but the construction of the sixteen-story World Building in 1890 was a harbinger of future heights. Yet, by far the most significant development occurred around City Hall Park. Three of the four buildings completed around the park were newspaper buildings—the World Building on Park Row at Frankfort Street, the thirteen-story Times Building on Park Row at Spruce Street, and the ten-story Mail and Express Building on Broadway at Fulton Street. The new Times Building was constructed on the same strategic site as the old one—a V-shaped lot at the intersection of Park Row and Nassau and Spruce streets (fig. 34). Immediately adjacent to it was the Potter Building, and to the east on Park Row were the Tribune and the World buildings.

Together, these four buildings created the first ring of tall structures to encircle an open space in New York. *King's Handbook* called the area around the City Hall Park "the grandest architectural square in America," and its prediction that "in time the City Hall Park will be surrounded with such buildings; the centre of incalculable activities" was proven correct.[13] In 1891 the Potter, Times, Tribune, and World buildings formed an ensemble of skyscrapers unequaled in the city. The new Mail and Express Building, together with the Western Union and Evening Post buildings, created a secondary cluster of tall buildings within the City Hall Park district. These three ten-story structures on Broadway between Fulton and Dey streets provided the first instance of linear development along Broadway, which was to become the dominant pattern of skyscrapers in New York.

The Washington and Welles buildings, which comprised the lower Broadway cluster in 1885, barely merited such a title at that time, but by 1891 lower Broadway had become a full-fledged tall building district. Five new buildings were constructed on Broadway south of Wall Street, and one, the Western Electric Building, was constructed to the west, on Greenwich Street. The resultant linear pattern of skyscrapers on Broadway created an impressive architectural display. A commentator in *Harper's Weekly* observed, "at frequent intervals on Broadway and adjacent streets roofs may be seen mounting in a way that amazes the returned wanderer."[14] By far the most spectacular development during this period, however, was the construction of the sixteen-story World Building at City Hall Park in 1890, the tallest building in New York for almost a decade. The World Building, in combination with the Times Building, reinforced the reputation of the City Hall Park district as the premier display area for the city's architectural achievements.

Between 1892 and 1897 major changes occurred in the development of tall buildings: the number increased fourfold (from twenty-five in 1891 to ninety-six in 1897); the height level was pushed to twenty stories; and the spatial extent of tall buildings moved northward to Fifth Avenue. The dramatic increase in the number of skyscrapers and in their heights was due, in part, to the acceptance by city officials and builders of the viability of steel for construction purposes. Although steel-frame construction was introduced in New York with the Tower Building in 1890, its use did not become widespread for several years.[15] The steel skeleton greatly simplified the construction of tall buildings and made feasible buildings that exceeded the thirteen-to-fourteen-story height limits of masonry construction.

The Wall Street cluster expanded from its original core in Wall Street north to John Street and south to Beaver Street. The eighteen new buildings that accounted for this expansion constituted twenty-five percent of all construction during this period. However, in contrast to City Hall Park, where the skyscrapers encircled the park, the

34. *(below)* The 1888 New York Times
Building attempted to compete with the
architectural and height standard
established by the adjacent Tribune
Building. (*Harper's Weekly*)

35. *(right)* The Postal Telegraph and
Home Life Insurance Company build-
ings, c. 1910. Added to the cluster of
skyscrapers surrounding City Hall Park
were the fourteen-story Postal
Telegraph and sixteen-story Home Life
Insurance Company buildings.
(Collection of the New-York Historical
Society)

Wall Street area was densely packed with tall buildings on its narrow streets in response to the high land values and limited space near Wall Street.[16]

Fourteen buildings were completed near City Hall Park by 1897, which accounts for nearly twenty percent of the construction of tall buildings during the period 1892–97. A group of four buildings appeared near Rose Street, east of the park, the tallest of which was the thirteen-story Metropolitan Realty Building at 20 Rose Street. More significant development, however, occurred on Broadway from City Hall to Canal Street, with six of the seven new buildings located on the west side of Broadway. Visible from the park areas were the fourteen-story Postal Telegraph and, next door, the sixteen-story Home Life Insurance buildings, between Warren and Murray streets (fig. 35), and at Chambers Street, the twin-towered twelve-story National Shoe and Leather Bank Building. Beyond the park were the thirteen-story Mutual Reserve, the nine-story Ayer Building, and the eleven-story Haggin Building, and, on the east side, the twelve-story New York Life Insurance Building. The Postal Telegraph, Home Insurance, and Shoe and Leather Bank buildings, which bordered the park, together with the earlier cluster of skyscrapers on Park Row (Potter, Times, Tribune, and World buildings) maintained the City Hall Park cluster as a major focus for tall building development.

During this time period, the lower Broadway cluster spread north and merged with the development around City Hall Park. Only ten buildings were built in the district, yet included in that group was the tallest building in the city, the twenty-story American Surety Building, on Broadway at Pine Street, and two seventeen-story structures, the Manhattan Life Insurance Building and the Bowling Green Building. The location of these three buildings along Broadway allowed for effective display of their architectural ornaments. Further north up Broadway, between Dey and Cortland streets, the thirteen-story Havemeyer Building was considered a prominent structure as much for its design by George Post as for its height.

The district that grew the most during this time period was that on Broadway near Washington Square. Nearly a third of all skyscraper construction in the city occurred in this district. In 1891, no tall buildings were located in this area; by 1897, twenty-two were spread along Broadway in two spatial patterns—a cluster just to the east of Washington Square, and a line along Broadway between Broome and Bleecker streets. The buildings in both groups ranged from nine to twelve stories, heights that were quite noticeable in relation to the surrounding five-story structures. Also significant during this time period was the construction of a group of seven buildings between nine and twelve stories on Fifth Avenue between Union Square and Madison Square.

By 1897, then, a pattern of tall building location was already established: clusters around Wall Street, City Hall Park, Washington Square, and Union Square; and a linear pattern along Broadway and Fifth Avenue. The linear pattern up Broadway was punctuated by two clusters of skyscrapers—one, on lower Broadway, was topped by the twenty-story American Surety Building, and the other, at City Hall Park, was dominated by the sixteen-story World Building. Wall Street was the most dense cluster, with twenty-nine buildings located between Nassau and William streets. Contemporary commentators could not help noticing this drastic change in the form of their city. One critic was somewhat alarmed by the overwhelming presence of commercial structures at the expense of other buildings:"The typical modern city is becoming an assemblage of gigantic commercial buildings, which overtop the loftiest church spire, and render insignificant the most ambitious and ornamental structures of an earlier time."[17] Those immense commercial buildings only grew larger as the city entered the twentieth century.

The Emergence of the Manhattan Skyline, 1898–1908

Although the spatial pattern of tall buildings was established in 1897, it was not until the last three years of the nineteenth century and the early years of the twentieth century that skyscraper development reached its peak (maps 6, 7). New York had 94 skyscrapers in 1897, 209 in 1902, and 366 in 1908.

Much of the construction of tall buildings occurred in the midtown area, on Fifth Avenue and Broadway north of Union Square. From a scattering of seven buildings in 1897, the area around Fifth Avenue north of Union Square was transformed by 1902 into a large cluster of twenty-eight tall buildings. Three buildings on the edge of Union Square were prominent—the eleven-story Hartford and Decker buildings and the nine-story Douglas Building. Although none of the skyscrapers in this area exceeded twelve stories in height, they stood out on the skyline, given the surrounding five- and six-story retail and residential structures. Along Broadway around Washington Square, twenty-seven new skyscrapers were completed. And, like the area surrounding Union Square, these buildings were not significantly tall—none were more than fourteen stories—yet they stood out and created an impressive skyline up Broadway.

Downtown, the pattern of skyscraper locations was relatively unchanged from 1897 to 1908. The twenty tall buildings constructed in the Wall Street cluster were located in tight groupings, with a particularly dense accumulation south of Wall Street near Beaver Street. Although the numbers of skyscrapers built near City Hall Park continued to increase during the period 1898–1902, the area's importance as a center of tall building construction was beginning to wane. The twenty-one buildings constructed in the area were located on Broadway north of the park, and in a tight cluster southeast of the Park Row. Most of these tall buildings were between twelve and fifteen stories, but five of them were over seventeen stories in height. Located near the

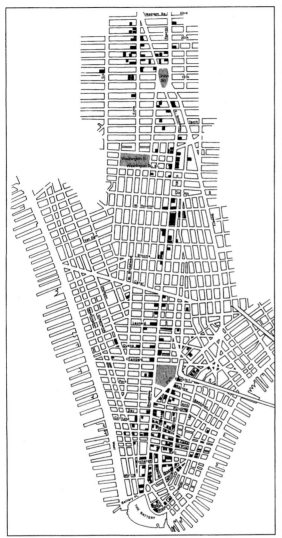 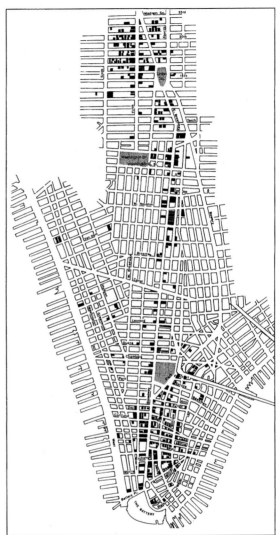

Map 6. Tall Buildings in Manhattan, 1902   Map 7. Tall Buildings in Manhattan, 1908

intersection of Broadway and Park Row were the thirty-story Park Row Building (the tallest in the city until 1906), the twenty-six-story St. Paul Building, and behind them on Nassau Street the twenty-two-story American Tract Society Building (fig. 36). On Broadway were several buildings ranging from seventeen to twenty stories in height.

The more than two hundred tall buildings that were located in Manhattan in 1902 created a profile markedly different from that of 1897. The cluster of tall buildings below City Hall Park became more dense, the height reached thirty stories, and the skeletal pattern up Broadway and over to Fifth Avenue was filled in and became a substantial backbone for the midtown skyscrapers. Development along Fifth Avenue was similar to that on Broadway—a linear pattern with breaks at the intersections with parks and squares. The tallest buildings in the city continued to be built on sites with high visibility, along the wide, well-traveled corridors and around open park areas.

Between 1902 and 1908, 166 skyscrapers were completed in Manhattan. This new construction was most visible north of Union Square, where tall buildings spread out from Fifth Avenue into the area between West 15th and West 23rd streets. The most significant development during this period was the dramatic increase in the size of these buildings. The tower of the Singer Building rose forty-one stories into the sky, making it the tallest building in the world in 1908, but only for one year until the Metropolitan tower was completed. The other office buildings over twenty-five stories that surrounded it provided New York with an unprecedented amount of office space.

Downtown, near Wall Street, twenty-six skyscrapers contributed to the density of tall buildings. Five buildings were taller than twenty stories, including the twenty-six-story building at 60 Wall Street and the twenty-five-story Wall Street Exchange Building. By 1908, then, the narrow streets in the area were lined with buildings over nine stories, with intersections marked by buildings of seventeen stories or more. Along lower Broadway twenty-one new skyscrapers were completed, with seven structures over nineteen stories. The Singer Building, the tallest building in the city, was among those seven buildings, as was the thirty-one-story City Investing Building. The skyscrapers completed near City Hall Park were dispersed throughout the area, and none surpassed the general twenty-five-story limit. Much of the space that could be used for display purposes already had skyscrapers built on it.

The cluster of skyscrapers along upper Broadway and Washington Square expanded north during this period and became more dense. The thirty-eight new buildings created a cluster on 10th and 11th streets between Fourth Avenue and East Broadway and filled in gaps along Broadway. None of these buildings exceeded twelve stories in height. Near Union Square, sixty-nine buildings were completed—the largest development during this period—accounting for more than forty percent of the total

Park Row, New York.

36. In 1902, the thirty-story, twin-towered Park Row Building (mid-foreground, with antenna) was the tallest in the city. Two other buildings complete the cluster of tall buildings—the twenty-six-story St. Paul Building (foreground) on the corner of Broadway and Park Row, and behind, the twenty-two-story American Tract Society Building.

skyscraper construction in the city. Only five of the buildings exceeded thirteen stories, but two of that five were twenty stories or more—the Bank of the Metropolis
Building on Union Square West and the Fuller or Flatiron Building, at the strategic
intersection of Broadway, 23rd Street, and Fifth Avenue (fig. 37). And under construction, on the northern edge of Madison Square, was what would make the building for a
time the tallest in the city: the fifty-story Metropolitan Life tower. Twenty blocks north,
at the intersection of Broadway and 42nd Street, the twenty-two-story Times Building
towered above the four- and five-story hotels and residences that surrounded it (fig. 38).

By 1908, 366 skyscrapers were located in lower Manhattan. These buildings formed
an impressive profile view and a readable spatial pattern—a dense cluster south of City
Hall Park, between Church and William streets, a linear pattern on Broadway north to
Union Square, and a midtown cluster focused around Fifth Avenue between 15th and
23rd streets. From both the New Jersey and Brooklyn shores, New York appeared as a
city of skyscrapers. The highest point of the fairly continuous profile that extended from
the Whitehall Building on Battery Place to the Flatiron Building at Madison Square was
the 612-foot domed tower of the Singer Building. Located on Broadway at Liberty Street,
the Singer Building, together with the thirty-two-story City Investing Building located
just to the north, served as the summit to the mountain range of New York's skyline.

This profile, which was to become the hallmark of the city, was the result of innumerable locational decisions that were based as much on site and potential for symbolic meaning as on the economic demands to profit from land. The basic linear pattern of tall buildings that characterized skyscraper locations along Broadway and Fifth
Avenue stands in contrast to the tightly clustered pattern around Wall Street. The skyscrapers in New York developed according to two locational logics: the first response,
to economic demands to be close to the point in the city that commanded the highest land rents, resulted in the tight dense pattern as characterized by the Wall Street
area and to some degree the lower Broadway area; the second response, to the
demand to be visible for promotional and expressive ends, resulted in loose clusters
around open areas and in a linear pattern on prominent and wide avenues, characterized by the pattern around City Hall Park and on Broadway (between Canal Street and
Madison Square) and Fifth Avenue. In practice, these two logics more than likely
worked together—decisions were made to locate, design, and build skyscrapers after
considerations of both symbolic needs and economic demands. In fact, often these
two demands were not separate—locating a skyscraper so that it could be seen meant
that it would be economically viable in the long term. But skyscrapers were not mere-
ly responses to land rents; they also fulfilled other needs of New York's upper classes.

37. Flatiron Building. Although originally called the Fuller Building, the shape of this building at the strategic intersection of Broadway, 23rd Street, and Fifth Avenue inspired the name "Flatiron." The distinctive shape and location of this building made it an icon for the new age of skyscrapers.

38. New York Times Building. The twenty-two-story building of the *New York Times*, located at 42nd Street, which was considered far uptown in 1903, towered above its neighboring structures. In this dramatic locational shift, the newspaper created an effective architectural statement and established the area as a new center of commercial activity.

The Commissioners

Individuals involved in the newspaper and life insurance industries were responsible for commissioning many of the first skyscrapers that were located for display
purposes.[18] The first industry to translate its promotional needs and notions of corporate imagery into tall structures was the newspaper industry. Daily newspapers
were a relatively new enterprise that relied on mass appeal to an urban audience, a
product of nineteenth-century American "city culture."[19] Also, the industry was dominated by a few strong magnates whose personalities were never opaque.[20] These
characteristics made the newspaper industry a likely exploiter of tall buildings. A
more detailed look at the history of the industry will clarify its relationship to the urban economy and the decisions of some of its practitioners to construct tall buildings.

A large and competitive market for daily newspapers of general interest developed almost immediately after the *New York Sun* began publishing in 1834. The
popularity of the metropolitan press was attributable to a new market created by
the urban masses' desire for identity. The metropolitan press pioneered journalistic
practices that satisfied people's needs for information about the bewildering place
they found themselves in, the other inhabitants, and themselves.[21] New York took the
lead, and by 1856, almost every New York family bought a daily newspaper.[22] The
national census of 1880 reported that the growth rate of the news industry was not
equaled by "any other phase of industrial development in the United States."[23]

Three of the six structures that constituted the first tall building cluster on Park
Row were directly associated with the newspaper industry. Park Row, which borders City Hall Park on the south, traditionally had been the site of the newspaper
industry in New York. Prior to the advent of mass communication systems like the
telephone and radio, an activity dependent on the rapid transmission of the news had
to be located near the sources of information. The newspaper industry, therefore,
was located between City Hall and the financial center at Wall Street. Park Row was
the most attractive location within this area because it fulfilled these spatial
demands and satisfied promotional and symbolic needs of the newspaper business.

The tallest structure in this first cluster of tall buildings was the Tribune Building.
The *New York Tribune* became a leading U.S. newspaper shortly after its inception in
1841.[24] It had occupied several different buildings near Park Row, but none gave such
obvious evidence of the achievements of the paper as the 1875 Tribune Building (fig.
39). The building was designed by Richard Morris Hunt in a style influenced by his
Parisian training, complete with mansard roofline and central tower.[25] It measured 260
feet from the sidewalk to the top of its iron and granite tower. In order to ensure the

association of the newspaper with the tall tower, the words "The Tribune" were cut into granite blocks on all four sides of the building at the top level. The tower with its spire clearly proclaimed the supremacy of the *Tribune* in the world of New York journalism.

As a pioneering structure, the Tribune Building provoked strong reaction. Most often, the building was heralded as an architectural marvel. The architectural critic Montgomery Schuyler commented, "The new Tribune Building was the wonder of New York that generation ago of which we were speaking…the wonder by reason of its altitude."[26] The author of an article entitled "The Palace-Building of the New York Tribune" called it "the most convenient and well-appointed edifice in the country."[27] The paper wasted no time in exploiting this attention. An advertising flyer used by the paper is graphic evidence of the promotional use of the new Tribune Building (fig. 40).

The success of the Tribune Building as advertisement and image maker inspired other newspapers to build tall. One of the most powerful statements of prestige was delivered by the home of Joseph Pulitzer's *New York World*, completed in 1889 on the corner of Park Row and Frankfort Street. Pulitzer had bought the paper in 1883 and changed the small press into an affordable and popular newspaper that had a record-breaking circulation of 250,000 by 1886.[28] Part of Pulitzer's successful formula was his switch to a sensational style of journalism and an expert handling of the visual possibilities of the newspaper through the use of large headlines, illustrations, and political cartoons. Therefore, when the *World* outgrew its old quarters on Park Row, Pulitzer was more than willing to spend the extra money necessary to make a visual impact and construct a building both finer and taller than the Tribune Building and the new Times Building, which had opened in 1888. The result was the sixteen-story World Building (fig. 41), designed by George Post in what could be referred to loosely as the French Baroque style. Post, who had studied under Hunt, was influenced by Hunt's Parisian training at the Ecole des Beaux-Arts.[29] The World Building towered six stories above any other building in the city, and its gold dome, topped by a flagpole, ensured the distinctiveness and dominance of the *World* on the New York skyline. Pulitzer made clear that he wanted his building to compare favorably to his competitors, and had written into George Post's contract a clause saying the building was to be at least as good as the Times Building:

> The finish of the building is something I know very little about. I want to be sure that no false economy or niggardliness will mar the building inside. I want the finish to be creditable at least, if no more, and first-class in every respect, as the contract with Post requires….How is the *Times* building finished? Have you ever been through it? Can anything be suggested by which our finish can be improved? You remember Post's contract requires it to be at least as good as that of the *Times*.[30]

THE NEW YORK TRIBUNE.

FOUNDED BY HORACE GREELEY.

THE BEST AMERICAN NEWSPAPER.

DAILY, $10 PER YEAR; SEMI-WEEKLY, $3 PER YEAR; WEEKLY, $1 PER YEAR.

THE NEW	TERMS OF
TRIBUNE BUILDING.	THE TRIBUNE.

ALL THE NEWS OF THE WORLD—FULL, FIRST AND INDEPENDENT.

THE TRIBUNE EXTRAS.

A LIBRARY FOR ONE DOLLAR.

THE TRIBUNE, New York.

Yet the prestige of creating the tallest structure in Manhattan was not sufficient for Pulitzer; he wanted his newspaper to be housed in a building that relayed a message more important than mere promotion. Pulitzer hoped that his World Building would serve as a monument to public service. The ninety-seven-page booklet published by the paper to celebrate the building's opening outlines more than forty acts of public service performed by the *World*, services that ranged from raising funds for the pedestal of the Statue of Liberty to helping to reform the debtor's law to providing free Christmas trees for poor children. According to this booklet, "The *World*, in a nutshell, is Public Service." In Pulitzer's message for opening day ceremonies, he made clear his intentions: "Let it ever be remembered that this edifice owes its existence to the public; that its architect is popular favor, that its moral corner-stone is love of liberty and justice, that its every stone comes from the people, and represents public approval for public services rendered."[31] With its classically inspired ornamented archways, columns, and pedestals, complete with four torchbearers representing Art, Literature, Science, and Invention, the World Building recalled the public structures of the nineteenth century and made it clear that the *World* was meant as a form of public "enlightenment." Thousands of New Yorkers came to the elaborate opening day ceremonies, and the building became a tourist attraction, with people riding the elevator to the top floor in order to view the

39. *(far left)* Richard Morris Hunt's Tribune Building, 1875, was considered an architectural marvel and symbolized the supremacy of the *New York Tribune* in the world of New York journalism. (*Frank Leslie's Illustrated Newspaper*, 1 May 1875)

40. *(left)* Advertising flyer for the *New York Tribune*. This promotional document gives clear evidence of the use of architecture as a symbol of business. In this case, the building's height is exaggerated in the visual image, leaving no doubt in the viewer's mind that the building was indeed the "highest on Manhattan Island." (Warshaw Collection of Business Americana, Archives Center, Museum of American History, Smithsonian Institution)

41. *(right)* The World Building. The sixteen-story building, designed by George Post for the *New York World* (owned by Joseph Pulitzer), was six stories taller than any other structure in the city when it was completed in 1889. Located along Park Row, the building was topped by a gold dome that assured its distinctiveness on the skyline. (Collection of the New-York Historical Society)

city from the highest vantage point. The World Building, therefore, succeeded as an advertisement to the mass market, as a monument to Pulitzer's success, and as a sign of the newspaper's legitimacy as a public institution. As was made clear in the pamphlet published by the *World*, the building was indeed the embodiment of Pulitzer's ideal— "along the illimitable lines of Progress *The World* must lead the van!"[32] The other leading newspapers joined the height competition, and their promotional motivations were only thinly disguised. As a commentator in *Scribner's* noted, "They [the newspaper buildings] rise, one above the other, in the humorous hope that the public will believe the length of their subscription lists is in proportion to the height of their towers."[33]

Newspapers exploited the tall building form for more than twenty years. In 1881, three of the four new tall buildings were directly or indirectly associated with newspapers. The Evening Post Building housed the newspaper founded by W. C. Bryant, the Morse Building was owned by R. C. and S. E. Morse, founders of *The Observer*, and the Bennett Building was built by James Bennett, the owner of the *New York Herald*. The three tallest buildings that were constructed over the next ten years were owned by newspapers—the Times and World buildings on Park Row, and the Mail and Express Building on Broadway.

Although all of these early tall buildings represented some type of innovation in building technology, they were consistently designed in the eclectic revival styles popular at the time. The urban entrepreneurs that commissioned them attempted to fit their symbols of commercial power into what they considered to be the current aesthetic dictates, in particular the Italian Renaissance style, in order to create symbols of power and impress what Barbara Rubin calls the "cultural elite."[34] For example, Joseph Pulitzer made very clear to George Post his intention that his new building be considered an architectural marvel. In its report of the opening of its new building, the *New York World* stated that Pulitzer had insisted that "the structure must be in every sense an architectural ornament to the metropolis; that it must be a magnificent business structure of the first order, embodying the very latest and best ideas in construction; that, to be worthy of the paper it housed, it must also be the best equipped newspaper edifice in existence."[35] Pulitzer was trying to legitimize his business by housing it in a structure that impressed the arbiters of good taste.[36] Yet these entrepreneurs also constructed buildings as a form of advertisement for the general public. To fulfill their first goal, they had their buildings designed as commercial palaces; to fulfill the second goal, they built tall, individualized structures. As is evident from the following review of the World Building in the *Record and Guide*, these two goals often conflicted:

But in a commercial building for a private owner who can tell whether the
obstacles to architectural success come from the alterations of the architects or

the freaks of the client?…It is not betraying anybody's secret to say that the dome is the obstacle to the architectural success of the World Building. The fact "jumps to the eyes" as the French have it, and it is fair to suppose that the client had imposed it.…But for thoughtful and refined design, one looks everywhere in vain, and the critic finds himself forced to follow the example of the designer—to "cuss the thing and quit it."[37]

The commercial impulse that led to individualized, tall buildings conflicted with correct aesthetic formulas. Yet the nouveaux riches did not have to forgo some of their commercial imperatives in order to please the cultural elite, not surprising in light of the fact that the cultural elite in New York were only one segment of a fairly heterogenetic and fragmented elite class. As Frederick Cople Jaher states, "New York, unlike Boston or Philadelphia, retained no single nineteenth-century group with the generalized hegemony necessary to form an upper-class structure; nor did any group in that city develop into an aristocracy by perpetuating a multifaceted urban leadership over several generations."[38] The very fact that skyscrapers developed without any checks on their spatial extent or height well into the twentieth century indicates that in New York the cultural elite had little, if any, political power. The impact of the cultural elite on skyscraper development seems to be limited to the design of the buildings, not to their form or location.

Despite their apparent failure as forms of cultural legitimacy, these early skyscrapers can be thought of as successful forms of recognition and display. As one commentator noted: "The commercial palaces grow more and more palatial with each decade. The little granite temples in which the banks of New York were housed forty years ago, and the iron sash frames which formed their façade twenty years ago, are alike giving way to buildings far larger and more luxurious, possessing, many of them, architectural individuality and interest."[39] The success of these early tall buildings as attention-getting devices seems to parallel their failure as signs of legitimacy, indicated by the dismissal of these buildings by New York cultural critics.

The life insurance industry took the place of newspapers as the leader in tall building construction.[40] Although built by newspapers, many of the first tall buildings housed insurance offices, and headquarters of insurance companies were located in the Bennett, Mills, and Potter buildings. By the 1890s, some of those companies decided to build their own tall structures, and more than twenty percent of the significantly tall buildings constructed between 1892 and 1896 were built by life insurance companies.[41] These included the American Surety, Home Life, Manhattan, Mutual Reserve, and New York Life insurance companies. Most of these buildings were located for functional and display purposes in the City Hall Park area, not in the Wall Street district, where other types of insurance companies were located.[42]

Like the newspapers, the life insurance industry was a product of nineteenth-century urban culture.[43] The period of extreme growth of the life insurance industry coincided with a time of massive immigration to American cities. These new arrivals, lacking family bonds and security, provided an untapped market for the industry. This new population, in combination with the more prosperous established urban dwellers who were willing to pay to insure their gains, explains the twelve thousand percent increase in the assets of the life insurance companies in the second half of the nineteenth century.[44]

With such wealth at stake, the competition among the leaders of the industry was fierce. The three leading companies—Mutual Life, Equitable Life, and New York Life—were continually striving for primacy. Unlike other insurance companies, however, the life insurance industry felt a need to justify itself beyond the chase for profits. The executives of the maturing life insurance companies shared an ideological commitment to public service. Equitable president James Alexander pinpointed that obligation: "Assuredly, an institution which exists for the benefit of widows and orphans…is one which ought not to be conducted on a low plane of competition."[45]

The industry built on this theme of social responsibility, identifying itself with missionary work and its leaders with prime ministers. This ideology of public service found appropriate expression in the home office buildings of the industry. Structures had to embody the tremendous economic power of the corporations and their newly found public stature. As a historian of the life insurance industry points out, "Men of great consciousness of place such as Hyde, McCurly, McCall, Dryden, and Hegeman [presidents of life insurance companies] looked for—and found in elaborate home offices—the sort of physical expression that their un-material business otherwise denied them." Investments in real estate and elaborate architectural forms fulfilled that need for material expression. For example, the entranceway of the classically inspired twelve-story annex of the New York Life Insurance Company was meant to resemble an ancient temple; it was, according to the company's historian, a "Temple of Humanity" (fig. 42).[46] *King's Handbook of New York*, a popular guide to the city, carefully documented all the life insurance companies and their home offices, with illustrations of the buildings and discussions of their design and height. An architectural competition for the new offices of the Home Life Insurance Company, a competition in "which the highest architectural talent was represented," resulted in a design by Napoleon LeBrun and Sons. The Italian Renaissance style building was fourteen stories tall, and, as the *Handbook* notes, the building was located where it could be seen: "In view of the most fortunate location of this building, fronting as it does on the City-Hall Park, it has the advantage of being so situated that its artistic merit is conspicuous, which is rarely the case on our city streets." The Mutual Reserve Fund Life Association Building on Broadway is a "masterpiece of architecture to its artistic aspect" and the nineteen-story Manhattan Life Insurance Building shades its "stately neighbors" as well as the "tall and graceful spire of Trinity Church" (fig. 43).[47]

The Metropolitan Life had been housed in three different structures in lower Manhattan before its move up to Madison Square. When the company began to outgrow its building at 32 Park Place, the president decided upon a new site for the expanded home offices—the corner of Madison Avenue and 23rd Street, facing Madison Square Park. In terms of real estate investment, the move was considered quite daring, because at the time Madison Square was known for its fashionable residences, not its business structures. In 1890, no office buildings were located north of 14th Street.[48] Napoleon LeBrun, who had renovated the company's building on Park Place, was commissioned to design the new Madison Square structure and created an eleven-story marble edifice that opened in 1893 (fig. 44).

When the Metropolitan Life Insurance Company moved into its new home at Madison Square in 1893, the structure was considered the most distinctive insurance building in New York. It "boasted a staircase inspired by the Paris opera, a president's office furnished at a cost of $90,000 and—by 1909—the famous tower then the tallest on earth" (fig. 45).[49] The Madison Avenue entrance led into a marble court with a vaulted ceiling three stories high.[50] Although the location was considered radical, the building itself was rather conservative in form and design. The structure was more akin to the Italian Renaissance style commercial palaces of the 1860s than the skyscrapers of the 1890s. Because the location of the building alone warranted attention, the company could choose a design that relayed a message more of culture than of commerce. *King's Handbook* noted the building as "a fine contribution to the architecture of the century, for which the Metropolitan Life-Insurance Company has the gratitude of all art-lovers. It covers one of the most conspicuous sites in the city, and its height makes it clearly visible across the whole of Madison Square, while its grandeur makes it a superb monument to the lovely park which it faces."[51]

By 1905, however, the company decided that it once again needed a new building, not only to house more workers, but also to continue to make an impact on the New York architectural scene. Metropolitan had grown enormously in the latter half of the 1890s, and in commissioning a new building the executives sought an appropriate material expression for their new economic power. The sons of the deceased Napoleon LeBrun were chosen as architects, and they designed a fifty-story tower to top the original eleven-story building (fig. 46). The completion of the tower in 1909 gave the Metropolitan Life Insurance Company the fame of having built the tallest structure on earth.

Apparently the idea of constructing a tower that would resemble the campanile of St. Mark's in Venice was initially that of the president of the company, John Hegeman. The final tower design included a clock that was visible more than a mile away, and, at the top, a beacon that Haley Fiske, the vice-president of the company, named "the light that never fails," a gesture that apparently was meant to compare the endurance and strength of the beacon with the company's new public stature.[52] A pamphlet published by the company after the tower's completion makes clear the symbolic intent: "High and lofty, like a great sentinel keeping watch over the millions of policy-holders and marking the fast-fleeting minutes of life, stands the Tower, its completion marking the culmination of this series of building operations which, commencing with the construction during the years 1890 to 1893 of the southwesterly section of the structure fronting on Madison Avenue, ended in 1909." The enormous hands of the clock (the minute hand is more than seventeen feet long, the hour hand more than thirteen feet) were illuminated at night and coordinated with the electric lantern at the top which, through a series of signals, flashed out the time.[53]

The image of the tower—with beams radiating out from its top, and, encircling the beams, the words "The Light That Never Fails," which became the logo for the company—appeared in advertising as well as public service pamphlets that it published.[54] The executives of the Metropolitan Life Insurance Company were very concerned with promoting the correct image for their business, an image that not only portrayed their economic power, but also conveyed a sense of their commitment to public ser-

42. *(opposite)* New York Life Insurance Company Building, 1906. Life insurance companies succeeded newspapers as the major investors in skyscrapers, creating such mammoth buildings as the home office of the New York Life Insurance Company. The company referred to the building as a "Temple of Humanity."

43. By the time the Manhattan Life Insurance Company moved into its offices on lower Broadway, the area was already taking on the character of steep canyons. This 1906 image of the building *(tallest in row)* depicts this canyon-like impression of lower Manhattan.

44. *(opposite, top)* Metropolitan Life Insurance Company Building, 1906. The decision by the company's executives to build their new home office at Madison Square was considered risky, since the area around Madison Square was occupied exclusively by fashionable residences.

45. *(opposite, bottom)* Interior of the Metropolitan Life Insurance Company Building. The entranceway to this building was complete with a vaulted ceiling three stories high, and marble arcades that led back from the entrance in background at right.

46. *(right)* Metropolitan Life Insurance Company Building. The addition of this fifty-story tower in 1909 gave the Metropolitan Life Insurance Company the distinction of having its home office in the tallest building in the city.

vice. A tower whose style harked back to the precapitalist, civic values of medieval Venice, and that was, in all aspects (even at night) quite prominent, served those purposes.

Like the newspaper industry, insurance companies were concerned with more than mere promotion; they also hoped their buildings would represent their cultural and civic status. As Barbara Rubin states, "The inventor-entrepreneur, on the other hand, despite his anarchic and individualistic approach to economic competition as manifested in his use of urban space in the late nineteenth century, entertained 'cultural' aspirations commensurate with his wealth."[55] The home offices of the life insurance industry were built as opulent displays of wealth, but also as symbols of civic virtues and common values; they were to convey a message of innovation in the business world, but also one of stability and security. These first tall buildings were attempts by this new economic class to fulfill two parallel goals—to find appropriate expression for their new power, and to legitimize that power by placing it within the constructs established by the more traditional elite.

By the turn of the century, as the technology for tall building construction advanced, the financial risks decreased and many construction firms and developers invested in skyscraper development.[56] Although the mammoth office structures built in lower Manhattan were not expressions of individual entrepreneurs, speculators continued to exploit the symbolism of height established by the first tall buildings. The real estate corporations that undertook these schemes assumed that the symbolic importance of height would induce professionals and corporate executives to pay a higher rent for a location in a tall office building, and they were eventually proven correct.

The pattern of tenancy of these new buildings reflected New York's changing economic position. New York's relative decline in manufacturing and trade near the end of the nineteenth century was more than compensated for by the increase in financial and professional service industries that concentrated in the city. By 1890, New York was the center for the offices of lawyers, engineers, and architects, as well as bankers and insurance sellers. In addition, New York had become the capital of American corporate headquarters. "By 1895 corporate offices were as disproportionately concentrated in the metropolitan region as were the banks and professionals. In that year Greater New York contained fully 298 mercantile and manufacturing firms worth more than one million dollars; Chicago, with a population about half as large, had only eighty-four, Philadelphia had sixty-nine, and Boston, sixty-four."[57] New York's economy experienced a shift in its work force from the productive to the nonproductive sectors. This large white-collar class occupied the offices of the speculative, new tall buildings. Yet the decision to locate in skyscrapers was based on the associations with height that had been established twenty years earlier. As the internal structure of business became increasingly more complex, and ownership became distanced from control, executives chose locations in tall buildings not as reflections of themselves or of their businesses, but because the symbolism of height with corporate power had become established in American society.

That symbolism had developed out of New York's particular socioeconomic context in the late nineteenth century. Because the elite class in New York was less cohesive than in other leading cities, the need for its new commercial powers to find appropriate physical expression was essential. For example, although Boston contained its share of ornamental skyscrapers, its cohesive and powerful elite class, which did not need this material expression of wealth, kept the height of those buildings in check and maintained an aesthetic climate that eschewed these symbols of unbridled commercialism.[58] By the latter half of the nineteenth century, Boston's elite were secure in their status. In addition, compared to New York, Boston was experiencing relatively little economic growth, and its position was set as a regional economic capital, rather than a national center. The city's economic competitiveness, therefore, did not fuel vertical expansion, nor did its elite class push their buildings skyward to create symbols of wealth and power. The only building in Boston of New York proportions and pretensions was the Mutual Life Insurance of New York Building, constructed at Post Office Square in 1875. The structure—a mansarded six-story classical revival building—was essentially no different from its neighbors, but it was topped by a clock-tower reminiscent of the Tribune Building in New York (fig. 47). The tower, with its iron flagstaff, contained a balcony from which the city and the harbor could be viewed. The New England Mutual Life Insurance Company Building of 1875 adjoined this structure but it had no tower, and the home offices of the John Hancock Company were kept within the general height levels of the business district.[59] Height restrictions were not enacted by the city until the 1890s, so this restraint was self-imposed. Boston's newspapers were located near the life insurance companies, further north and west on Washington and Milk streets. Although described as occupying "tall, costly, well-appointed buildings," the buildings of the *Transcript, Herald, Journal, Globe, Advertiser,* and *Record* did not compete in the height competitions that kept their New York counterparts so busy (fig. 48). The Globe Building, described as "one of the finest and largest in Boston," was a very simple eight-story structure, with little ornamentation or design initiative, except for a flagpole at the top, and an insignia of a globe inscribed over the doorway.[60] The Ames Building, completed in 1890 at the corner of Washington and Court streets, was twelve stories in height and was by far the tallest building in the city at the time. Yet instead of inspiring other tall structures, the building served as a warning to the city and was the main catalyst for the enactment of height limitations.

In contrast, New York's new entrepreneurs of the late nineteenth century, seeing an opportunity to express their commercial success, and a chance to lend an air of

47. Post Office Square, Boston. The towered Mutual Life Insurance Company Building is quite similar to the tower of New York's Tribune Building. However, the building did not set off a trend in tall building construction, as the Tribune Building did in New York.

legitimacy to that status, did not hesitate to build the tall structures that distressed the more staid elite classes. Writing in "Architectural Aberrations," a regular feature section of the journal *Architectural Record*, one commentator described Broadway as

> an architectural Babel, a confusion of tongues. The present development of it corresponds to the latest phase of immigration, as attested by the names on the signs, which still further variegate and vulgarize its architecture, and bespeak not only an Anglo-Saxon and a Celtic and a Teutonic but a Semitic and a Slavonic population. Indeed, it is the heterogeneousness of the part of Broadway of which we are speaking that makes this mile from Canal Street to 10th Street perhaps the most horrible stretch of architecture on the face of the earth. Everything has conspired to make it so, but most of all the facility which the steel frame has afforded of carrying buildings twice as high as it used to be possible to carry them.[61]

New York's skyscrapers related a clear message of the diversity and heterogeneity of New York's entrepreneurial class (fig. 49). Yet for many that message was unacceptable. In the next several decades, New Yorkers would wage a battle over who controlled the city's landscape—the culture critics or the business class. Ultimately, a new aesthetic that we now refer to as modernism, and a new vision of urban order called

48. Newspaper Row, Washington Street, Boston, 1889. As in New York, newspaper buildings clustered together, but they did not engage in a significant height and architectural competition. (Courtesy of the Bostonian Society/Old State House)

49. Skyline by night, New York City. By the first decade of the twentieth century, the skyline had become an important icon, symbolizing all the excesses and dynamism of the city.

the City Beautiful movement with its concomitant land use regulations such as the first zoning ordinances, would resolve the issue.[62] The corporate world that came to dominate New York's economy in the first decades of the twentieth century was not particularly concerned with symbols of personal or corporate status. Instead, it was interested in the built environment as a means of promoting a corporate image and facilitating the transportation and communication systems that were essential to its functions and profits. The new design and planning professions, imbued in the ideology of the City Beautiful movement, which favored utility and the rational ordering of space, found symbols of rampant rivalry inappropriate and unacceptable. But with the new corporate world, such symbols were no longer necessary. The age of unbridled competition that was symbolized by the skyline was slowly coming to an end, to be eclipsed by the modernist glass boxes of the corporate world.

4 Developing Boston's Back Bay

It is all very rich and prosperous and monotonous, the large lower level [the Back Bay]—
but oh, so inexpressibly vacant! A bourgeoisie without an aristocracy to worry it is, of
course, a very different thing from a bourgeoisie struggling in that shade, and nothing
could express more than these interminable prospects of security the condition of a community leading its life in the social sun.

—Henry James, *The American Scene* (1907)

Boston's refined Back Bay district, the upper-class enclave of the late nineteenth century, was not immune to the biting analysis of Henry James. Those "interminable
prospects of security" were indeed inhabited by Boston's bourgeoisie, a group that
not only did not have to struggle with an aristocracy, but had self-consciously made
itself into its own aristocracy. Compared to the rich and prosperous houses of New
York's Fifth Avenue, the Back Bay was monotonous. Its houses did not cry out for
individual attention but instead expressed group solidarity. Its "stately dwelling-houses"
and "magnificent squares," as contemporary commentators described them, were
meant to impress; they were, indeed, manifestly symbolic, conveying specific messages
to themselves, the city, and the nation.

In the only comprehensive study of the Back Bay, Bainbridge Bunting suggests the
nature of these messages: "In planning Commonwealth Avenue in 1856 as a great

boulevard and in constructing in the early sixties blocks of impressive brownstone mansions akin to those being built in Paris in the same years, Boston expressed her will to assume a place among the great cities of the world."[1] To be considered among the great cities of the world is a fairly high ambition for a city that ranked at best second in a country that barely was making its way out of the periphery of the western world. Bostonians, however, were able to create a district that, although small in size, impressed European visitors. Yet Bunting ignores some vital points here by focusing on the symbolism of the Back Bay within its national and international context, for the Back Bay is assuredly a statement meant for local consumption as well. It represented, both in the manipulation of the urban land market that made its development possible and in its planning and overtly symbolic design, the consolidated control of an elite class. In this sense, the story of the construction of the Back Bay reveals how the nature of Boston's social structure shaped the city's most extensive nineteenth-century land development, and how the resultant domestic enclave that was created actively represents the values of the elite group who controlled that social structure. I shall document the physical construction and development of the Back Bay before turning to an analysis of its design and the development process.

The Construction of the Back Bay

The Back Bay refers to the waters that lay to the west of the Boston peninsula until the middle of the nineteenth century, separating the city from the mainland, except for a narrow strip of land that connected the two, aptly called the Neck. In 1821 the Boston and Roxbury Mill Corporation constructed two dams: a long mill dam extending west of Beacon Street, separating the tides of the Charles River from what came to be called the Mill Pond, and another dam that ran perpendicular to the mill dam. This Cross Dam divided the Mill Pond into two fairly equal parts. The two bodies of water were kept at differing levels, allowing for water power to be generated at the Cross Dam, where a series of mills had been constructed.

By the 1840s, however, the stagnant enclosed waters of the Back Bay had become a noxious eyesore, and the city's department of health had deemed the Mill Pond and Dam unhealthy. The bay waters served not only as the city's dump site, but also as the end point of the city's common sewer. These smells and sights deterred development around the area, and the atmosphere was of particular concern to Boston's elite who lived on Beacon Hill. The Mount Vernon Proprietors, developers of most of the housing on Beacon Hill, had expanded their interests west along Beacon Street, building several granite houses along the north side of the street west of River Street.

In the 1840s, several other houses were built along Beacon Street opposite the Public Garden (see fig. 9). These houses were perilously close to the Mill Pond, and, unless something was done about the site, further elite expansion west was blocked (fig. 50).

Yet expansion west seemed the only possible solution for Boston's elite. The city districts to the east were of decreasing symbolic and economic importance. Much of the wealth of the upper class was based in towns outside of the city, while, at home, Boston's streets were becoming crowded with people of different ancestry and value systems. Even in the elite enclave of Beacon Hill, commercial activities were encroaching from the southeastern edge, and, on the north slopes, a working-class residential district was becoming more dense.[2] In addition, the "old" South End, the first elite enclave in the city, was facing encroachment from commercial activities. The elegant homes on the slopes of Fort Hill retained their air of propriety and wealth up to the mid-nineteenth century, yet the area was in sight of the docks and wharves along the water and, perhaps even worse, was dangerously close to the buildings that housed Irish immigrants.[3] Given these circumstances, it is not surprising that the Boston elite took the opportunity afforded by the possible development of a large area within the city proper to stake an undisputed claim for their own protected enclave.

The leaders of the Boston elite in the 1840s were men who had made their fortunes in the textile towns of Waltham, Lowell, and Lawrence, and they looked to the city not as a site of productive economic activity, but as a domestic and cultural retreat. Yet they had no distinctive landscape expression in the city. Both the "old" South End and Beacon Hill were, after all, primarily built for and associated with the previous generation of elite.[4] The Boston Associates, as this wealthy and powerful group of men who controlled the Lowell-Waltham system were called, wanted their own expression in the urban landscape, and the Back Bay provided the perfect opportunity. With elite residences already in place along the west end of Beacon Street, it seemed only natural that westward movement would continue and that the Back Bay would be filled to provide land for an elite enclave.

When completed, the filling of the Back Bay added 450 acres to the city's original 783 acres and effectively incorporated the city into the mainland.[5] Yet before the technical aspects of filling such a large expanse of water could be tackled, the more pressing concern of land disputes had to be settled. The land rights in the area were held by various institutions and individuals, including the Boston and Roxbury Mill Corporation, the Boston Water-Power Company, the city of Boston, and the Commonwealth of Massachusetts. In 1852, the state legislature appointed a body called the Commissioners on Boston Harbor and the Back Bay (in 1855 and after simply the Commissioners of the Back Bay) to resolve the land disputes. In 1856, the commissioners devised a scheme that divided the land three ways. The Boston

50. Beacon Hill and the construction of the Back Bay (*midground, left*), c. 1875. This photograph was taken looking west from the cupola of the State House. Arlington Street borders the far side of the Public Garden, and the beginning of Commonwealth Avenue can be seen running perpendicular to it. Beacon Street extends into the background, linking the city to the hills of Brookline, and dividing the waters of the Charles River (*right*) from the bay. (Courtesy of the Bostonian Society/Old State House)

and Roxbury Mill Corporation were deeded the rights to the water flats north of the Mill Dam, the commonwealth had rights over the area between Beacon Street to the north, Boylston Street to the south, and a line drawn irregularly between Exeter and Fairfield streets to the west. The Boston Water-Power Company was granted the rest of the Back Bay. The city was apparently considered uncooperative in the dealings, and was not granted any land rights.

This settlement cleared the way for filling the land granted to the common-wealth. And yet the state legislature was not willing to grant any funds for the actual filling procedures, which promised to be expensive because there was no local source of fill materials available. Much of Boston's land expansion throughout the eighteenth century had occurred through landfill taken from the hills of the city. By the mid-nineteenth century, however, those hills were already densely settled and could not be mined for landfill material. Fill for the Back Bay, then, would have to be found outside the city and brought in. The commissioners secured a contract with the firm of Munson and Gross, who would receive four blocks of land in exchange for filling the bay west to Clarendon Street.[6] The actual construction and develop-ment costs would be paid for by selling the house lots gradually, thus obtaining funds from one sale to be used to develop the next area.

The filling procedure, which lasted twenty years, was quite a technological feat. Railroad lines crossing the Back Bay brought in fill from Needham, nine miles away. The fill was obtained with the use of the newly invented steam shovel, and it was esti-mated that an entire train of thirty-five cars was filled in ten minutes.[7] Several of these trains were in use at one time, so that one train arrived at the Back Bay every forty-five minutes. At the peak of the process, it was estimated that two house lots were filled each day. By 1861, the original contract was completed, and the area was filled to Clarendon Street. The Boston Water-Power Company also contracted to fill its lands, and the district was completed by 1876.

Private Interests and Public Plans

The filling and subsequent development of the Back Bay proceeded mainly on public financing supported by the state. This, of course, had not always been the case in Boston. Most of the other filling procedures in the city, including that along the shoreline near Long Wharf, the original Mill Pond, and the Mill Dam across the Back Bay had been undertaken as commercial endeavors, although city officials and com-missioners were involved.[8] Yet the Back Bay development was different. The decision to develop the area as a public project was based partly on the difficulties of that process—involving complex legal battles over land ownership and expensive, time-consuming landfill procedures. Yet such a process could have been secured by private investors and speculators with strong incentives for development. Members of the Boston elite, who were looking to expand west from Beacon Hill, could have proceeded as a private body to buy up the land rights in the Back Bay, or do so in conjunction with the Boston and Roxbury Mill Corporation, and develop the area themselves. That the upper class chose not to let private interests shape the new district had as much to do with their outlook on society and economy as on the material realities of construction. To develop the area privately would have conflicted with their ideological concern to create a benevolent society and with their need to see themselves as public servants. The Commissioners of the Back Bay, the group appointed by the Massachusetts legislature to oversee the development process, summarized this position in their 1857 report:

> There are obvious advantages in the execution of this policy, at least in its preliminary stages, by the state rather than by private individuals. If the territory in the Back Bay were exclusively private property it might be "improved" in accordance with the dictates of a narrow-minded and short-sighted policy, which should seek to secure the most rapid return of money for the least original outlay, without regard to the higher considerations of permanent value and public welfare which the state is bound to cherish.[9]

Those "higher" considerations that were to benefit the city as a whole also benefited the Boston elite, which could secure its investments and contribute to civic "welfare" at the same time.

As a civic project funded with public monies, the Back Bay development was inherently political; it required conscious decision making in a public arena and therefore had to involve the confrontation and arbitration of conflicting interests. What were those interests, and how were they accommodated in the final decision?

Significant progress on the filling of the Bay was not made until the 1850s, and only in the late 1870s was the filling completed. In the intervening years, particularly prior to the construction of houses in the late 1850s, many plans for the area were conceived and rejected. All but one of the documented plans assumed that the main focus of the new area was to be residential—the variations in the plans concerned design issues, such as whether a body of water should be left in the district for scenic appeal.[10] The documented plan for the Back Bay that differed from the others envisioned a commercial focus for the area. This plan of 1850 suggested the use of the Back Bay area as an extended wet dock, such as those that existed in

London and Liverpool. The report by the commissioners investigating the issue makes quite clear how the interests represented by their scheme conflicted with others:

> The demand for land is, in a great degree, an individual demand,—the demand of companies engaged in speculations, while the demand for water is a demand of the public,—a demand of commerce,—in which the State and nation have a deep and vital interest. When such claims come in competition, that of the public should prevail....It may be some inconvenience to the merchant to reside out of the city,—but it would be a greater one to have his vessel compelled to anchor out of the harbor.[11]

The commissioners suggest here that the best use for the area would be as a wet dock for commercial ships. That "demand of commerce," they suggest, is at the heart of public interest. To fill the area and turn it into residences is seen as a private demand that will not help the city's commercial position.

The argument here, that the public is best served by promoting commerce, is one that was increasingly heard in Boston throughout the mid-nineteenth century. This 1850 scheme reflects the fear among Boston's merchant community concerning the commercial well-being of their city, as well as the apparent disregard with which the city's more established economic elite was viewing the city's relative mercantile decline. It also points to the schism between Boston's established elite, whose economic interests at this point focused on industrial endeavors, and merchants, whose interests were exclusively commercial. This new industrialist class and members of the old mercantile community who had joined the world of industry saw their city primarily as a financial center, and as a place of leisure and culture. Their industrial activities were kept outside the city borders, while their economic interests in the city proper focused on real estate opportunities. They therefore envisioned the Back Bay as a residential and cultural retreat whose rising land values would provide ample occasion for lucrative land speculations. In contrast, other less powerful merchants were interested in increasing the city's commercial capacities, and therefore envisioned the Back Bay as a potential wet dock area. The figures indicating the relative decline of Boston's share of coastal and international trading, as well as diversified manufacturing, are well documented and indicate the material conditions in which Boston's merchants found themselves.

As early as 1825, Boston merchants were recognizing the failure of their city to compete with the port of New York. It was argued, for example, that Boston needed to establish a packet line with Liverpool because merchants were sending their goods through New York instead of Boston: "Observing men have noticed a diminution of our shipments since the New York packets have been in operation, and they discern a rapid increase of exportations from that favoured city."[12] In 1860, the Boston Board of Trade contended that Boston was losing trade because of its lack of good transportation to the South, and it argued that a steamboat line to New Orleans would help Boston compete with other major cities for the southern trade: "In the rivalry between the principal Lines of Rail, inland, and of Steamers, on the sea-coast, we are daily losing some of our customers at the South and West, and retain others only by assurances of changes for the better, or, by submitting to the humility and expensive condition of delivery in New York, the goods purchased here, at our own charge of conveyance." It was clearly unsatisfactory for Boston's merchants and new industrialists to have to ship their goods to New York before having them conveyed to the South. So, the Board of Trade hoped to raise the money for these steamships by appealing to "retired capitalists" (referring, of course, to the Boston Associates) and owners of real estate. "We cannot but believe that the gentlemen who own our dwellings, warehouses, and wharves, and who are large stock-holders in our rail roads and factories, are quite as *much* interested, to say the very least, in preserving and in extending the business of this City, as are our merchants: and hence, our appeal to the retired capitalists, for help in the emergency."[13]

By 1860, however, the Boston Associates had little economic interest in the development of such trade networks. Indeed, their investments in transportation were strictly limited to rail lines that supported the Lowell-Waltham system. Investing their money in trade was considered not only risky and a poor investment, but also ideologically incorrect. Involvement in trade was considered too narrow, too focused on the small details of the economy, and too subject to its vagaries. It did not allow time to pursue other activities that were considered crucial to the legitimacy of a ruling elite—public service and philanthropy. Amos Lawrence, one of the wealthiest merchants and financiers in Boston, wrote in 1826 that the concerns of business were taking far too much of his time and emotional energy: "I now find myself so engrossed with its cares, as to occupy my thoughts, waking or sleeping, to a degree entirely disproportioned to its importance....Property acquired at such sacrifices as I have been obliged to make the past year costs more than its worth; and the anxiety of protecting it is the extreme of folly."[14] By 1830, both Amos and his brother Abbott had invested large sums of money in Lowell, and, by advising others of the safety of such an investment in industry, raised enough capital to organize three new manufacturing corporations there.[15] The Lawrences, and the many friends they encouraged to invest in Lowell, accumulated fortunes from their investments in the textile factories and from sale of the city's land and water power. Thirty years later, with their fortunes secure, the Boston Associates had neither need for nor interest in commerce. Investing in a steamship line to New Orleans was both unnecessary and superfluous to their new world view. Their interest in improving the city had shifted from economic investment to cultural enrichment.

Otis Clapp, a bookstore owner and civil servant, voiced the fear and frustration of Boston's merchants in reaction to the lack of concern by the Boston Associates.[16] In a letter that was published in 1853, Clapp addressed two of the most prominent members of the elite, Abbott Lawrence and Robert G. Shaw.[17] The issue at hand was why the Western Railroad had failed to secure the western trade, and Clapp was bold enough to suggest that this was due to the Boston elite's inflexibility in sticking to a policy that favored high profits for the few over smaller profits but increased volume of business for the many: "We are now reaping the fruits of the inflexible workings of this policy; a policy based upon the idea of doing a comparatively small amount of business at a large profit, instead of a large amount of business at a small profit. What but the workings of this policy has kept the commerce and growth of Boston nearly stationary for several years, while the other Atlantic cities are increasing with giant strides?"[18] That Clapp found it necessary to make this appeal publicly indicates the urgency that some of Boston's merchants felt regarding their economic future. As Dalzell has shown, the Boston Associates supported a policy that favored high freight rates, which made it exceedingly difficult for Boston's merchants to maintain a competitive edge.[19] That Clapp addressed the letter not to fellow merchants, or to the public at large, but to two members of the Boston elite, suggests that he put responsibility for the problem directly in their hands. Lawrence and Shaw and their associates had sufficient control over the city's economy to dictate economic policy.[20] Clapp also makes clear in the letter that he feels the public had been deceived into believing that the benefit of the few was somehow in their best interest. The public, he said, have been "mesmerized and impressed with its truth." Clapp therefore felt it his duty to make public what was happening to Boston's economy. It was this conflict in interests that was represented by the alternative scheme for the Back Bay. The new merchants were looking for a plan that promoted commercial, economic growth—the wet docks—benefiting the public at large, whereas the other proposal, for merchant residences, benefited only the few.

The possible plans for the Back Bay developed within this context of competition between two distinct economic groups with different visions of the future of Boston's growth, yet where one vision was clearly dominant. The city's established elite, led by the Boston Associates, were able to control the design and sale of the lands of the Back Bay, ensuring both monetary rewards and an exclusive domestic enclave for themselves. Much of that control was carried out by the commissioners of the Back Bay, who had close ties to the Boston Associates.[21] The immediate economic interests of the Associates are evident in their ownership of much of the prime real estate.[22] The established elite had a very strong economic and social stake in the development and construction of the Back Bay, and, since they effectively controlled those processes, there was little doubt that the area would fulfill their vision of an elite enclave. The plan for the wet docks was forgotten, apparently never having received much serious attention. The merchants representing this alternative scheme were not in a position to challenge Boston's elite seriously. By the mid-1850s, then, the commissioners decided that the Back Bay was to be developed as a public process instead of a private one, and that those to benefit would be Boston's established elite.

The Experience of Lowell

The notion of planning a completely new environment, and of making money from the control of real estate, was not foreign to the core members of Boston's elite, for they had a long history of planning new environments, beginning with the textile towns of Waltham and Lowell from about 1800 to 1820, and then Lawrence in the 1840s. Many of the Boston Associates had years of experience in large-scale real estate transactions that they put to use in Boston. Historian Robert Spalding has shown that after the Boston Associates' original fortunes were secured in textile production, their main source of income shifted to the control of real estate, water power, and machinery, particularly in Lowell.[23] They continued to draw large profits from their textile factories, but by the 1830s their commercial maneuverings were focused on buying and selling land and water rights along their canals and rail lines.

This savvy arrangement was accomplished by a rather complex business maneuver. During the planning and start-up of the new mills at Chelmsford (later called Lowell), the investors developed a scheme to separate control of the actual mill operations from its auxiliary needs—land, water power, and machine shops. The Waltham mills were funded through a joint-stock arrangement, where investors bought shares in the Boston Manufacturing Company, which ran the entire operation. The idea of setting up a new town, building and furnishing mills, and administering the water power was considered too complex, and the scale of undertaking too massive, for this simple stockholder arrangement. Patrick Tracy Jackson, one of the original Lowell investors, devised a plan whereby the Proprietors of the Locks and Canals of the Merrimack River, originally a navigation corporation, would take over from the Merrimack Company (the major mill company) control of its machine shop and all real estate and water power in Lowell. Stock in this new company was owned, by and large, by the proprietors of the Merrimack Company. This meant that any new enterprise opening in Lowell would have to negotiate with the owners of the Locks and Canals for land, water power, and machinery. Most of the financiers shifted their stock holdings from the manufacturing firms to the Locks and Canals, assuming that real estate, utilities, and equipment would be more lucrative. Unfortunately for the town of Lowell, the Associates' economic stake was not necessarily in its improved productive capacities, but rather in more and more companies locating there, because that expansion would fuel stock prices in the Locks and Canals.

In the long term, this led to overexpansion and overproduction and to disastrous drops in the prices of textiles, but in the short term, investment in the Locks and Canals was incredibly lucrative. The original 1821 purchasing price was $100 an acre in Lowell; in 1844, a lot in the center of town sold for $21,780, and another lot further away from town, $15,240. According to Spalding, the average annual return rate on stock in the Locks and Canals between 1825 and 1845 (when the company was liquidated) was 25 percent. For each $500 share of stock purchased in 1825, the total earnings were $3,004 in 1845. Spalding estimates that Nathan Appleton (a primary investor in Lowell and one of the wealthiest members of the Boston elite) made $124,210 on his investments, and that much of the Lowell family fortune was made by buying and selling this lucrative stock.[24] By the time the Back Bay was being considered for development, the Boston Associates had already shifted much of their attention away from mercantile and even industrial endeavors and had turned to investing in and controlling real estate.

Creating industrial complexes in Lowell, Waltham, and Lawrence also gave the Boston Associates familiarity with the mechanics of developing a new environment in a way that ensured continued economic gain. These towns were designed for a specific purpose—to produce cotton textiles—and, in each town, distinctions of social status and the separation of economic functions were expressed clearly in the developers' respective overall plans and architectural designs. In Lowell, large sections of land along the canals were designated for each of the manufacturing plants, and then subdivided into factory areas, housing for skilled and unskilled labor, and a separate residential area for the managers.[25] Ideals of social order were made manifest in these designs, where each class of persons and economic functions had a clearly prescribed place. This spatial segregation was essential for stable land values and profitable real estate ventures.

Spatial segregation was used in the design of the Back Bay, for the Boston Associates must have known that, to insure their real estate investments, the Back Bay had to be a planned and orderly environment, with separate commercial and residential districts. Unlike Lowell, Boston was not neatly segregated into distinct areas, and the threat from a mingling of classes and from residential and commercial mixture was evident. The old elite enclaves of Beacon Hill and the "old" South End were being encroached upon by commercial interests, and invaded by lower-class housing. The Back Bay development, then, promised to be one of the few opportunities to plan and control a residential enclave for the elite in the city of Boston.

The Design of the Back Bay

The design of the Back Bay was the result of a series of plans that had evolved over time. The original vision by architect Arthur Gilman centered on a major boulevard that was to serve as the focus of a series of residential streets laid out in a grid pattern. That vision was maintained, although the actual surveying and the problems of fitting the street network into the existing pattern meant that Gilman's ideas were modified and altered. The commissioners that were selected each year from 1852 onward, originally to organize and monitor the complex legal decisions regarding land ownership, took on a much larger degree of control over the actual plan of the area in the 1860s and 1870s. The final gridded residential plan centered on Commonwealth Avenue, which connected the new area to the Common and Public Garden (fig. 51). Architectural historian Bainbridge Bunting has pointed out that the final plan was based on Haussmann's plan for Paris, where the attention was drawn to long boulevards, instead of the English model of small enclosed residential squares from the Georgian period. The design for the Back Bay centered on a long, impressively wide avenue, flanked by rows of uniform housing blocks. The Parisian model of boulevards, however, was based more on the Baroque notion of a star-shaped pattern than a grid pattern, with boulevards serving as major thoroughfares bisecting the city. Boston's Back Bay was designed as an elite enclave, and Commonwealth Avenue was meant as its centerpiece, not as a major thoroughfare. The new French style, brought to Boston by several architects trained in Paris, had more of an influence on the eventual look of the district, particularly in terms of the housing styles.[26]

Evidence suggests that Gilman's plan for the Back Bay was based on English precedents. Gilman apparently formulated the plan while on a visit to England, where he was shown around the city of London by several of its more famous architects.[27] Much of the new development in London at the time was in the West End, particularly in Bayswater (north of Hyde Park) and Kensington (south and west of the park). These areas were not laid out in small, enclosed squares, but rather were designed around grand boulevards. The most imposing boulevard in Bayswater was Westbourne Terrace.[28] Although no definite proof exists, it seems likely that Gilman toured these new areas of the city. At the time of his tour in 1844, Westbourne Terrace led from a park (Hyde Park) out toward land not yet developed. It was intersected by a series of parallel streets, creating an overall gridlike pattern similar to the plan for the Back Bay. What

51. Bird's-eye view of Boston, 1870. The grid plan of the Back Bay used Commonwealth Avenue as its main axis. The Back Bay development bordered the Public Garden and Common, providing both a playground for the elite living in the area and a buffer from the commercial areas of the city. (Courtesy of the Trustees of the Boston Public Library)

is of particular interest about Westbourne Terrace is its width and the central, tree-lined promenade that runs down its center, surrounded by the smaller passageways in front of the homes. A similar central promenade forms the focus of Commonwealth Avenue (fig. 52). Given the general cultural climate in Boston, and the direct emulation of London's fashions and literary tastes by the Boston elite, it seems likely that the layout of the Back Bay was fashioned after the model of the new West End in London.

This style seemed particularly appropriate for Boston. The scale and sense of grandeur of the boulevards of London and Paris must have appealed to Boston's elite. The boulevards acted as material forms for group representation—arenas for display of civic power and group wealth. The Champs-Elysées, for example, with its Arc de Triomphe, was a monument to national power and civic institutions, at the same time that it symbolized elite control over the city and its inhabitants.[29] Such a double meaning was apparent in the Back Bay's design.

Commonwealth Avenue was designed to be the grand boulevard, uniting the heart of the city, the Common, with the Back Bay and surrounding suburban areas. The house lots along its eastern end were the first sold in the district, and, if land prices are any indication, the most prestigious. Most of these houses were designed in the French Second Empire style, with mansard roofs all of an even height (fig. 53). The stylistic conformity was the result of both legal restrictions on land use and the dictates of the changing aesthetic climate. Bainbridge Bunting has outlined the sequence of styles that characterized the houses of the Back Bay, including styles influenced by the Beaux Arts tradition and other, less discrete Victorian styles like the Gothic and Romanesque Revival. Many houses were designed in the Federal Revival style, recalling the era of Boston's mercantile glory nearly a century earlier.[30] But because of the land use restrictions and the similar lot sizes, most of the houses followed several simple floor plans.

This conformity presented an image of stability and solidity, emphasized by the rigid layout of the street and lawn areas. Each house on the avenue opened up to the tree-lined grassway as a common front yard, just as the whole district opened up to the Public Garden and the Common. These public areas of the city served as the entranceway to the Back Bay and were incorporated into the district, where strollers on Commonwealth Avenue could walk, greeting their friends and business colleagues on their way to their offices or while playing with their children. The prohibitions and ordinances that regulated Back Bay development were established to create a district that was safe from commercial encroachment, that presented a culture and civic-minded image, and that secured the elite's investments. The original plan called for a width of the street and grassway that would leave one hundred and seventy feet between houses. The written decision by the commissioners to extend the width of Commonwealth Avenue and the grassway in 1857 made many of these motivations clear:

52. Commonwealth Avenue, looking east from Dartmouth Street, c. 1880. Commonwealth Avenue was designed as the grand boulevard of the Back Bay, with a distinctive tree-lined promenade that ran down the center. The stylistic conformity of the houses along the avenue reflected the stability of Boston's elite class. (Courtesy of the Boston Public Library Print Department)

53. Houses on Commonwealth Avenue, 1990. Many houses in the Back Bay were designed in the Federal Revival style, a fairly conservative style that harked back to Boston's mercantile days a century earlier.

We were convinced that this feature would make this territory attractive and
desirable as a place of residence, to an extent, which, in the first place, would
enhance the prices of the lands, and facilitate sales; and in the second place,
would confer a lasting and permanent benefit upon the public by providing a
broad and ornamental avenue connecting the Common and public garden in
Boston with the picturesque and pleasing suburban territory.[31]

Commonwealth Avenue was a symbol of the grandeur of Boston, but a grandeur
based on the control of a small elite; it was a sign of civic improvement that was also
supposed to make money for the state; it was to serve the public, but in reality was
only meant for a small portion of that public. And, of course, the avenue would
make Boston famous as a city of refined taste (fig. 54). If New York was famous as
the economic capital, Boston could stake its claim as the cultural capital. Guidebooks
and promotional material on the city made it clear that the Back Bay was meant to
express the "higher" culture of the city: "Probably there is no city neighborhood in

54. Commonwealth Avenue, looking east, c. 1885. Commonwealth Avenue was the architectural showpiece for the city and a symbol of the refined lifestyle of Boston's elite classes.

this country wherein are more exquisite collections of those trifles of art and taste which bespeak a higher order of civilization and thorough cultivation than to be found in this section—the Belgravia of the 'hub,' the center of its fashion and splendor, the home of its merchant princes."[32] And Commonwealth Avenue was easily recognized as the center of this ornamental district:

> Commonwealth Avenue, especially, presents an unbroken array of splendid dwellings and noble churches, with here and there a hotel, and many of the structures in this long line of costly domiciles possess marked beauty of architectural design and are built in massive blocks, chiefly of brown stone. To describe in detail the many objects of interest to be seen on this avenue would require more space than we have at command. It may be appropriately remarked in this connection that an inquisitive visitor should, on taking a stroll through the Back Bay, be accompanied by a herald, a mercantile register, an elite directory, and a wise old club man with his stores of personal and family gossip.[33]

The commentator was accurate in his portrayal of the Back Bay as the elite enclave. A study of fifty randomly chosen house lots on Commonwealth Avenue in 1900 found that forty of the fifty resident families were listed on the Social Register, and that those forty belonged essentially to the same clubs and the same churches.[34] In addition, seventeen of the fifty families had members who had attended Harvard— usually the undergraduate college, but also the medical college and law school. That this fairly consolidated and stable elite class inhabited the central avenue of the Back Bay was apparent from the area's design and reputation.

The design of the area, focused on Commonwealth Avenue, served the elite's dual purpose. It set the elite off from the commercial city—the grid pattern was in visible distinction to the organic maze of streets in the older portions of the city, and the Common acted as an effective barrier—while enabling them to remain close enough to the downtown to exercise control. The elite did not flee the central portion of the city en masse, as the upper class in most cities was doing at the time. Instead, just as they kept their textile mills at a distance, they kept the commercial city, with its noise and turbulence, and the lower classes, far enough away not to disturb them, but close enough to maintain control.[35] In this way, they were able to maintain a strong presence in the city, without giving up any of the amenities of a domestic refuge.

Speculation on land in the district was originally kept to a minimum by the Back Bay commissioners who controlled sales. Lots were sold by public auction as the land was filled and was deemed ready for development. But during times of economic slumps, when it became apparent that decent prices could not be obtained for the lots, they were held back from sale. The commissioners' report of 1865 makes this clear: "It has not been the policy of the Commonwealth to encourage a speculative demand for lands in the Back Bay, but rather to maintain permanent and substantial improvements. The Commissioners have not, therefore, attempted to force the sale of these lands, but have put into market a quantity deemed sufficient to meet the expenses of filling and improvement for the current year."[36] This argument was used frequently in subsequent years to control speculative bidding for Back Bay land, thereby insuring an "orderly" pattern of growth in the district.[37]

The Back Bay Commissioners established strict controls over the use and design of the area, formulating policies that presaged twentieth-century zoning legislation.[38] According to Bunting, property restrictions that were written into the deeds included strictures that prohibited any manufacturing in the area, limited the types and locations of commercial activities that were allowed, and guaranteed uniform heights for the buildings.[39] In addition, the terms of sale for the first lots to be sold guaranteed that the houses would be "first-class" dwellings without stables, that they would be set back from the street twenty-two feet, that there would be a sixteen-foot wide passageway at the rear of the dwelling, and that the cellars would not be lower than four feet below the level of the Mill Dam.[40] These conditions ensured the homogeneity of the area and protected land values.

As part of the mid-nineteenth-century aesthetic milieu, the designers of the Back Bay interspersed residences with park areas containing ornamental shrubbery and trees.[41] Altogether, the Commonwealth of Massachusetts set aside forty-three percent of the area for streets and parks.[42] The Public Garden was given due consideration as an area for horticultural display, at one point containing even a botanical garden (see chapter 5).[43]

Land was reserved for the construction of public and educational institutions, thereby adding the desired element of cultural fulfillment to the list of amenities that the Back Bay could offer. Yet this was not part of the original plan and was adopted only after a group of petitioners representing such institutions of "science and art" as the Natural History Society and Horticultural Society informed the legislature of the approximate amount of money the commonwealth would make on the higher cost of land bordering the space reserved for public use. "In other words, on these conditions the sales of the adjacent lots would not only re-imburse the state for the land reserved, but would add to the public treasury nearly $80,000."[44] The legislature was convinced and in 1861 set aside several areas for public use, the first of which was a square bordered by Berkeley, Clarendon, Boylston, and Newbury streets, and, later, a triangular area that was to become Copley Square (fig. 55). The Back Bay Commissioners reported in 1863 that the value of lands opposite the first building of the Massachusetts Institute of

55. Copley Square looking east, 1889. The cultural center of the Back Bay, this area was set aside by the state legislature for public use. In the foreground is the construction site of the Boston Public Library, with Trinity Church located just across the triangular lot. (Courtesy of the Bostonian Society/Old State House)

56. Boylston Street, junction of Huntington Avenue and Clarendon Street, 1877. The first movement of public buildings into the Back Bay is evident in this image, depicting the Rogers Building of the Massachusetts Institute of Technology, in the large building in the center, and just to its right, the Boston Museum of Natural History. The Back Bay Commissioners figured that these buildings had doubled the value of the land opposite them. (Courtesy of the Bostonian Society/Old State House)

57. Beacon Street, looking east, 1883. The mansard roofs of many of the houses in the Back Bay indicate the French influence in the design of the area. Beacon Street is fairly characteristic of the area and conveys the stability and propriety that the district was meant to represent. (Courtesy of the Bostonian Society/Old State House)

Technology and the Natural History Museum had already doubled, providing proof of the economic viability of using some of the Back Bay lands for cultural institutions (fig. 56).[45]

These decisions created a residential enclave that, on the one hand, was a secure investment, and, on the other hand, embodied the Boston elite's vision of a benevolent society (fig. 57). These two goals were far from contradictory. As with their plans for the creation of Lowell, the Boston Associates devised a system whereby they could insure economic return and create a cultural experiment at the same time. Both in its two-dimensional plan and three-dimensional form, the Back Bay district embodied the elite's ideological views and reinforced their imperatives. They legitimized the construction and development of the area just as they had their economic control of the city—by aligning their private interests with those of the public. Using culture to justify the checks on unlimited growth, they successfully proscribed speculative development of the district. And the homogeneous, discrete, and ornamental environment that they created was an unambiguous statement to the city, and to outsiders, of their ideological commitment to culture and commerce. Boston's elite simultaneously secured its investments and created a cultural heritage.

In contrast to the Victorian styles that dominated the rest of the country, particularly New York City, the discreet style of the Back Bay homes was a direct expression of the city's stable and conservative elite class. As Bainbridge Bunting states:

> Without question life in Boston had less of the willful, noisy, self-assertive vigor
> that one finds elsewhere in the country. In architectural terms this quality is
> demonstrated by the houses of the Back Bay. Compared to the energetic but
> sometimes splendid monstrosities produced by Victorian builders in other parts
> of America during the last half of the century, the architecture of polite Boston
> is remarkably discreet. Among the fifteen hundred houses constructed in the
> Back Bay district, there are not more than a half a dozen "shockers."[46]

New York's elite residential district on Fifth Avenue was anything but discreet. In contrast to the planned community of Boston's Back Bay, the development of Fifth Avenue as a residential district was governed strictly by the forces of the land market. The grid pattern, which had dictated New York's spatial growth since the 1811 Randall Plan, was in no way altered to accommodate an alternative urban vision. The grid had proven an economical and practical way to divide and develop land and was never seriously challenged by alternative conceptions of urban space. New York's spatial expansion was controlled by real estate speculators, not public officials or planners. In effect, Fifth Avenue was not a district in the same sense as the Back Bay, but was simply the extension of the elite movement north out of the central business district that had begun in the 1820s (see chapter 1). The decisions that led to the development of the district were private, not public; individuals chose to live in the area based on their wealth and social standing. Although private decisions were certainly involved in the movement to the Back Bay, the district had been shaped by the political decisions of a controlling body. While Boston's elite was able to control the shape of the city, New York's was far too splintered for such a coordinated effort.

The lack of controls in New York and the effects of private decision making are evident in the architecture of the Fifth Avenue mansions. The architects, including George Post, Stephen Hatch, and Richard Morris Hunt, used the latest eclectic styles to decorate their masterpieces and no ordinances stood in the way of expressing their egos or those of their clients. As a result, the Fifth Avenue streetscape was one of disorder, with buildings of different shapes and sizes intermingled. The houses of, for example, William H. Vanderbilt and his sons Cornelius and William K. on Fifth Avenue were each designed in different European Revival styles (fig. 58). John Snook designed two brownstone mansions at 51st Street for William H. and his daughters, Richard Morris Hunt was responsible for William K. Vanderbilt's French Renaissance mansion at 52nd Street, and George Post designed the French chateau for Cornelius at 57th Street.

Boston's conservative architecture directly contrasted with the spirit that invaded New York, where architects emphasized the ostentatious expression of wealth and luxury. The Back Bay had some of the finest urban residential buildings in the country, designed by such architects as Arthur Gilman and John Sturgis and the architectural teams of Peabody and Stearns and McKim, Mead, and White.[47] The area's homogeneity and continuity of style presents the "most significant surviving example of Victorian architecture and planning in the country."[48] Although several examples of the chateau style were constructed in the district, they constituted the exception, not the rule. Bunting points out that these exceptions illustrate that New York's "idea of magnificence" had little effect on Boston.[49]

This contrast in both the two-dimensional pattern and three-dimensional form of the Back Bay and Fifth Avenue can be understood in its relation to each city's social structure. Boston's elite class had enough political clout to dictate its version of culture in the form of a planned residential enclave. Those plans effectively prohibited commercial land use, thereby insulating the area from the undesirable effects of business expansion and allowing the area to remain exclusive and residential. As a unified and stable social group, Boston's elite did not need to use housing ornamentation as an outward sign of individual status. The fragmented elite class of New York did not have enough consolidated power to control urban design, and, as an unstable group, used housing to display economic status. Yet the two elite classes were not completely different in their intentions. Both elite classes benefited from investments in their housing as real estate, but in Boston that money was made by keeping the land values of the Back Bay consistently high,

58. The Vanderbilt mansions, Fifth Avenue, c. 1884. Individual architectural statements were more characteristic of New York than Boston. Here, the eclectic revival styles of the Victorian period are evident in the homes of the Vanderbilts, which occupied an entire block along Fifth Avenue.

whereas in New York fortunes were made by speculating on new land developments. And, in the end, many of the houses built in the later years of the Back Bay development look surprisingly similar to New York's brownstones of the Upper West Side and East Side.

The Completion of the Back Bay

H. G. Wells wrote of Boston in 1906: "The capacity of Boston, it would seem, was just sufficient but no more than sufficient, to comprehend the whole achievement of the human intellect up, let us say, to the year 1875 A.D. Then an equilibrium was established. At or about that year Boston filled up."[50] The year 1875 witnessed the filling up not only of the Boston mind, but literally of its land—that date represents a midpoint in the construction of the houses of the Back Bay after the landfill procedures had been completed.[51] And, in many ways, the Back Bay represents this "filling up" of Boston, this closing of the Boston mind. In its enclaved, ordered form, the Back Bay represents the failure of the Boston elite to create what they considered a responsible society. Despite the rhetoric of public service, the Back Bay was not very different from the upper-class enclaves built in other cities—it served as an elite residential retreat from an emerging industrial downtown.

The life of Abbott Lawrence and his relationship to the Back Bay illustrates this point. Abbott Lawrence entered the Boston economic scene as a parvenu—his older brother Amos had come to Boston from Groton in 1807 to make his way as a dry goods merchant. After some early success, Amos sent for Abbott to join his firm in Boston. Together, they made a formidable team and benefited from clever business transactions. For example, Amos sent Abbott to England as soon as the War of 1812 was over, and Abbott returned to Boston in a record eighty-four days with plenty of English textiles that were sold off at enormous profits.[52] Their wealth accumulated, but money alone could not make them part of Boston's social elite, which consisted of a small group of people whose fortunes had been made on long-distance trade—so mere merchants were not considered worthy of the honor that accrued to those whose wealth had been made in the "noble" enterprise of shipping. Yet the amount of capital the Lawrence brothers had accumulated was difficult to ignore, particularly in times of economic downturn, when even the established elite class needed financing. The Lawrences began to invest their money in real estate and to lend it to troubled manufacturing firms. Soon they were allowed into some of the institutions controlled by the Boston elite, particularly after Nathan Appleton, one of the group's main gatekeepers, saw in the Lawrences a source of capital. Amos and Abbott were co-founders of the Suffolk Bank in 1818, which was to become the central bank of New England and the main supplier of capital to the Lowell-Waltham system, and were prominent stock-holders in the Massachusetts Hospital Life Insurance Company, which acted primarily as an investment house for the Boston Associates.[53] But the Lawrences were not members of the textile-owning elite. They had invested in small manufacturing plants, but it was not until the Lowell proprietors needed a way to finance their expansion in the late 1820s that Lawrence money was allowed into the closely knit circles of Boston's aristocracy. The Lawrences set up three new manufacturing enterprises at Lowell, as well as being allowed to purchase stocks in the Locks and Canals.[54]

Their money opened the doors not only to new investments, but also to a new social class. Abbott took the appropriate step by marrying Katherine Bigelow, the daughter of a member of the established elite, and spent much of his energies in politics, serving as a congressman and, later, as ambassador to England. But his influence went much further than that, for he used his money to exert considerable influence on politicians and political issues.[55] His philanthropic efforts were much heralded, in particular his large contributions to Harvard to establish a scientific school.[56] To perfect his pedigree, he became partners with William Appleton in a firm involved in the China trade, thereby linking him with the seagoing ancestors of Boston's established elite. As Josephson comments, "Not only were these ventures at sea profitable, but they gave Lawrence a social cachet in Boston merchant circles which all his other successes had failed to obtain."[57]

Abbott and his brother also took great interest in urban real estate, and although all of those interests were pecuniary, it was only after Abbott had been granted status in elite circles that his position concerning the development of the city of Boston was aligned to theirs. For example, in 1824, Abbott was involved in a project to construct some buildings on the lower end of Boston Common. As he wrote to his brother Amos, however, that project was rejected by the city's aristocracy:

> The question upon the subject of building at the bottom of the common has been submitted to a Committee of twenty-five to report—I do not think anything will be done, as Mr. Clough and Orator Adams are both opposed to it—their opposition with those of their peculiar feelings, together with what has been called the Aristocracy of the town will without doubt stifle this speculation in embryo—all seem to agree who are opposed to building upon it, that the best move that can be adopted will be to fill the Marsh and make an elegant lawn or Park of the whole.[58]

He also had invested in the Roxbury and Boston Mill Dam Company, a company that was responsible for noxious industrial activity close to the Common and Beacon Hill. But with his acceptance into the aristocracy, Abbott's real estate investments became more outwardly conservative. In 1831, he wrote to Amos that he was looking for a new house, preferably one near the Common.[59] In 1835 he purchased 8 Park Street, originally part of a row of homes designed by Charles Bulfinch, and previously owned by Jonathan Amory, Jr., a member of the "aristocracy."[60] With an aristocratic wife, and a home bordering the Common, just half a block from the State House, Abbott Lawrence had made it into the inner circles of power. His home was described by a contemporary commentator as "adorned with finished taste, no vulgar display of overloaded magnificence, but that subdued elegance and exquisite attention to comfort which the most refined of French authors describes as the chief attractions of luxury; books and sculpture are here the constant every day companions of the dwellers in those pleasant halls; and every domestic arrangement is faultless."[61]

As a full member of the Boston elite, Abbott made sure that his children's marriages solidified his social standing. Three of his children (Abbott, James, and Katherine) married into old Boston families that had become firmly established as cultural sponsors and public servants. And Abbott Lawrence the younger, after spending time in London in a post arranged by his father, returned home and moved into his new dwelling on Commonwealth Avenue. According to the catalogue of land sales, the Lawrence family owned several valuable lots in the Back Bay, not only on Commonwealth Avenue, but also on Marlborough Street and Beacon Street.[62] The symbolism of such a statement was clear—the Lawrence family was itself part of the aristocracy.

And yet this class that Lawrence and his family had so successfully joined now closed itself off from any new blood. Having consolidated its wealth and power, the mid-nineteenth-century Boston elite turned inward. As Jaher has shown, after the Civil War, the Boston industrial elite suffered from a lack of leadership and business acumen. Their conservative business practices, tied to the maintenance of trust funds, did not serve them well in a rapidly expanding and changing economy. And the Lowell-Waltham system that had furnished their economic base had gone into a long-term decline. Jaher suggests that this elite class failed to regenerate its textile industries for two reasons: "It no longer admitted self-made men or developed and dominated emerging enterprises."[63] The post–Civil War elite did not reach out to the late nineteenth-century equivalent of Abbott Lawrence—those who had new capital and ideas to invest. In effect, the controlling class closed itself off from the new economic realities.

Local political power ebbed along with this relative economic decline, and, by the 1880s, the first Irish Democrat was elected mayor.[64] And in national politics the Associates' influence waned, although the group did produce several prominent politicians, including Henry Cabot Lodge. But coincident with this decline of commercial and political power was a turn to culture and style. Jaher observes of the elite at this time, "No longer able to dominate the corporation or the government, it still rules the muse-

um, the academy, the dinner table, and the club."[65] And so the Boston Associates retreated into the world of culture and art, dictating the manners and morals of Boston's social
world, but no longer able to control its economy or government. And through the chan-
nels of culture, the elite were able to express their distaste for the new industrialists,
using, for example, the *North American Review* as a device to attack the vulgarity of
the new Republicans and all those who participated in coalition and party politics.

This cultural hegemony, so well symbolized in the orderly and homogenous Back
Bay, continued as a powerful force throughout the latter half of the nineteenth century. Eben Jordan, co-founder of the city's largest department store, tried desperately to
legitimize his wealth and join the Boston elite by investing in the city's culture enterprises. Jordan founded the New England Conservatory of Music, while his son donated
the money for a new auditorium to the Conservatory and paid for the construction of
the Boston Opera House and its operating costs.[66] Jordan participated in the cultural
world established by the old Boston elite in order to try to fit in, and yet he was never
successful. He, and the many other parvenu merchants and industrialists who may have
tried to fit cultural norms, were nevertheless kept out of the elite—at this point closed
to anyone without the right pedigree. Yet while the elite controlled the cultural scene,
they had lost control of the real power in the city. Jordan owned large chunks of Boston
real estate, and invested heavily in the Back Bay, owning in the 1870s entire blocks along
Marlborough and Beacon between Dartmouth and Fairfield streets.[67] He was able to do
this because the controls on land speculation that the Back Bay Commissioners had
instituted lasted only until the end of the 1860s—after that, speculation in the Back Bay
was rampant. Jordan was happy to invest in the lucrative Back Bay, putting his money
behind the safe walls of the modestly designed homes, and taking advantage of the land
use restrictions devised originally by the Boston Associates. So, even within the Back
Bay, behind the discreet façades symbolizing the culture of Boston, the city's parvenus
manipulated the land market just as the Boston Associates had before them.

The espoused values of the Boston elite involved a commitment to create a moral
society, one that provided cultural amenities for its citizens and in which all classes
participated in a common cultural system. And during the first half of the nineteenth century, the elite did promote activities and expend funds to fulfill that commitment. The civic and cultural improvements of the early nineteenth century, such
as Quincy Market and the Public Library (in the original building on Tremont Street)
were situated in the commercial heart of the city, meant to beautify and serve the
entire metropolis. But the landscape of the Back Bay speaks of different commitments, and tells a story that includes far less heroic deeds. Many of the city's philanthropic and cultural institutions were located at Copley Square, deep in the Back

Bay, not readily accessible to the city at large. Most of the cultural improvements of the late nineteenth century were meant only for the elite, who had symbolically and physically retreated into the Back Bay. The Boston upper class found it difficult if not impossible to incorporate the Irish immigrants, who now threatened the society they had created, and so the elite retreated from a city over which they no longer had absolute political and economic control. The conservatively styled house of the younger Abbott Lawrence, reminiscent of Boston's eighteenth-century heritage, was on Commonwealth Avenue in the Back Bay, close to cultural amenities but not to the commercial and political heart of the city. His father's house on Park Street had been half a block from the State House and half a block from the edge of the financial district. Abbott Lawrence had retreated into the world of culture, of history, of art; he, like others of his time, withdrew into the Back Bay. As Martin Green says of this generation, "The Yankees found themselves taking up a stand more and more simply over-privileged, reactionary, on the defensive, withdrawn."[68] The Back Bay can be seen as a statement of the retreat of this once powerful elite from a world that was no longer of their making.

This story of the Back Bay also reveals the elusive and ephemeral nature of the distinctions between commercial and cultural, private and public, civic and personal. The Back Bay was developed and paid for with public monies, yet it was controlled by private interests; it was spoken of as a civic improvement, yet it represented the interests of a select group of individuals; and the cultural institutions it incorporated were constructed for commercial as well as philanthropic reasons. Henry James's "interminable prospects of security" were far from "inexpressibly vacant"—behind those prospects was a community that led a commercial life as active as its social life, and the shade that community was struggling with was not that of an aristocracy, but of the Irish proletariat who, in the end, re-created the city in its own image.

5 Preserving Boston's Common and Planning Its Park System

The Common is, without doubt, the most noble place of the kind which had yet been laid out in any of our cities. It is indeed, with its fine trees, its crystal crescent, and its adjacent scenery, almost all that we could desire it to be.

—*The Boston Common, or Rural Walks in Cities* (1838)

That wide open expanse of land known as the Common was, by 1838, already a source of pride for the Boston elite. Originally a cattle grazing area owned by the city, by the mid-nineteenth century Boston Common and its adjoining Public Garden had become the city's parade ground and open-air focus. They served as the front yard for the Boston elite, who lived around its edges, on Beacon Hill, on Park Street, or on Tremont Street. Yet the Common occupied valuable land that could have been commercially developed, and, throughout the nineteenth century, attempts were made to erect buildings on the Common and encroach upon its borders with commercial structures. An 1842 commentator assessed the situation thus: "It seems to some, no doubt, a great waste to withhold so much land from building lots. We cannot say how many speculators have in their own minds laid out the Common for houses and shops. But let them despair."[1] Although assuredly those speculators found outlets for their investments elsewhere, they did despair when it came to developing the Common. Through legislation and other land use controls the Boston elite kept the Common free from commercial encroachments. While the preservation of the Common provided a welcome relief from the densely built city and separated the commercial and working classes from the more commodious parts of town, it also provided a display ground for the Boston upper classes and served as an expression of their cultural aspirations. In this sense, these open areas were indeed "front lawns," the Boston elite's inscription of self-representation on the land. The Common and adjoining Public Garden were arenas of social display meant for internal consumption—for leisurely strolls and aesthetic appreciation—and for external consumption—for projecting an image of Boston as a cultured city, with a sense of history and civic awareness. As Walter Firey has argued, "although the Common is but a tract of waste land so far as economic utility is concerned, it nonetheless has a very real function in renewing and revitalizing the sentiments of communal solidarity."[2] Firey suggests that the strict adherence to preserving the Common and keeping its forty-five acres out of economically productive uses can be explained by examining the symbolic uses of the Common area. The Common, he argues, is associated with important events in Boston's history, and as such has engendered sentiments and feelings of attachment from the city's inhabitants. Furthermore, Firey argues, the Common has taken on fetishistic characteristics, that is, the actual events that the Common symbolizes to people have receded in importance, so that the Common itself, not its history, has become the end value. "The idea of the symbol comes to usurp the idea for which the symbol originally stood." As a result, the Common carries a varied array of meanings for the people of Boston, meanings not necessarily related to each other, nor to the actual historic events from which the original meaning was derived. As Firey argues, "The dramatic events which lent to the Common its original affective significance, while by no means absent from people's consciousness today, are less apparent in the imagery which it elicits than are other more generalized sentimental responses."[3]

Throughout the nineteenth and twentieth centuries, the Common took on a wealth of symbolic meanings, representing the civic consciousness, historical attachments, and cultural values of the city. Yet it is difficult to suggest that the events that "lent to the Common its original affective significance" were "dramatic." As we will see, the Common was originally preserved not because of its historical associations but because it served the economic and ideological interests of the Boston elite, which had enough power in the city to protect its interests. New York's City Hall Park had its share of historical associations, but the city's fairly fragmented elite class was too busy establishing new and more fashionable residential squares uptown to take any interest in what must have seemed a relatively futile effort—that is, stopping the commercial spatial expansion downtown. But the powerful Boston elite, with their elegant homes bordering the Common and their industrial interests located outside the city, protected their real estate investments and expressed their communal solidarity by preserving as parkland forty-five acres of prime commercial real estate.

Long before the urban park movement of the second half of the nineteenth century mobilized the middle classes around the issue of preserving open spaces in their cities, Boston's ruling classes protected their Common and Public Garden. At first, they were able to do so by direct political control of the city, but later they used less obvious means for the same ends. In the late nineteenth century, the social movement associated with urban parks took its particular form in Boston under the guidance of the city's elite class. In this chapter I shall trace the relationship of Boston's elite class, whose membership base was the families that controlled the textile industries in New England, to the preservation of the Common and Public Garden, and to the development of the city's nineteenth-century park system. An understanding of the values and ideology of that elite class illuminates the reasons for the preservation of the Boston Common. By keeping the Common free from commercial infringement, and thereby inhibiting the spatial expansion of the city's commercial areas, the elite effectively shaped their urban landscape to reflect and legitimize their belief in Boston as a cultural city. The "noble place" of the Common was a direct reflection of Boston's aristocracy.

The Common and the Public Garden

Like many other towns in seventeenth-century America, Boston owned land that was used communally by its citizens. The original proprietor of all the acreage on which Boston stood, William Blackstone, sold to the town in 1640 his last forty-five acres of land as he fled from the Puritan stronghold.[4] The treeless land became public property and was used primarily for grazing cattle. Yet because this 45-acre expanse stood significantly north and west of the main focus of the town throughout most of the seventeenth and eighteenth centuries, its use was not of particular concern to most of the town's citizens. The city's merchants did not worry about a fairly remote piece of land when civic improvements and real estate investment were so necessary and lucrative in the city center, close to the bustling wharfs and counting houses.

Yet, in the mid- to late eighteenth century, Boston's spatial expansion was pushing beyond its original core, and, typical of a mercantile city, the city's wealthy began looking for residential locations somewhat removed from the commercial focus of the docks and warehouses, near State Street and Long Wharf. This movement was precipitated by a fire in 1794 that destroyed the city's ropewalks (long, covered walkways used for manufacturing rope) between Pearl and Atkinson streets. That destruction had two immediate effects. First, it opened up a large area for elite residences in what was called the South End, close to the area that was already under construction by Bulfinch, the town's favored architect and developer. Second, a new location for the ropewalks had to be found, as the manufacture of rope was essential for a city reliant upon shipping. The city granted to the ropewalk owners the mud flats at the foot of the Common near where it receded into the Back Bay to build their covered walks, on condition that they also construct a seawall to keep the water from intruding onto the land (fig. 59).[5] This seawall effectively closed off the Common from the water for the first time, allowing for the area to have a defined perimeter. A year later, after learning of the plans to build the new State House on the slope of Beacon Hill, the Mount Vernon Proprietors, a group of wealthy merchants, bought John Singleton Copley's adjoining property, a large expanse of hilly land that sat just to the north of the Common.[6] With such development, the Common was beginning to be seen as more than a barren, remote land. The construction of the State House and elite residences along one edge suggested that the Common was beginning to serve as an ornamental focus for the wealthy of the city.

Charles Bulfinch was partly responsible for the change. He returned to Boston in 1787 from his European tour much impressed with the grand architectural designs and plans of the European capitals, particularly with the Georgian style in London and the parks and promenades of France. Bulfinch became the favorite architect of the city's elite, designing the new State House, building mansions for the wealthy in the South End, and designing many of the homes of the Mount Vernon Proprietors on Beacon Hill and, in the early years of the nineteenth century, homes along Park and Tremont streets (fig. 60). Familiar with the residential squares and city parks of London and Paris, Bulfinch understood the potential of the Common for architectural design and as civic improvement. He labored to give the unkempt Common at least the appearance of propriety, hoping to turn this grazing land into pleasant vistas and promenades. Two sides of the Common had already been lined with trees; a long promenade known as the Mall was edged by trees on both sides and ran along Tremont Street, and a smaller tree-lined promenade faced Park Street (fig. 61). Yet the other three sides of the Common were little more than mud roads. In 1803, Bulfinch was able to raise enough money, mostly by private contributions from the Beacon Hill proprietors, to create a promenade of trees along Beacon Street and around the corner onto Charles Street up to the ropewalks. In 1816, the city gave Bulfinch funds to lay out a wide avenue connecting Charles Street to Tremont Street.[7] Thus, Bostonians could now walk the perimeter of the Common, making it a true parade ground.

It seemed only logical that when the city regained use of the land that had been temporarily granted for ropewalks, the ornamentation of the Common's border would

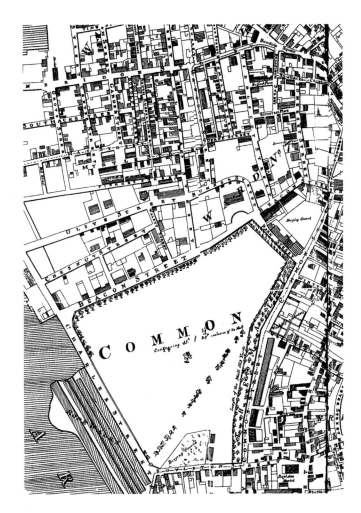

59. Detail from J. G. Hales's 1814 map of Boston. The ropewalks, extending from the Common into the waters of the bay, were moved here after the fire of 1794 had destroyed their covered walkways between Pearl and Atkinson streets. The seawall that the proprietors of the ropewalks had built was the first effective barrier between the Common and the waters of the bay.

be maintained. And because residences surrounded the Common on the other sides, enterprising speculators saw a chance to develop the last remaining area bordering the Common. The construction of fine homes, like those on Tremont and Park streets, was on the minds of men like Abbott Lawrence, who proposed to the city council that they adopt a plan for laying out roads and houselots on the disputed acreage. The committee that examined the matter agreed with Major Quincy that such action ran counter to the refined spirit of Boston: "To recommend its adoption, would be to suppose that, instead of the lone improvement, we had imbibed a spirit of desolation; that we had become retrograde in civilization; that instead of the intelligence and refinement of a polished and cultivated age, the barbarism of Gothic rudeness was revived, regardless, as it is ignorant, of everything beautiful in nature, or elegant in art."[8] In reaching its con-

60. Beacon Street and the Common, c. 1811. Beacon Hill mansions were lined up along Beacon Street, extending down the hill from the State House and facing the Common, the area's symbolic front yard.

61. Park Street, looking from the State House toward Tremont Street, c. 1858. The tree-lined promenade along the Park Street border of the Common indicates that the Common was seen as an ornamental park space for the elite whose residences surrounded it. The house of Abbott Lawrence (*second from left*) is just steps from the State House and the Common. (Courtesy of the Bostonian Society/Old State House)

clusions, this committee consulted a group of "five eminently discreet persons" that included three prominent Boston Associates: Patrick T. Jackson, Ebenezer Francis, and Peter C. Brooks.[9] These men were presumably the "aristocrats" that Abbott Lawrence referred to when he wrote to his brother Amos of his unsuccessful bid for the land. With one dissenting vote, this group recommended that the city buy the contested land from the owner of the ropewalks for $55,000 and not sell the land for private development.

Alarmed by this attempt at development close to the Common, Boston's voting citizens legislated in 1824 that the land known as the Common "should be forever thereafter kept open, and free of buildings of any kind, for the use of the citizens."[10] This statute mandated that the Common would be kept free from commercial encroachment, yet the fate of the land on which the ropewalks had stood was still unclear. The city had decided not to sell it for housing lots, but finding a proper use for the land remained a problem.

In 1836, a group of private citizens petitioned the city for the right to use the land as a public botanical garden. Horace Gray was the leading advocate of the group, and in 1837 he and his associates were granted permission to use the land for horticultural purposes. Gray hired John Cadness, a gardener from London, to take charge of the plans, but the work was difficult because the land was only partially filled.[11] However, with Cadness's expertise and Gray's money, work on the garden proceeded; a greenhouse was constructed, and a large building converted into a conservatory was filled with various imported exotic plants. The project came to an unexpected halt with the failure of Gray's business in 1847 and therefore the loss of the garden's funding. Charles Francis Barnard, a minister at the Warren Street Chapel, became a trustee of the Public Garden in 1847, and took over from Gray as champion of its cause. Very much interested in horticulture, and familiar with English gardens, Barnard had taken a long-standing interest in the garden. Based on his knowledge of English gardens, he laid out a plan for plantings and an arboretum in the Public Garden. The plans for the arboretum were never realized, but his efforts did result in the first decorative plantings.[12] But without adequate funding, Gray's optimistic plans for the garden languished, and the area seemed to some an eyesore. With the gardens in disarray, some city leaders were apparently coming to see the benefits of what Lawrence had proposed earlier—that is, selling the land for housing. The city's Committee of Aldermen recommended in 1850 that the 25 acres of land be laid out in streets and sold for private residences, citing the expense of maintaining the area and the benefits of more housing. The report also mentioned the poor condition of the Public Garden, suggesting it was neither public nor a garden: "In its present condition, it is far from meriting the name it bears,—is seldom resorted to by the public, and wholly unworthy to be considered one of the public grounds of the city. If pointed out to the stranger, it is always with an apology for its uninviting aspect; and from its proximity to our noble Common, even despoils it of some of its grandeur and loveliness."[13]

Despite the "uninviting" appearance of the area, no immediate action was taken on the plan to build houses on the land, giving Barnard time to arouse public opinion to the potential of the garden. Barnard used the press to show the benefits of the public garden for the health, morality, and education of the city's inhabitants. He wrote articles in a publication of his own, "The Gazette of the Public Garden," describing the public gardens of Europe, quoting doctors and naturalists speaking of the virtues of natural recreation.[14] Citing merchants in England who had pursued interests in horticulture, Barnard suggested indirectly that Bostonians could do the same: "The vacant land at the foot of the Common of our city, together with the Common itself, afford an invaluable opportunity for decorative landscape planting, that, improved at a small expense, would in a few years form a public park and arboretum worthy of a great and wise nation."[15] His vision of the public benefits of an arboretum with walkways and flower beds, rather than the more specialized botanic garden, finally proved successful. He was given permission by the city to surround part of the area with a wooden fence and to build a conservatory for the public sale of flowers.[16] The matter, however, was not finally settled until the land disputes concerning the entire Back Bay area had been resolved. In their 1858 report, the Back Bay Commissioners declared their intentions of preserving the garden as part of the Back Bay:

> We have observed that it has been proposed by the City Council of Boston to sell a portion of the Public Garden for building purposes: and also, to lay out a street through the Public Garden, in continuation of the central avenue of the Commonwealth. We cannot but regard either or both of these measures as contemplating the ultimate conversion of the whole Public Garden to buildings purposes, and detrimental to the interests of the Commonwealth in the Back Bay, as well as to the best interests of the city of Boston.[17]

Again, plans were being considered to build on the Public Garden, and again they were thwarted. Several competing institutions had claims to the water and land rights in the area (see chapter 4), and it was not until 1859, with a final settlement, that a legislative act ensured the preservation of the Public Garden. The act outlined the area to be called the Public Garden and allowed for building on it only if the structure were to be used for horticultural purposes or if the city ever wanted to build a City Hall there. The act called for a vote of the city's citizens, and in the public flier that announced the proposed act, the intentions of the city's ruling class were made clear:

> No one supposes now that this favorite spot will ever be sold. Public sentiment is undoubtedly opposed to any such course. While New York, and Philadelphia,

and Baltimore are expending enormous sums in laying out magnificent Parks, Squares and Commons, and are ornamenting them at great cost, it would be an act of vandalism for Boston to sell the Public Garden, or to diminish its proportions a single inch. But it is desirable to have it understood now, to what uses it may be put hereafter, inasmuch as any uncertainty on this point is sure to deter persons from erecting splendid mansions on the new land, and the danger is, that an inferior class of buildings may be first erected, and this would be injurious to the whole improvement.[18]

At this point, then, the Public Garden was seen as a well-established public improvement, one that was to be expected of a major American city. It was to be kept free from commercial development to serve as a park, but also to ensure that it would be an ornament to the Back Bay housing development that was under way just to its west. The future inhabitants of those "splendid mansions" being built in the Back Bay might be put off if the Public Garden were allowed, for example, to be commercially developed. This would, of course, put a damper on the larger plans for the Back Bay "improvement." The Public Garden, then was finally mandated only after the future plans for the Back Bay were in place.

Meanwhile, the movement to protect the Common from commercial encroachment similarly used recourse to the public interest as a justification for that protection. In 1843, the Boston and Providence Railroad Company sued the city, claiming that part of the Common just north of its depot was public land that could be sold. The legal opinion that declared such a sale to be illegal was based on the long-term use of the Common lands for public uses: "It will be observed that I [the lawyer, Franklin Dexter] do not found my denial of the right of the City Council to sell these lands upon the prohibition contained, by implication, in the City Charter, but upon the prior dedication to public uses, which it would require all the powers of the Legislature to revoke."[19] Like the Public Garden, the legality of the Common's existence was based on its previous public uses (fig. 62). Those who wished otherwise, like the Boston and Providence Railroad proprietors, found it impossible to fight the city's ruling class.

This trend continued throughout the nineteenth century. An 1869 permit to construct a building on the Common for a musical festival was met with such negative popular feeling "that the managers of that enterprise deemed it injudicious to accept the grant, and the building was placed upon land further south and west." The agitation that accompanied the proposal to widen Tremont Street for tracks for a horse-drawn railway in 1873 led to an 1875 legislative act that prohibited any roadway from being constructed on any public common or park unless approved by a vote of the citizens of the city.[20]

By the 1870s, however, the Boston elite no longer had absolute control over the city's political machinery. It was able to achieve its desired ends by appealing to the public nature of the Common and Public Garden and by indirectly influencing political decisions. In 1877, business interests directly lost to other, less mercenary ideals when a proposal to construct an exhibition hall on the Common for the Massachusetts Charitable Mechanics' Association was turned down after much debate. The association requested permission to construct a temporary building for its triennial exposition of industry and art, a fairly benign request given the willingness of the association to submit to the regulations of the Committee on Common and Squares and to guarantee that the building would be removed when the exposition was over. Those supporting the proposal included many representatives of Boston's newer commercial and industrial ventures, including its department stores, several piano manufacturing companies (one of Boston's most prolific industries), and a representative of one of the largest construction firms in the state.[21] The petition was referred to the Committee on Commons and Squares, which unanimously recommended granting permission for the exposition hall. Yet when the committee reported to the city's Board of Aldermen, they were presented with a document, signed by "citizens of and tax-payers in Boston," that opposed granting such permission. The issue then went back to the committee, with instructions to hold a public hearing on the matter.

62. Boston Common, c. 1835. This artist's view depicts the Common as the leisure space for fashionable Bostonians.

This public discussion did not go well for the petitioners. During the hearing the secretary of the Mechanics' Association answered questions about his group's proposal that pertained to the building and to whether the group would continue to ask permission to hold the exposition on the Common every three years: "That is, out of any given three years, you propose to occupy the Common more than one-sixth of the time, and practically take it every third summer?" This somewhat exaggerated argument seems to have carried weight, because the hearing was adjourned for one week, during which time those who opposed the petition formed a committee to "consult about the best course in defence of the Common."[22] Chosen as a member of this committee to defend the Common was Abbott Lawrence, whose father had attempted to purchase the lands of the Public Garden for private development fifty-three years earlier. A second public hearing was held at which this committee presented a petition opposing the exposition, with two hundred and forty-four signatures, including members of the Brooks, Lowell, and Jackson families—some of Boston's oldest and wealthiest. Despite these pressures, the Board of Aldermen supported the petition, but it was stalled permanently in the city's common council. Permission was not granted for the exposition that year, but the possibility of future commercial displays on the Common remained. Alarmed by this possibility, the committee that represented opponents of the petition thought it "best to attempt to procure a law, which should define and protect the rights of the public."[23] The act, which disallowed any building of more than six hundred square feet from being built on any public common or park, was passed in May 1877.

This well-documented example of how the Common was protected from commercial encroachment suggests how Boston's established elite class manipulated the city's politics. Despite the fact that by the 1870s the Boston Associates had already lost direct political control, they still directed many of the city's policies. In this example, both the Committee on Commons and Squares and the Board of Aldermen voted to allow the construction of the exhibition hall on the Common. Yet, by mobilizing enough public support and speaking in terms of public interest, the Boston elite protected its Common. As in the Back Bay, the Boston elite legitimized its position by aligning it with the "public good." Abbott Lawrence, living in the Back Bay with a secure income, had little interest in using the Common for an industrial display. The Common had been his playground, and now it stood as a buffer from the commercialized areas of the city. A horticultural display that offered recompense for its use of the Common in the way of culture and cultivation was acceptable to Lawrence and his colleagues, but an industrial exposition was simply out of the question. Industry and cultivation were not to be mixed; each was to be kept in its own place in the city.

By the late nineteenth century, the cause of preserving the Common had become firmly entrenched in the Boston mind-set. In Walter Firey's terms, the Common had become a fetish, and its preservation was attached not to specific events, but to a host of values and sentiments that were linked to civic commitments and the public good. The debates that arose in the 1890s over the construction of a subway under Tremont Street show the degree to which the Common had taken on the symbolic weight of the city's heritage. Traffic congestion along Tremont Street had apparently reached acute levels in the early 1890s, and several remedies were put forward by private transit companies and the city transit commission, including an extension of trolley tracks across the Common to connect Tremont Street to Columbus Avenue or Commonwealth Avenue, and the widening of streets that adjoined the Common (fig. 63).[24] These proposals were not approved, but a public referendum finally allowed construction of a subway under Tremont Street, despite the potential disturbance to the Tremont Street Mall. Even this compromise plan met with some disapproval. And efforts to widen streets near the Common continued into the early years of the twentieth century, often backed by Boston's department store owners, although they too were defeated.[25]

As a result of the preservation of the Common and limited transport routes around it, Boston's commercial districts were kept from spatially expanding westward. Given what we know of late nineteenth-century urban development in general, the strict adherence to the noncommercial use of the Common contributed to the relatively small and atypical pattern of spatial expansion of Boston's retail district (fig. 64). As Firey has pointed out, the Common stood directly in the path of expansion for Boston's commercial district.[26] If the Common had not been protected from commercial development, it is likely that it would have been encroached upon by an expanding retail district. By the 1860s, Boston's retailing district had begun to move north onto Tremont Street. In 1865, R. H. White and Company, a prominent dry goods store in the city, was located at 32 Winter Street, just a half block from Tremont, and by 1875 it was joined by Stearn's, which was located just around the corner at 131–132 Tremont Street, and Houghton and Dutton, further east at 55 Tremont Street. The stores' move north makes economic sense, because their best customers, the middle and upper classes, had moved from their earlier enclaves in the old South End to Beacon Hill and thence to the Back Bay. Yet this trend did not continue. By 1885, R. H. White had moved south onto Washington Street, joining Jordan Marsh and Hovey and Company, and Stearn's moved off Tremont Street; and by 1895 it was clear that the retailing district would remain centered on Washington Street.[27] The city's middle and upper classes had stabilized their locations in the city, and, with the Common and Public Garden protected from development, retailers consolidated their locational position along Washington Street (map 8).

63. Tremont Street, looking toward Scollay Square, 1893. The congestion along Tremont Street, as indicated here by the pedestrian, carriage, and streetcar traffic, led some in the city to call for a widening of the street, although that proposal was blocked. (Courtesy of the Bostonian Society/Old State House)

64. Tremont Street, looking north to Park Street, c. 1892. The commercial areas of the city, including the retailers along the east side of Tremont Street, were stopped from expanding west by the presence of the Common on the west side.

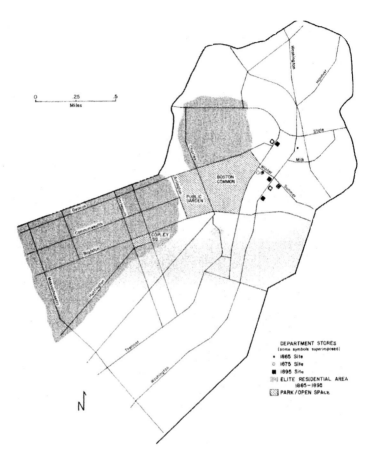

Map 8. Major Department Stores and Elite Residential Areas in Boston, 1895

Although numerous retailers campaigned for commercial expansion near the Common, by the 1880s it was clear that attempts to alter the Common in any way were destined to fail. Several retailers supported the petition by the Massachusetts Charitable Mechanics'Association to build an exhibition hall on the Common, but their support did little to allow even this relatively minor commercial incursion. Given the support of retailers for intra-urban transportation networks found in other cities, it seems likely that these retailers were also supporters of the petitions to widen Tremont Street for horse-car traffic, but again, that support had little effect against the still powerful Boston elite class. Boston's retailing district, therefore, expanded slowly and incrementally along Washington Street and surrounding side streets but did not significantly alter its locational focus. By the turn of the century, smaller commercial establishments, facing increasing congestion, did move out of the district, but were forced to stretch themselves out in an elongated fashion around the Common. This pattern was not the most optimal for shopping, because, as Firey has suggested, "businesses of a given type may be found scattered over a distance much too great for the average shopper who is interested in comparing similar merchandise at different places."[28]

In contrast to Boston, New York's retailing district moved north up Broadway without any barriers to commercial expansion (see chapter 2), and its downtown public spaces were not protected from development. The equivalent to Boston's Common was New York's City Hall Park, which was used first as a common area and later for public architectural displays throughout the nineteenth century. But in contrast to the Common, its history is one of development. The park itself is only a small portion of what had been the original common area in the eighteenth century. Little by little it had been encroached on all sides, first by civic structures, and later by New York's expanding commercial districts. Constructed in the park through the nineteenth century were an almshouse, the Hall of Records, City Hall, a city and county courthouse, and a post office.[29] Its borders were gradually encroached with retail stores along Broadway in the 1850s, and then newspaper and other office buildings on Park Row and Broadway in the 1870s (fig. 65). By mid-century, its role as a "front lawn" had vanished—the elite had abandoned it for more commodious areas to the north, and if the park can be considered a display ground, it was for architectural displays of commercial wealth, not social strolls (fig. 66). It was uptown that a "lawn" was needed, and New York's upper classes ensured that it was to be the grandest display of civic pride in the country: the story of the design and construction of Central Park is a long and complicated one, involving massive political maneuvering and exchanges of capital. But the point is that, unlike Boston, New York's Central Park was completely separate in conception and execution from the city's earlier smaller squares and parks.

No attempt was made to preserve City Hall Park until after the turn of the century, when the City Beautiful movement began to have an impact on urban planners. At that time, members of the Municipal Art Society of New York formulated a plan for the park inspired by their desire to create a civic center worthy of a world metropolis.[30] In other words, the first organized efforts to plan for the park grew out of a concern for civic aggrandizement—not preservation, as was the case in Boston.[31] In addition, these efforts occurred nearly a century later than those in Boston, and they were motivated by a national trend toward planning, not by internal pressure. Moreover, New York had no equivalent to the consolidated elite class of Boston. Throughout the nineteenth century, the economic elites did not seem to support anything that could possibly have hindered their expansion, nor did the cultural elites have enough power to control that expansion.

65. City Hall Park and Newspaper Row. New York's City Hall Park was gradually reduced in size throughout the nineteenth century as it was overrun by civic and commercial land uses. By the end of the century, only the relatively small expanse in front of City Hall remained open.

66. Broadway at City Hall Park. The elite had abandoned the areas around City Hall Park in the early years of the nineteenth century, and by the end of the century, the park was an anomaly amid the tall commercial and financial office buildings.

Ornamentation and Cultivation

But why did the Boston elite fight so vociferously for the Common and Public Garden? The Public Garden's horticultural uses point to some specific explanations. The original pleas to not build on the land that became the Public Garden were driven by an interest of the elite to represent themselves as civilized and beyond the base instincts of commercial gain. The proposal to use the land for horticultural purposes, therefore, was amenable to their goals. Thus, the designation of the Public Garden as a botanical garden was another manifestation of the Boston's elite ideological commitment to legitimizing its commercial wealth and the authority it conferred. In the search for a means of expressing its status, and for legitimation of power in a republican society, Boston's elite created landscape symbols rife with the symbolism of a cultured life. Tamara Plakins Thornton observes that the Boston elite from 1830 to 1860 "enjoyed economic, social, cultural, and political power as never before. Yet if one consequence of class consolidation was increased strength, another was a growing tendency to self-preoccupation, self-examination, and hence a need for self-definition and self-justification. In this generation, as in those that preceded it, the rich symbolism of rural pursuits answered the subtly changed needs of Boston's elite."[32]

Interest in rural pursuits, particularly those associated with the scientific advancement of farming and horticulture techniques, was one of the many interests of the Boston elite throughout the nineteenth century, and was used as a form of self-legitimation for the group.[33] Rural pursuits were seen as a higher stage of civilization than commerce—they were not associated with luxury and decadence, the foreseen results of a civilization marked by commercial interests alone.[34] If commerce served a higher plane of activity, such as the betterment of life through scientific learning, then it, and the power it conferred on individuals, could be legitimized. And the associations of a botanical garden that had been established by the London elite (through the founding of the Horticultural Society in 1804) conferred a high moral status—as a way of advancing learning, of providing a healthful life, particularly in the middle of the city. Horticulture provided distance from unabashed commercialism, an alternative to complete separation from the commercial city. As Daniel Bluestone has shown in his analysis of nineteenth-century Chicago, horticulture was an important symbol of living a gentile, cultivated, and urbane life.[35] And, as in Chicago, Boston's gentlemen horticulturists organized a society in 1829, eighteen years earlier than their Chicago counterparts. The Massachusetts Horticultural Society, modeled after the Horticultural Society of London, gave institutional form and added legitimacy to this "cultivating" activity. As Thornton states, the formation of the society became a symbol of the gentility of the Boston elite.[36] Abbott Lawrence, in a speech to the horticultural festival in 1842, spoke of this "higher" state: "The exhibition here to-night, altogether, is the best proof that can be presented of a high state of civilization and refinement."[37]

Horace Gray, who inherited a large fortune from his father, William, a shipping merchant, and who had made his own fortune in manufacturing, was advocating the interests of his class when he promoted a botanical garden for Boston. His father was head of one of the wealthiest families of Boston and, after his initial mercantile success, became involved in banking, serving as head of the State National Bank of Boston. Like many other Boston merchants in the early years of the nineteenth century, he was also politically active, serving twenty years in the state house and senate, thereby helping to consolidate much of the power of his mercantile class.[38] Two of Horace's brothers, Francis and John, pursued cultural interests and were not engaged in commercial endeavors. John Chipman Gray, working from a summer estate in Cambridge, was a member and served as president of the Massachusetts Society for Promoting Agriculture, as well as a founder and vice-president of the Massachusetts Horticulture Society.[39] Francis Gray was described as an "accomplished scholar" who did not engage in business matters.[40]

So, by controlling the "public" arena of politics and economics, the upper class was able to protect a public space for its private use. In addition, by so doing, it was also able to fulfill its ideological commitment to public service as its attempts to protect the Common were couched in terms of helping the citizenry and the public good. Wasn't it for "public uses" that the Common was being preserved? Or, would the public have been better served if part of the Common had been sold off for an expanded retail district or for wider streets for better horsecar service?

Urban Parks

The construction of the Back Bay and the waning of the power of the Boston Brahmin class altered the reasons for protecting the Common. With increasing immigration, and the relative decline of economic and political power of the Boston ruling class, such public spaces as the Common could not be controlled so easily. The Common began to function less as a private residential square and more as an urban park. People from all classes began to use the space for promenading and recreation. As early as 1842, keen observers noticed class distinctions operating within the Common. Apparently promenading in the Mall had become the ordinary course taken by the working classes (fig. 67), while the fashionable elite had taken to using the brick sidewalk (fig. 68):

> The brick side-walk around the Common is at present a more fashionable promenade than the beautiful mall with its arched avenue of trees. In the propensity of cultivated and fashionable life in our republican country to separate itself from the

common and plebeian world, it is interesting to notice a different method of effecting its object from that in which an established nobility separates itself from the people. Nobility has its parks and terraced walls from which the public and cattle are excluded; but in this country the common people are peers of the realm, and the genteel, in order to maintain a separateness in their unavoidable union with them in certain enjoyments, given an artificial vogue to a place or thing which is obviously inferior to a thing of the same kind which the common people enjoy. This is probably the reason for the fact, which it is true we have no court calendar to confirm, but which is sufficiently obvious, that it is considered more genteel to promenade on the brick side-walk, outside of the Common, than in the mall.[41]

Here, the Common is more than the elite's front yard—it is being taken over by the "plebeian" class. With the large increase in immigrant population in Boston in the mid-nineteenth century, particularly the Irish, the idea that the Common was public space took on a different meaning. The Common provided the only expanse of open space for the immigrants living in crowded tenement districts in the North End and South End, and therefore served a vital function for expanding population.

67. Tremont Street Mall, c. 1881. The Common contained many different areas for leisure activities, including tree-lined promenades.

68. Park Street Church, Tremont Street Mall, c. 1890. By mid-century, it was considered more fashionable to promenade along the new sidewalks than along the malls. Many in Boston fought attempts to widen Tremont Street in order to preserve these promenades. (Courtesy of the Bostonian Society/Old State House)

Yet many of the Boston elite still maintained their residences in the downtown area bordering the Common, and such uses of their front yards must not have been welcome. The working classes needed recreational space, but the Common itself was not meant to serve such purposes. By the 1860s, the Boston elite shifted some of its attention to alerting the public of the need for a park system.

The elite classes in many other American cities were doing the same thing—with cities in social and economic turmoil, the idea of urban parks as antidote to the evils of the city was a particularly appealing notion. As David Schuyler has shown, the social movement to create urban parks participated in an ideology that incorporated various streams of thought—the sanitary reformers' attempts to bring open spaces into the congested city, the need for relief from the often gridded urban form of the commercial city, the democratic appeal of a public urban space where all classes could participate equally, and the need to uphold the grandeur of the new nation in light of urban developments in Europe, England in particular. The park was meant to bring the country into the city, to display the natural within the urban. "The park, then, embodied a new urban symbolism—the curvilinearity of the natural landscape—and stood in sharp contrast to the straight lines and rigid angles of the gridiron, a pastoral counterpoint to the urban environment."[42] That natural landscape, of course, was far from unaltered, for the nineteenth-century urban park was a humanized landscape: planned, designed, and structured for specific purposes. It was in this sense no different from the commercial areas of the city, except that it was meant to fulfill quite different functions.

Neither the Common nor Public Garden had been designed along the naturalistic aesthetic. The shape of the Common had evolved over several centuries and was not the result of conscious planning. Its borders were not curvilinear but were rather straight, and its five sides met at hard angles. The layout of the interior portions of the Common did not follow naturalistic principles—many of its walkways followed functional paths. This was to be expected, of course, in a park whose original function was as an extension of the urban areas surrounding it, not as a counterpoint to those areas. The Common had served the city not only as its original cattle grazing area, but also its military parade-ground and site of public executions. Its natural topography was quite hilly, and each of its four hills was named, with anecdotes attached to each. A portion of one of the hills was called "smokers' circle" because, according to chronicler Nathaniel Shurtleff, its circle of elm trees formed comfortable seats for those "persons who indulge in the use of tobacco."[43] Most of its small ponds or bog areas had been filled in by the 1850s, except for the Frog Pond, whose edges had been lined with stones in the 1820s (fig. 69). The Common, therefore, did not contain the picturesque walkways and water areas of the naturalistic parks. Yet attempts were made throughout the mid-nineteenth century to make the area more commodious.

By the 1880s, the Common was encircled with an iron fence, and was laced with asphalt paths lined by wooden fence rails, surrounded by carefully pruned trees (fig. 70).[44]

The Public Garden was slightly different from the Common in that it had been laid out in the 1850s and 1860 and therefore had not evolved as part of the original urban fabric. In 1859 the city selected George F. Meacham, a Harvard graduate and architect of several Back Bay homes, to design the garden, and his plans combined formal, French-inspired elements with naturalistic features. The design included a linear axis and geometric flower beds, but also an irregularly shaped pond and pathway system.[45] As David Schuyler comments, the plan "was closer in intent to Fort Greene Park [in Brooklyn] and to Downing's Washington [D.C.] Mall than it was to a naturalistic landscape. It was really more an extension of the city than an escape from it."[46] Yet it had never been the intent of the Boston elite to use the Common and Public Garden as an escape from the city. These open spaces represented instead the commitment of the elite to the city, to maintaining cultivated spaces within the disarray of the urban chaos. During the formative years of these parks, the Boston elite had little to fear from the urban scene—they controlled both its economy and society. Yet, by the 1870s, that was no longer the case, and an urban park system that provided an outlet for the city's working population must have become more appealing.

The Boston Common, then, became the starting point for a new metropolitan park system. The story of the creation of Boston's "emerald necklace," as the series of parks throughout the metropolitan area came to be called, shows the continued, although somewhat indirect, control of the Boston's established elite over the city's use of space. As Roy Rosenzweig and Elizabeth Blackmar have pointed out, the construction of urban park systems in America has always involved, and at least initially represented, the interests of the urban elite. For example, the decision to build Central Park, "although clothed in democratic rhetoric, was fundamentally rooted in the interests of New York's wealthiest citizens—its gentlemen and ladies."[47] Boston was no different, although what is remarkable about the development of the Boston park system is the degree to which the early nineteenth-century elite still were successful at maintaining their interests in the late nineteenth-century city.

Prodded by the example of New York's Central Park, many of Boston's elite discussed plans for the city's future park system throughout the 1860s and 1870s and held public forums to solicit opinions on how many and what kinds of parks the city needed. That these parks were important for the working classes was made clear in an 1869 report: "A public park, planted with the proper trees, and set apart for re-creation; that is the proper term, and signifies the object and purpose of a park, set apart for the re-creation of that class in the community who have not the means of riding round

69. The Frog Pond, Boston Common. Because the Common predates by two centuries the naturalistic park movement in America, many of its original features were modified to fit into the new aesthetic, such as attempts to beautify the Frog Pond.

70. Beacon Street Mall, Boston Common. The Boston Common was "beautified" in the last decades of the nineteenth century with asphalt walkways lined by carefully pruned trees.

Beacon St. Mall Boston Common.

the suburbs of this city."[48] Boston's leaders began soliciting the views of the nation's prominent landscape architects, including H. W. S. Cleveland and Robert Morris Cleveland, who in addition to Olmsted, presented proposals for a Boston park system in the late 1860s and early 1870s.[49] All the designers agreed that the city, with such limited space, would have to design a park system that was metropolitan in scope and scale, thereby including the suburban areas, although they disagreed as to the extent of that system. Olmsted, in a lecture at the Lowell Institute in 1870, made it clear that in planning a park system for Boston, the city's future growth into suburban regions would have to be considered. Just three months after his lecture, the state legislature passed an act establishing a metropolitan park system. However, the measure failed to get the support of a majority of the city's voters, and therefore was not enacted. Apparently, Boston's working-class residents feared that they would be taxed to pay for these new park spaces, many of which would be located in the new suburban areas that were relatively inaccessible to them.[50] Yet the idea continued, and was pursued by Mayor Samuel Cobb, who appointed a commission to study the issue, and soon thereafter, a municipal park commission. The mayor chose three prominent members of the Boston elite as the first park commissioners—William Gray, Jr., T. Jefferson Coolidge, and Charles H. Dalton—and these men spearheaded efforts for a municipal park system.[51] They held public hearings and eventually devised their own comprehensive plan.[51] The commission verified earlier suggestions that the city did indeed need more park space, citing the relative lack of acreage devoted to such uses in Boston as compared to New York, Philadelphia, and Chicago. It also concurred that a series of parks would be more appropriate than one large park: "We need in Boston no single large 'Central Park'; the shape of the city forbids it, nor would it answer our purposes. We need many open spaces in every part; a series of parks, of various sizes and shapes, where the land may be found best fitted for them, connected by broad driveways."[52]

The problem of public land acquisition, complicated by the fact that this proposed park system assumed access to suburban lands, prevented any immediate action. The city, however, had already begun to annex many of its suburban communities, and by the late 1870s had asked Olmsted to begin to design and implement a park system. He began plans for Franklin Park, in West Roxbury, dividing the park into two areas, one to be designed with naturalistic scenery, the other to include more active, recreational spaces such as a playground and music concourse.[53] The more comprehensive plan for a metropolitan park system, however, was still hampered by the problems of political borders and lack of a metropolitan planning commission with control over land. The metropolitan system was finally made a reality in the 1890s, under the leadership of Charles Eliot, a landscape architect and the son of the president of Harvard. Eliot attended school with Olmsted's son and became a colleague of Olmsted senior, who had settled in suburban Brookline. He worked with both Olmsteds on the plans for and implementation of Franklin Park, the Arnold Arboretum, and the Fens, before leading his own crusade for a metropolitan park system. Eliot garnered public support from his publications proclaiming the cause of a metropolitan system of public parks, and he established a metropolitan park commission, that, through the powers of the State General Court and legislature, had authority that transcended local town boundaries.[54]

Under Olmsted's direction, the Emerald Necklace began to take shape. After his work on Franklin Park and then Harvard's Arnold Arboretum, Olmsted continued with a large-scale design to construct a series of green spaces that would connect the Common and Public Garden to Franklin Park. He solved the problem of how to continue Commonwealth Avenue westward without crossing the Boston and Albany Railroad tracks, by changing the direction of the avenue from west to northwest at West Chester Park, and his plan for converting the flats of the Muddy River into a naturalistic park that became the Fens succeeded as a decorative link to the parks further west and south. Under Eliot's supervision, Olmsted's design for the Riverway and Jamaica Park was completed, thereby connecting this coordinated system of parks.

However, according to Albert Fein, the success of Olmsted's plan had as much to do with the social climate of Boston as with its aesthetic climate:"Olmsted's record of achievement in Boston after his defeat in New York City [due to political differences, Olmsted's service to the Department of Public Parks was terminated in 1878] was owing to the social and political support he found there. Boston, unlike New York, still retained an effective intellectual and social elite committed to large-scale environmental planning."[55] As in the fights to protect the Common and Public Garden, the Boston Brahmins had always found effective means of shaping their city's built form. In this case, the formation of a metropolitan park system was due to their direct intervention. The city's park commissioners were all directly related to the Boston Associates. William Gray, Jr., was the great-grandson of one of the wealthiest merchants in eighteenth-century Boston and member of the Boston Associates. Gray, the treasurer of the Atlantic Cotton Mills, spent much of his time as a member of the Massachusetts Horticultural Society and was elected its president in 1878. T. Jefferson Coolidge, treasurer of the Lawrence and Amoskeag Manufacturing Companies, also descended from one of the city's first families. Charles H. Dalton was a treasurer of the Manchester Print Works but served the city mainly as one of its prominent physicians, involved in Massachusetts General Hospital and the establishment of McLean Hospital, two institutions closely associated with the Boston elite.[56]

In addition, Olmsted's original invitation to Boston came on the behalf of the Lowell Institute, an institute completely controlled by the Boston Brahmins. Begun with an endowment by John Lowell, Jr., in 1836, and offering free lectures to the general public, it appeared that the institute served the public education needs of the city. Yet, according to historian Ronald Story, that seemingly democratic goal was illusory. With its single trustee (who was always a member of the Lowell family) and strict lecture format, the institute did not "allow for democratic control or audience participation." Despite this elitism, or perhaps because of it, the institute had become by 1845 a major force in Boston's cultural community, and by 1860, "it had displaced or absorbed most of the competing lecture organizations in the Boston area."[57] Thus, Olmsted's lecture at the Lowell Institute was sure to have both a properly educated audience and a particularly influential one. And Olmsted's visions fit well with the Brahmin ideology of public service and culture. The park plans would provide a cultural adornment to the city, a place for the working classes to re-create, and an appropriate environment for the pursuit of individual contemplation of nature, a goal befitting proper late nineteenth-century gentlemen and gentlewomen.

The elite apparently made quite public their support for Olmsted's plans. In 1876, at one of the public hearings concerning the establishment of a park system, one of the speakers pointed out which citizens in particular were interested in the park system:

> My friends, I need not tell you that this matter has excited the interest of our philanthropic and public-spirited citizens, and especially of the medical faculty, to whom it is, in its sanitary aspect, a matter of most important practical interest. And, through their representatives to the city government and to the state legislature, a bill was brought before the legislature, which I had the honor myself to report in the House of Representatives a little more than a year ago, and which was passed by large majorities in both houses, authorizing the city of Boston to purchase and to take lands within its own limits for laying out public parks, and to co-operate with adjacent towns in laying out conterminous parks for the common benefit and advantage of citizens on both sides of the line.[58]

"Philanthropic" and "public-spirited citizens" can refer only to the Boston elite, who—particularly those "of the medical faculty"—not only showed great interest in the park, but also were active politically in authorizing the city to purchase lands for public parks.

The reference to the medical faculty is of particular interest here. Urban parks were often legitimized as necessary for the health and sanitation of urbanites, but rarely have the people responsible for health been so aligned with an urban elite.[59] The major medical institution in Boston, Massachusetts General Hospital, was completely controlled by the Boston elite. As Story has pointed out, almost all officials of the hospital, as well as most of the physicians and surgeons, were from the city's leading families.[60] This control by the elite over the medical profession extended beyond the walls of the hospital. According to Jaher, the Brahmins also dominated Harvard Medical School and the Massachusetts Medical Society, a group that set standards of medical practice and education. These institutions "licensed physicians, educated the prominent doctors, decided criteria for professional conduct, conferred the highest medical posts, and assessed the validity of and awarded the honors for medical accomplishments."[61] Thus, when the medical faculty favored and politically maneuvered for public parks, it reflected the interests of the Boston elite class.

However, even with the consolidated support of the elite, it was not until the 1890s, under the leadership of Charles Eliot, that the metropolitan park system was finally put into place. Eliot's father, Charles W. Eliot, declined an offer to become superintendent of the Merrimac Company's Lowell Mills, and instead pursued a career in the academy, eventually becoming one of the most prominent of Harvard's presidents.[62] His son pursued another "civilized" career, that of a landscape architect. During the time he served as the commission's landscape architect, Eliot created a plan for America's first metropolitan park system, which, according to Schuyler, represented the "culmination of the evolution of the naturalistic urban landscape in nineteenth-century America."[63]

What Eliot finally created, however, was quite different from what his predecessors in the 1860s and 1870s had envisioned. The original notion of urban parks serving recreational and health needs of the city's inhabitants, so well expressed by the "medical faculty," had been superseded by a rationale for urban parks based on the contemplation of natural scenery. As Schuyler states, "the conception of the park evolved from an associational and educational space that was essentially an extension of the city into a naturalistic landscape that in its very rusticity was the antithesis of the urban environment."[64] This logic led Eliot to form the Trustees of Public Reservations, a private organization whose goal was to buy up and thereby preserve what was left of the region's "wilderness."

Wilderness preservation was certainly a far cry from the early nineteenth-century attempts to preserve the Common, which was then an integral part of the city, similar in purpose to private residential squares. It was protected from commercial uses by the elite class, who had a large personal as well as financial stake in the residential property surrounding the Common, and whose commercial real estate interests were located outside the city, in Lowell and Lawrence. The horticultural aspects of the Public Garden were seen as legitimate uses for open space in the city, because the science of cultivation was considered of high moral stature, fitting the ideology of the Boston elite. But by mid-century, the "private" space of the Brahmins' Common had been invaded by people not of their ancestry and who did not share their value system. With many of the elite still residing in Beacon Hill and the Back Bay, the Common and Public Garden continued to serve an ornamental function for their elite enclaves (fig. 71), but increasingly these open spaces also offered the elite a type of buffer from the commercial activities of the downtown, and from the Irish, many of whom lived in the North End. Yet the need to find recreational and healthful outlets for the working classes was felt more urgently as the elite were losing much of their direct control over the city's economy and politics. An urban park offered the elite a chance to provide such recreational spaces for the city, and their support for the park system eventually led to the realization of Olmsted's plan for Boston's metropolitan park system. And under the supervision of Eliot, that park system took on new dimensions, fulfilling the goal of providing what was considered by this time a necessary escape from the city—places for the contemplation of spiritual and intellectual goals. As with its development of the Back Bay, the Boston elite shifted its energies from investing in the city to escaping from it. Inhabiting a city over which they no longer had direct or certain control, the elite retreated into the world of cultivated nature in their park system, and cultured urbanity in their homes and cultural institutions.

71. The Public Garden, c. 1881. This view, from the corner of Beacon and Charles streets looking south, and west toward the Back Bay, portrays the area as a leisure space for the fashionable classes. The naturalistic design of the garden is evident in the irregular shape of the pond and the connecting network of curvilinear walkways.

Conclusion

> New York began to regulate the shape of tall buildings only after they had already transformed
> many of the streets into permanently sunless canyons, whereas Boston laid down in advance reg-
> ulations against what were considered excessive building heights; which showed the effect of his-
> torical tradition rather than the relative chances of profit and loss in the two cities.
> —*New York Panorama* (1938)

This study has attempted to show the power of "historical tradition" in shaping the
nineteenth-century landscapes of New York and Boston. This is not to suggest that
decisions based on profit and loss were not integral to the processes of landscape creation—indeed, as we have seen, real estate speculation, for example, was as important
to the Boston elite in their decisions concerning the location of cultural institutions,
as it was to New York businessmen in choosing to build skyscrapers. Yet those important decisions were not left up to relative chance; each determination was based on
specific considerations, including the particular predilections of individuals, the social
structure in which those individuals operated, and the general outlook on society and
culture that was prevalent at the time. This is what I take to mean historical tradition.
And by examining historical tradition in the shaping of the nineteenth-century land-

scape, I have tried to give meaning to those landscapes, to fill in the gaps that separate the two-dimensional maps of urban patterns from the three-dimensional, complex reality that we encounter in the streets.

The Nature of the Modern City

The middle and upper classes of nineteenth-century New York and Boston were as concerned with creating cultural products as material wealth. In fact, culture and commerce were seen as complementary rather than opposing. In this way, architectural displays and grand boulevards were as important in these classes' self-identity and self-representation as were their factories and offices and warehouses. A member of the ruling class in Boston or New York looked at the city as a cultural map, where classes distinguished themselves by the clothes they wore, the shops they frequented, the parks they strolled in, and the houses they inhabited, and where the boundaries delineating areas on that map were constantly shifting.

This was a particularly precarious world. With most of the upper-class wealth of relatively recent vintage, the need to protect and legitimize it was acute. The creation of landscape was vitally important, since built forms were used not only to generate and consolidate wealth, but equally or even more to legitimize it and the people who had created it. And this legitimizing landscape was not constituted of workers and working-class housing, of factories and warehouses, of, in short, what many geographers think of as critical to the nineteenth-century city. By the first half of the nineteenth century, the middle and upper classes of cities like New York and Boston had consolidated their economic positions enough that they could readily employ resources to create landscapes of self-representation that could display and legitimize their status. This, then, was a city of shopping and leisure districts, of exclusive residential enclaves, of parks and boulevards, and of ornamental architectural displays. These elements constituted the cultural map of the nineteenth-century city.

In this sense, one can trace strong lines of continuity between the city of the nineteenth century and the late twentieth century. David Harvey's description of the postmodern urban landscape as an "architecture of spectacle, with its sense of surface glitter and transitory participatory pleasure, of display and ephemerality" could apply equally well to Stewart's stores, or Pulitzer's World Building, or the Neoclassical façades of Boston's cultural institutions.[1] The elaborate Olmsted park systems that encircled many of our nineteenth-century cities, the ornate mansions, decorative commercial buildings, and revival style skyscrapers were as much display-oriented and image-laden as are our gentrified residential areas, and Disney-like festival settings.[2] To go shopping in Stewart's cast-iron palace or in Berlin's arcades was as much a spectacle and arena for display as is shopping in South Street Seaport or on Rodeo Drive.[3]

In addition, the decline of public space in the city that is being mourned as a casualty of the postmodern era also has its roots in the nineteenth-century city.[4] Many of the "public" arenas in nineteenth-century New York and Boston were privately controlled and highly manipulative spaces. Boston's Common, for example, in the first decades of the nineteenth century was a private residential square, and the urban park system that was built in the last half of the century represented the private interests of the city's elite. The city's Back Bay project, although carried out as a public process, in the end created a private and elitist residential area. And the so-called public spaces for women in the retailing district of New York were privately controlled and maintained so that women would adhere to appropriate gender ideology. The nineteenth-century city, therefore, has much to teach us about the nature of modernism, and by implication, about our present postmodern world.

Interpreting the Landscape

The cultural maps of nineteenth-century cities could differ in dramatic ways, however. Analyzing large-scale economic transformations in nineteenth-century America and the impact of those changes on class and gender relations is important in order to understand the structural framework for the production of built forms, but it does little to explain how those transformations were translated into action in specific circumstances. New York and Boston took different trajectories in the nineteenth century, at least in part because of particularities of each city's socioeconomic structure. Although the middle and upper classes in each city were struggling with a similar dilemma—how to control their landscape, keep it livable for themselves, and use it to legitimize their status—the particularities of each city's elite class meant that the dilemma was negotiated on different terms. Because of the degree of control Boston's upper class maintained, they were more successful in creating a group identity for themselves based on their need for cultural legitimacy. Their factories were kept out of the city and were set up as paternalistic enterprises, fitting their ideological stance. They prevented commercial encroachment of the Boston Common and the Back Bay, where they maintained architectural standards in the best of taste. New York's upper classes were constantly struggling to assert that control, because the boundaries of the cultural and economic map of their city were changing rapidly. To project a cultured and therefore legitimized image of themselves required constant vigilance, with the battle never securely won. As a result, the landscape they created was more an arena for the display and exchange of cultural capital, than an expression of group identity. Despite their efforts, their ostentatious department stores and skyscrapers spoke of unabashed commercialism and competition, not civic commitment and cultural legitimacy. And the particular structures of each city's middle and upper classes that gave shape to the urban landscape were themselves products of certain socioeconomic conditions. The relatively stagnant economic growth of Boston allowed the elite classes to stabilize, and therefore maintain control over much of the city's political and economic processes. New York's explosive economic growth never allowed for the consolidated control of one powerful class, thereby preventing one class's interests from prevailing. Interpreting the urban landscape, therefore, required analysis of the particular elements that comprised each city's historical trajectory.

This analysis may not yield a knowledge that is easily generalizable to other situations, but it will reveal the complex set of relationships that supply a logic of landscape creation and construction. I hope that this study has made some relationships more clear and contributed to that ongoing discussion concerning the nature of urban visions and urban form in nineteenth-century America.

Notes

Introduction

1. M. Christine Boyer, *Manhattan Manners: Architecture and Style, 1850-1900* (New York: Rizzoli, 1985), 1.

2. Embedded in most theoretical constructs of urban geography is an assumption that cities generally follow similar courses of spatial expansion coincident with stages of economic development. See, for example, James E. Vance, Jr., *The Continuing City* (Baltimore: Johns Hopkins University Press, 1990); Harold Carter, *An Introduction to Urban Historical Geography* (London: Edward Arnold, 1989); Maurice Yeates and Barry Garner, *The North American City* (New York: Harper and Row, 1976).

3. Denis Cosgrove and Stephen Daniels, eds., *The Iconography of Landscape* (Cambridge: Cambridge University Press, 1988).

4. Mona Domosh, "A Method for Interpreting Landscape: A Case Study of the New York World Building," *Area* 21 (1989): 347-355.

5. Donald J. Olsen, *The City as a Work of Art* (New Haven: Yale University Press, 1986).

6. Robert Darnton, *The Great Cat Massacre and Other Episodes in French Cultural History* (New York: Vintage Books, 1985), 6.

7. Marshall Berman, *All That Is Solid Melts into Air* (New York: Simon and Schuster, 1982).

8. See John Agnew, John Mercer, and David Sopher, eds., *The City in Cultural Context* (Boston: Allen and Unwin, 1984); Marwyn Samuels, "The Biography of Landscape," in *The Interpretation of Ordinary Landscapes*, ed. D. W. Meinig (New York: Oxford University Press, 1979); Anthony D. King, ed., *Buildings and Society* (London: Routledge and Kegan Paul, 1980); John A. Agnew and James S. Duncan, eds., *The Power of Place: Bringing Together Geographical and Sociological Imaginations* (Boston: Unwin Hyman, 1989).

9. Denis Cosgrove and Peter Jackson, "New Directions in Cultural Geography," *Area* 19 (1987): 95–101; Denis Cosgrove, "A Terrain of Metaphor: Cultural Geography 1988-1989," *Progress in Human Geography* 13 (1989): 566-575.

10. For exceptions, see James Duncan, *The City as Text* (Cambridge: Cambridge University Press, 1991); Denis Cosgrove and Stephen Daniels, eds., *The Iconography of Landscape* (Cambridge: Cambridge University Press, 1988); Kay Anderson and Faye Gale, eds., *Inventing Places: Studies in Cultural Geography* (Melbourne: Longman Cheshire, 1992); James Duncan and David Ley, eds., *Power/Culture/Representation* (London: Routledge, 1993).

11. Richard Walker, "The Transformation of Urban Structure in the Nineteenth Century and the Beginnings of Suburbanization," in *Urbanization and Conflict in Market Societies*, ed. Kevin Cox (Chicago: Maroufa Press, 1978); David Gordon, "Capitalist Development and the History of American Cities," in *Marxism and the Metropolis*, ed. William Tabb and Larry Sawer (New York: Oxford University Press, 1984).

12. See, for example, Raymond Murphy and James E. Vance, Jr., "Delimiting the CBD," *Economic Geography* 30 (1954): 189-222; and Martyn J. Bowden, "Downtown Through Time: Delineation, Expansion, and Internal Growth," *Economic Geography* 47 (1971): 121-134.

13. See, for example, David Ward, *Cities and Immigrants* (New York: Oxford University Press, 1971), and Sam Bass Warner, *Streetcar Suburbs* (New York: Atheneum, 1976).

14. Michael Conzen, "The Maturing Urban System in the United States, 1840-1910," *Annals of the Association of American Geographers* 67 (1977): 88-108; David Meyer, "Emergence of the American Manufacturing Belt: An Interpretation," *Journal of Historical Geography* 9 (1983): 145-174; Allan Pred, *The Spatial Dynamics of United States Urban Industrial Growth, 1800-1914* (Cambridge: MIT Press, 1966).

15. Frederic Cople Jaher, "Nineteenth-Century Elites in Boston and New York," *Journal of Social History* 6 (1972-1973): 33-77; Jaher, "Style and Status: High Society in Late Nineteenth-Century New York," in *The Rich, the Well Born and the Powerful*, ed. F. C. Jaher (Urbana: University of Illinois Press, 1973); Jaher, *The Urban Establishment: Upper Strata in Boston, New York, Charleston, Chicago and Los Angeles* (Urbana: University of Illinois Press, 1982); Martin Green, *The Problem of Boston* (New York: W. W. Norton, 1966); Paul Goodman, "Ethics and Enterprise: The Values of a Boston Elite, 1800-1860," *American Quarterly* 18 (1986): 436-451; David C. Hammack, *Power and Society: Greater New York at the Turn of the Century* (New York: Russell Sage Foundation, 1982); Brett Howard, *Boston: A Social History* (New York: Hawthorn Books, 1976); Robert Rich, "'A Wilderness of Whigs': The Wealthy Men of Boston," *Journal of Social History* 4 (1971): 263-276; Ronald Story, *The Forging of an Aristocracy* (Middletown, Conn.: Wesleyan University Press, 1980).

16. For examples of surveys, see Henry-Russell Hitchcock, *A Guide to Boston Architecture, 1637-1954* (New York: Reinhold, 1954); Ada Louise Huxtable, *The Architecture of New York: A History and Guide* (Garden City, N.Y.: Doubleday, 1964); Douglas S. Tucci, *Built in Boston* (Boston: New York Graphic Society, 1978). For thematic analyses, see Bainbridge Bunting, *Houses of Boston's Back Bay* (Cambridge: Harvard University Press, 1967); Paul Goldberger, *The Skyscraper* (New York: Alfred A. Knopf, 1982); Winston Weisman, "Commercial Palaces of New York: 1845-1875," *Art Bulletin* 36 (1954): 285-302; Weisman, "The Commercial Architecture of George B. Post," *Journal of the Society of Architectural Historians* 31 (1972): 176-203; Weisman, "A New View of Skyscraper History," in *The Rise of an American Architecture*, ed.

Edgar Kaufman (New York: Praeger, 1974); Robert B. Rettig, *The Architecture of H. H. Richardson and His Contemporaries in Boston and Vicinity* (Philadelphia: Society of Architectural History); Charles Lockwood, *Manhattan Moves Uptown* (Boston: Houghton Mifflin, 1976).

Chapter 1. New York and Boston in the First Half of the Nineteenth Century

1. Edward Spann, *The New Metropolis* (New York: Columbia University Press, 1981), 426.

2. Quoted in Martin Green, *The Problem of Boston* (New York: W. W. Norton, 1966), 47.

3. Frederic Cople Jaher, *The Urban Establishment: Upper Strata in Boston, New York, Charleston, Chicago and Los Angeles* (Urbana: University of Illinois Press, 1982); John S. Hekman and John S. Strong, "The Evolution of New England Industry," *New England Economic Review* (March-April, 1981): 35-46.

4. John F. Kasson, *Civilizing the Machine: Technology and Republican Values in America, 1776-1900* (New York: Penguin Books, 1976).

5. Robert F. Dalzell, Jr., *Enterprising Elite: The Boston Associates and the World They Made* (Cambridge: Harvard University Press, 1987), 79.

6. Ibid, chapter 2.

7. Thomas Dublin, *Women at Work: The Transformation of Work and Community in Lowell, Mass., 1826-1860* (New York: Columbia University Press, 1979)

8. Kasson, *Civilizing the Machine.*

9. Quoted in ibid., 71.

10. Hekman and Strong, "New England Industry," 39.

11. Dalzell, *Enterprising Elite*, 79-80.

12. Jaher, *Urban Establishment*, 87-97.

13. Edward Pessen, *Riches, Class and Power before the Civil War* (Lexington, Mass.: D. C. Heath, 1973), 224-225; Jaher, *Urban Establishment*, ch. 2.

14. For example, in 1857, only 7.8% of America's exports and 15.3% of its imports went through the port of Boston, compared to 36% of exports and 63% of imports for New York. Boston's relative standing in terms of tonnage of vessels entered in foreign trade diminished throughout the latter half of the nineteenth century. See Hamilton Andrews Hill, *Boston's Trade and Commerce for Forty Years, 1844-1884* (Boston: T. R. Marvin and Son, 1884); Pliny Miles, *The Advantages of Ocean Steam Navigation, Foreign and Coastwise, to the Commerce of Boston, and the Manufactures of New England* (Boston: Emery N. Moore, 1857). For an analysis of the relative decline of Boston's position in national politics, see Dalzell, *Enterprising Elite*, particularly chapter 6.

15. Green, *Problem of Boston*, 56.

16. Ronald Story, *The Forging of an Aristocracy* (Middletown, Conn.: Wesleyan University Press, 1980); Jaher, *Urban Establishment.*

17. Ronald P. Formisano and Constance K. Burns, eds., *Boston 1700-1980: The Evolution of Urban Politics* (Westport, Conn.: Greenwood Press, 1984); Frederic Cople Jaher, "The Politics of the Boston Brahmins: 1800-1860" in ibid.

18. Robert Rich, "A Wilderness of Whigs: The Wealthy Men of Boston," *Journal of Social History* 4 (1971): 63-276.

19. Frederic Cople Jaher, "Nineteenth-Century Elites in Boston and New York," *Journal of Social History* 6 (1972-73): 33-77.

20. *Report of Mr. Sturgis's Committee to Twenty-eight Manufacturing Companies* (Boston: William Chadwick, 1852).

21. For example, by 1851, Abbott Lawrence, who throughout his life had pursued every means of expanding his material wealth, was warning his nephew against such practices: "We must wait a little before we take up new things, we must be careful how we move, for we cannot afford experiments that

may become expensive." Abbott's brother Amos told his son, "you must be the literary and perhaps philanthropic head of your family, perhaps of our name." Quoted in Jaher, *Urban Establishment*, 78.

22. Boston's population more than doubled between 1870 and 1890, as did the number of retail establishments. See *Boston's Growth* (Boston: State Street Trust, 1910), *The Boston Directory* (Adams, Sampson, 1865), and *The Boston Directory* (Sampson, Murdock, 1895).

23. Dalzell, *Enterprising Elite*, 112; Jaher, *Urban Establishment*.

24. Robert G. Albion, *The Rise of New York Port, 1815-1869* (New York: Charles Scribner's Sons, 1967).

25. Robert Murray Haig, *Major Economic Factors in Metropolitan Growth and Arrangement, Regional Survey of New York, Vol. 1* (New York: Regional Plan of New York, 1927).

26. Allan Pred, *The Spatial Dynamics of United States Urban Industrial Growth 1800-1914* (Cambridge: MIT Press, 1966); Michael P. Conzen, "The Maturing Urban System in the United States, 1840-1914," *Annals of the Association of American Geographers* 67 (1977): 88-108.

27. David C. Hammack, *Power and Society: Greater New York at the Turn of the Century* (New York: Russell Sage Foundation, 1982).

28. Spann, *New Metropolis*, 14.

29. Ibid., 15.

30. Alfred D. Chandler, "Patterns of American Railroad Finance," *Business History Review* 28 (1954): 263.

31. Jaher, "Nineteenth-Century Elites," 32-33.

32. Spann, *New Metropolis*, 23-24, 430.

33. Hammack, *Power and Society*, chapter 10; Jaher, *Urban Establishment*, chapter 3.

34. Spann, *New Metropolis*, chapter 5.

35. Hammack, *Power and Society*, 36.

36. Ibid., 77.

37. Ibid.; Jaher, *Urban Establishment*.

38. Jaher, *Urban Establishment*, 256.

39. Spann, *New Metropolis*, 283.

40. For an overview of the emergence of economic districts in large cities, see Martyn J. Bowden, "Growth of Central Districts in Large Cities," in *The New Urban History*, ed. L. Schnore (Princeton: Princeton University Press, 1975).

41. See James E. Vance, Jr., "Land Use in the Pre-capitalist, Capitalist and Post-capitalist City," *Economic Geography* 47 (1971): 101-120.

42. Spann, *New Metropolis*, 10; Charles Lockwood, *Manhattan Moves Uptown* (Boston: Houghton Mifflin, 1976), 104.

43. Paul Goldberger, *The City Observed: New York* (New York: Vintage Books, 1979), chapter 1.

44. Douglas T. Miller, *Jacksonian Aristocracy: Class and Democracy in New York, 1830-1860* (New York: Oxford University Press, 1962), 74.

45. Kenneth A. Scherzer, *The Unbounded Community: Neighborhood Life and Social Structure in New York City, 1830-1875* (Durham: Duke University Press, 1992), chapter 6.

46. Charles Mackay, *Life and Liberty in America* (New York, 1859), 20. Quoted in Miller, *Jacksonian Democracy*, 162.

47. Spann, *New Metropolis*, 148.

48. Walter Muir Whitehill, *Boston: A Topographical History* (Cambridge: Belknap Press of Harvard University Press, 1968), 96-98.

49. Edward Stanwood, "Topography and Landmarks of the Last Hundred Years," in *The Memorial History of Boston*, ed. Justin Winsor (Boston: James R. Osgood, 1881).

50. Douglass Shand-Tucci, *Built in Boston* (Amherst: University of Massachusetts Press, 1988), 6. The crescent was torn down in 1858 and the theater in 1852 to make way for the expansion of commercial areas.

51. Harold and James Kirker, *Bulfinch's Boston: 1787–1817* (New York: Oxford University Press, 1964), 136.

52. The plan of the square closed it off from the northern slope. According to Carl Weinhardt, "the two streets connecting Pinckney Street with the North Slope were closed, and the north side of Pinckney Street was laid out in an unbroken line of uniform lots from Anderson to West Cedar Street. This protected the new development from the dissimilar area to the north." See Carl J. Weinhardt, Jr., *The Domestic Architecture of Beacon Hill, 1800–1850* (Boston: Bostonian Society, 1973), n.p.

53. Whitehill, *Topographical History*, 122.

54. Oscar Handlin, *Boston's Immigrants: A Study in Acculturation, 1790–1880* (Cambridge: Harvard University Press, 1959), 56.

55. Tamara Plakins Thornton, *Cultivating Gentlemen: The Meaning of Country Life among the Boston Elite, 1785–1860* (New Haven: Yale University Press, 1989).

Chapter 2. Creating New York's Retail District

1. Gunther Barth, *City People* (New York: Oxford University Press, 1980), 146.

2. M. Christine Boyer, *Manhattan Manners: Architecture and Style, 1850–1900* (New York: Rizzoli, 1985), 43.

3. Ibid., 44.

4. Stuart Blumin has documented the growth of this middle class, and the relationship of this new class to new urban spaces and the values of consumption. See Blumin, *The Emergence of the Middle Class: Social Experience in the American City, 1760–1900* (New York: Cambridge University Press, 1989).

5. William R. Taylor, *In Pursuit of Gotham: Culture and Commerce in New York* (New York: Oxford University Press, 1992).

6. The development of the department store, and its relationship to nineteenth-century urban life, have been discussed elsewhere. See Michael B. Miller, *The Bon Marché: Bourgeois Culture and the Department Store, 1869–1920* (Princeton, N.J.: Princeton University Press, 1981); Barth, *City People*; Susan Porter Benson, *Counter Cultures: Saleswomen, Managers, and Customers in American Department Stores, 1890–1940* (Urbana: University of Illinois Press, 1986); Elaine S. Abelson, *When Ladies Go A-Thieving: Middle-Class Shoplifters in the Victorian Department Store* (New York: Oxford University Press, 1989); David Chaney, "The Department Store as a Cultural Form," *Theory, Culture and Society* 1 (1983): 22–31; William R. Leach, "Transformation in a Culture of Consumption: Women and Department Stores, 1890–1925," *Journal of American History* 71 (1984): 319–342.

7. For specific stores and locations, see John Crawford Brown, "Early Days of Department Stores," in *Valentine's Manual of Old New York*, ed. Henry Collins Brown (New York: Valentine's Manual, 1921); *Through the Years* (New York: Arnold Constable, 1950); *John Wanamaker's Centennial Book, 1823–1923* (New York: John Wanamaker, 1923); Edward Hungerford, *The Romance of a Great Store* (New York: Robert M. McBride, 1922); *The History of Lord and Taylor* (New York: Lord and Taylor, 1927).

8. The effects of mass production on the establishment of the middle classes has been well documented, most notably by Stuart Blumin. See Blumin, *Emergence of the Middle Class*.

9. Chaney, "Department Store," 27, 24.

10. Rosalind H. Williams, *Dream Worlds: Mass Consumption in Late Nineteenth-Century France* (Berkeley: University of California Press, 1982).

11. *New York Herald*, 22 September 1846, 2.

12. *New York Herald*, 26 September 1846, 2.

13. Blumin, *Emergence of the Middle Class.*

14. Iver Bernstein, *The New York City Draft Riots: Their Significance for American Society and Politics in the Age of the Civil War* (New York: Oxford University Press, 1990).

15. Deborah S. Gardner, "'A Paradise of Fashion': A.T. Stewart's Department Store, 1862-1875," in *A Needle, A Bobbin, A Strike: Women Needleworkers in America*, ed. Joan M. Jensen and Sue Davidson (Philadelphia: Temple University Press, 1984).

16. James D. McCabe, Jr., *Lights and Shadows of New York Life; Or, The Sights and Sensations of the Great City* (1872; reprint, London: Andre Deutsch, 1971), 144.

17. Ibid., 143.

18. Abelson, *Ladies Thieving*, 40.

19. See, for example, Leonore Davidoff and Catherine Hall, *Family Fortunes: Men and Women of the English Middle Class, 1780-1850* (Chicago: University of Chicago Press, 1987); Peter Stallybrass and Allon White, *The Politics and Poetics of Transgression* (Ithaca, N.Y.: Cornell University Press, 1986).

20. Sally Shuttleworth, "Female Circulation: Medical Discourse and Popular Advertising in the Mid-Victorian Era," in *Body/Politics: Women and the Discourses of Science*, ed. Mary Jacobus, Evelyn Fox Keller, and Sally Shuttleworth (New York: Routledge, 1990).

21. *New York Herald*, 26 September 1846, 2.

22. E. L. Godkin, *Nation* 22 (1876): 259.

23. Brown, "Early Days."

24. Data concerning the locations of New York's department stores was derived from city directories and historical atlases. *Trow's New York City Directory* (New York: Trow City Directory, 1865, 1875, 1885, 1895); *Atlas of the City of New York* (Philadelphia: G. W. Bromley, 1879, 1891, 1902, 1908).

25. I use the location of department stores to indicate the general spatial pattern of retailing. As the establishments with the largest stakes in real estate, department stores have been recognized as the prime shapers of retail expansion and tend to act as anchors for smaller retail establishments. The locations of department stores indicate the central portion of the retail districts, but do not indicate the full areal extent. Smaller and often more specialized retailers are often located on the fringes of the district. What is being described as the location of department stores is the central portion of the retail district. See Martyn J. Bowden, "Downtown Through Time: Delimitation, Expansion, and Internal Growth," *Economic Geography* 47 (1971): 121-134; David Ward, "The Industrial Revolution and the Emergence of Boston's Central Business District," *Economic Geography* 42 (1966): 152-171.

The rapid movement and expansion of New York's retail district can be contrasted to the rather limited expansion of Boston's retailing area. By 1895, Boston's retailing area had expanded approximately five blocks from its core area near Milk and Pearl streets in the 1840s to the intersection of Washington and Winter streets. New York's retailing area during the same time period moved more than forty blocks north from its original core area. Boston's relatively small retail expansion was due to many factors, but primarily was the result of legislation that prevented commercial encroachment of the Common and Public Garden, the fact that the city's upper classes did not move out of the city rapidly, and the proportionately smaller retail trade in Boston. In essence, Boston's retailing area did not make any significant locational shifts throughout the latter half of the nineteenth century, nor did the area alter its appearance greatly. For example, Boston's leading department store, Jordan Marsh, moved into a building on Washington Street in 1861, and expanded by adding smaller structures to the original brownstone building. It was not until 1907 that the owners constructed an entirely new building, on an adjoining lot and connected to the older structure. Data on the location of Boston's department stores was derived from *The Boston Directory* (Adams, Sampson, 1865); *The Boston Directory* (Boston: Sampson, Davenport, 1875 and 1885); *The Boston Directory* (Boston: Sampson, Murdock, 1895); *Atlas of the City of Boston* (Philadelphia: G. W.

Bromley, 1895). See also Richard H. Edwards, Jr., *Tales of the Observer* (Boston: Jordan Marsh, 1950); John William Ferry, *A History of the Department Store* (New York: Macmillan, 1960).

26. McCabe, *Lights and Shadows*, 375.

27. "Yellow Houses," *Real Estate Record* 25, 3 April 1880, 311. Quoted in Boyer, *Manhattan Manners*, 101.

28. Boyer, *Manhattan Manners*, introduction and chapter 1.

29. Allan Nevins, ed., *The Diary of Philip Hone, 1828–1851*, vol. 2 (New York: Dodd, Mead, 1927), 896. Quoted in *Manhattan Manners*, 45.

30. Martyn J. Bowden, "Growth of Central Districts in Large Cities," in *The New Urban History*, ed. Leo Schnore (Princeton, N.J.: Princeton University Press, 1975).

31. Brown, "Early Days," 106.

32. *Through the Years* (New York: Arnold Constable, 1950), 11.

33. *The History of Lord and Taylor* (New York: Lord and Taylor, n.d.), 36.

34. McCabe, *Lights and Shadows*, 385.

35. Ibid.

36. Robert Hendrickson, *The Grand Emporiums* (New York: Stein and Day, 1979); Ferry, *History of the Department Store*.

37. Harry E. Resseguie, "A. T. Stewart's Marble Palace—The Cradle of the Department Store," *New York Historical Society Quarterly* 48 (1964): 131–162.

38. Miller, *The Bon Marché*, 3.

39. Resseguie, "A. T. Stewart's."

40. It is unclear exactly who designed the building. Records show that Stewart hired an Italian marble cutter to design the marble façade, but it is not clear if he had anything to do with the actual design of the building (Winston Weisman, "Commercial Palaces of New York: 1845–1875," *Art Bulletin* 36 [1954]: 288). However, a more recent analysis of the books of their architectural firm makes a strong case that Joseph Trench and John Snook were involved in the design of the original building and were the architects of its subsequent additions. See Mary Ann Smith, "John Snook and the Design for A. T. Stewart's Store," *New York Historical Society Quarterly* 58 (1974): 18–33.

41. *History of Architecture and the Building Trades of Greater New York* (New York, 1899), 139, quoted in Weisman, "Commercial Palaces," 286.

42. Nevins, *Diary of Philip Hone*, quoted in Resseguie, "A. T. Stewart's," 139.

43. Resseguie, "A. T. Stewart's," 9.

44. Weisman, "Commercial Palaces," 286.

45. Ibid., 289.

46. *Evening Post*, 21 September 1846. Quoted in Smith, "John Snook," 25.

47. Boyer, *Manhattan Manners*, 90.

48. *New York Herald*, 18 September 1846, 1.

49. William Leach, *True Love and Perfect Union: The Feminist Reform of Sex and Society* (New York: Basic Books, 1980), 222–242.

50. Stewart's successful formula included sound financial policies, strict control over his employees, and overriding interest in getting the best prices for the goods he purchased. To do so, he acquired a controlling interest in several textile mills, thus insuring a constant and cost-controlled supply of dry goods to his store. See Resseguie, "A. T. Stewart's," and Smith, "John Snook," 18.

51. *Harper's New Monthly* 9 (1854): 261.

52. *New York Herald*, 22 September 1846, 2.

53. Ferry, *History of the Department Store*.

54. *Golden Book of the Wanamaker Stores* (Philadelphia: John Wanamaker, 1911).

55. *John Wanamaker's Centennial Book.*

56. Resseguie, "A. T. Stewart's," 126.

57. Barth, *City People*, 127.

58. Boyer, *Manhattan Manners*, 92.

59. P. B. Wight, "A Millionaire's Architectural Investment," *American Architect and Building News* 1, 6 May 1876, 148.

60. For a discussion of the Victorian idea that architecture could be used to stimulate particular conceptions in people's minds through association with certain laudable elements of the past, see James A. Schmiechen, "The Victorians, the Historians, and the Idea of Modernism," *American History Review* 93 (1988): 287–316.

61. Quoted in Boyer, *Manhattan Manners*, 94.

62. Godkin, *Nation*, 259.

63. *Sibyl*, 1 November 1856, quoted in Leach, "Culture of Consumption," 232.

64. D. J. K., "Shopping at Stewart's," *Hearth and Home* (9 January 1869): 43.

65. Leach, *True Love and Perfect Union*, 232.

66. Abelson, *Ladies Thieving*, 21.

67. Leach, *True Love and Perfect Union*, 232.

Chapter 3. Constructing New York's Skyline

1. The exact criteria that define a building as a skyscraper are debated by architectural historians. The height of a building, whether measured by number of stories or in feet, is favored by Henry-Russell Hitchcock and Montgomery Schuyler. See Henry-Russell Hitchcock, *Architecture, Nineteenth and Twentieth Centuries* (Baltimore: Penguin Books, 1958), and Montgomery Schuyler, *American Architecture and Other Writings*, ed. William Jordy and Ralph Coe (New York: Atheneum, 1964). There are two technological definitions of skyscrapers: J. Carson Webster and Francesco Mujica insist on steel-frame construction, whereas Carl Condit and Winston Weisman emphasize the passenger elevator. See J. Carson Webster, "The Skyscraper: Logical and Historical Considerations," *Journal of the Society of Architectural Historians* (1959): 126–139; Francesco Mujica, *History of the Skyscraper* (New York: Da Capo Press, 1977); Carl Condit, *American Building Art, the Nineteenth Century* (New York: Oxford University Press, 1960); Winston Weisman, "A New View of Skyscraper History," in *The Rise of an American Architecture*, ed. Edgar Kaufman (New York: Praeger, 1970). I have used a simplified criterion of nine stories in height to define a skyscraper in order to be as inclusive as possible, particularly in the first years of skyscraper development when complex technical considerations are difficult to decipher.

2. Studies of the central business district have located the changing intersections with peak land value in several cities and have pointed out the correlation with tall buildings. See, for example, Martyn J. Bowden, "The Dynamics of City Growth," Ph.D. diss., University of California, Berkeley, 1967, and James E. Vance, Jr., and Raymond Murphy, "Delimiting the CBD," *Economic Geography* 30 (1954): 189–222.

3. In 1890, land values around City Hall Park were approximately $150 per square foot, compared to $350 per square foot on Wall Street. See Richard Hurd, *Principles of City Land Use* (New York: The Record and Guide, 1903), 158, and Michael Mikkelsen, "A Review of the History of Real Estate on Manhattan Island," in *A History of Real Estate and Architecture in New York City* (1898; reprint, New York: Arno Press, 1967), 123–125.

4. David Hammond, *Power and Society: Greater New York at the Turn of the Century* (New York: Columbia University Press, 1987), 81.

5. Daniel Bluestone, *Constructing Chicago* (New Haven: Yale University Press, 1991), 140, 123.

6. Urban economic theory assumes that location in cities is based on competition to be close to the

point that is the most accessible in the city. For standard works on urban economic theory, see W. Alonso, *Location and Land Use: Toward a General Theory of Land Rent* (Cambridge: Harvard University Press, 1964); Maurice Yeates and Barry Garner, *The North American City* (New York: Harper and Row, 1976); Richard U. Ratcliff, *Urban Land Economics* (New York: McGraw-Hill, 1949); Homer Hoyt and Arthur M. Weimer, *Principles of Urban Real Estate* (New York: Ronald Press, 1948).

7. Ibid., 301-302.

8. For a discussion of the replacement of churches by commercial buildings as important icons of the American city, see Christopher Tunnard and Henry Hope Reed, *American Skyline* (New York: Mentor Press, 1956).

9. Building activity in the United States did not regain its pre-1875 level until 1882. See J. R. Riggleman, "Building Cycles in the U.S., 1875-1932," *Journal of the American Statistical Association* 28 (1933): 174-183, and Mikkelsen, "Review of the History of Real Estate."

10. Historical atlases were used to determine the locational pattern of New York's first tall buildings. Five cross sections were taken of lower Manhattan between the years 1881 and 1908, and the locations, heights, and, if applicable, names of all buildings nine stories or more in height were recorded. E. Robinson, *Atlas of the City of New York* (New York: E. Robinson, 1885); G. W. Bromley, *Atlas of the City of New York* (Philadelphia: G. W. Bromley, 1891, 1897, 1902, 1908). Because the 1891 atlas failed to provide information on the heights of the buildings, assessment records were consulted: *Record of the Assessments, City of New York, First Ward* (New York: 1891). Sanborn atlases were difficult to use because those extant today were updated frequently but often in an irregular pattern.

11. Hurd, *Principles of Land Use*, 158.

12. For a discussion of the social and cultural significance of the Brooklyn Bridge, see Alan Trachtenberg, *Brooklyn Bridge: Fact and Symbol* (Chicago: University of Chicago Press, 1979).

13. *King's Handbook* (New York: Moses King, 1893), 824.

14. Amos Wright, "Seeing the Metropolis Grow," *Harper's Weekly* 34 (1890): 81.

15. Several framing types represent transitions from masonry to full steel-frame construction. Buildings that incorporated some elements of steel framing in their construction were built in New York before the Tower Building. See Mujica, *History of Skyscraper*.

16. Land values in the Wall Street area were approximately $400 per front foot, compared to $200 in City Hall Park. See Hurd, *Principles of Land Use*.

17. Barr Ferree, "The High Building and Its Art," *Scribner's* 15 (1894): 279.

18. An analysis of city directories provided information on the activities associated with constructing tall buildings. *Trow's New York City Directory* (New York: Trow City Directory, 1886, 1892, 1898, 1903, 1909).

19. Gunther Barth, *City People* (New York: Oxford University Press, 1980). Newspapers in New York prior to the 1830s were mercantile newspapers sold by subscription and devoted entirely to news sought by merchants. It was only after the development of daily newspapers of general interest in the 1840s and 1850s that newspaper companies required large buildings to house their staffs. James Crouthamel, "The Newspaper Revolution in New York, 1830-1860," *New York History* 45 (1964): 91-113.

20. For studies of some of those individuals and the papers they owned, see George Juergens, *Joseph Pulitzer and the New York World* (Princeton, N.J.: Princeton University Press, 1966); James Wyman Barrett, *Joseph Pulitzer and His World* (New York: Vanguard Press, 1941); Allen Churchill, *Park Row* (Westport, Conn.: Greenwood Press, 1958); Elmer Davis, *History of the New York Times* (New York: New York Times, 1921); Augustus Maverick, *Henry J. Raymond and the New York Press* (1870; reprint, New York: Arno Press, 1970); Meyer Berger, *The Story of the New York Times* (New York: Simon and Schuster, 1951); Willard Grosvenor Bleyer, *Main Currents in the History of American Journalism* (New York: Houghton Mifflin, 1927).

21. Barth, *City People*, 59.

22. Crouthamel, "Newspaper Revolution," 103.

23. S. N. D. North, "History and Present Condition of the Newspaper and Periodical Press of The United States, with a Catalogue of the Publications of the Census Year," in U.S. Department of the Interior, Bureau of the Census, *Tenth Census* (Washington, 1884), 51, quoted in Barth, *City People*, 59.

24. Crouthamel, "Newspaper Revolution," 101–102.

25. Architectural historian Sarah Bradford Landau refers to this style as "commercial neo-Grec," since it is characterized by segmental arches and flat, hard-edged decorative motifs. See Landau, "Richard Morris Hunt: Architectural Innovator and Father of a 'Distinctive' American School," in *The Architecture of Richard Morris Hunt*, ed. Susan R. Stein (Chicago: University of Chicago Press, 1986), 47–78.

26. Montgomery Schuyler, "Some Recent Skyscrapers," *Architectural Record* 22 (1907): 4.

27. "The Palace-Building of the New York Tribune," *Potter's American Monthly* 5 (1875): 538.

28. Bleyer, *Main Currents*, 329.

29. See Stein, *Architecture of Hunt*, 54–60.

30. Quoted in D. C. Seitz, *Joseph Pulitzer: His Life and Letters* (New York: Simon and Schuster, 1924), 175.

31. *The New York World, Its History and New Home* (New York, 1890), 54, 3.

32. Ibid., 4.

33. Richard Harding Davis, "Broadway," *Scribner's Magazine* 9 (1891): 588.

34. Barbara Rubin, "Aesthetic Ideology and Urban Design," *Annals of the Association of American Geographers* 69 (1979): 342.

35. "The Pulitzer Building," *New York World*, 10 December 1890.

36. In New York, those arbiters consisted of what Frederick Cople Jaher calls the Old Guard, a group of economic elites that were losing power in the late nineteenth century. This group turned to cultural concerns as a way of combating the nouveaux riches. "Aristocratic sponsorship became a weapon against materialistic vulgarity, a means of separating the Old Guard from the nouveau riche, and a compensation for displacement in other aspects of leadership" (Frederick Cople Jaher, *The Urban Establishment, Upper Strata in Boston, New York, Charleston, Chicago, and Los Angeles* [Urbana: University of Illinois Press, 1982], 234).

37. "The New World Building," *Record and Guide*, 14 June 1890, n.p.

38. Jaher, *Urban Establishment*, 259.

39. "A New Commercial Palace," *Harper's Weekly* 29 (1880): 78.

40. The life insurance industry had been interested in material forms of display since mid-century: witness the various guises of the Equitable and Mutual Life buildings. The argument here is that the industry did not get involved in development of skyscrapers (i.e., buildings of nine stories or more) until after 1890.

41. For exact heights, see Mona Domosh, "Scrapers of the Sky: The Symbolic and Functional Structures of Lower Manhattan," Ph.D. diss., Clark University, 1985.

42. Unlike other types of insurance companies such as fire and marine insurance, which needed to be central to financial activities, the life insurance industry was not directly linked to the financial district and could afford to move out of the area and seek cheaper locations. As an established display focus, City Hall Park became a desirable location.

From the 1890s on, life insurance companies were found in the tallest buildings in the city. In 1891, two life insurance companies were in the sixteen-story World Building, two in the eleven-story Potter Building, and one in the thirteen-story Times Building. In 1908, four life insurance companies were located in the twenty-six-story St. Paul Building, and three in the fifty-six-story Singer Building. Other types of insurance companies apparently felt no need to locate in the most prominent structures, and located as close to Wall Street as was possible. For example, only three fire insurance companies were located in buildings over nineteen stories in 1908, and those buildings (the German American Insurance Building at 19 Liberty Street, and the Kuhn, Loeb Building at 52 William Street) were within the Wall Street district. Most of the fire insurance companies were located in medium-height structures. For example, in the Wall Street district in 1908, ten fire insurance companies were in the sixteen-story Royal Insurance building at 84 William Street, thirteen in the ten-story building at 45–49 Cedar Street, nine in the twelve-story building at 92 William Street, and seven in the thirteen-story Woodbridge Building at 100 William Street.

43. For studies of individual life insurance companies, see: Marquis James, *The Metropolitan Life* (New York: Viking Press, 1947); Shepard B. Clough, *A Century of American Life Insurance* (New York: Columbia University Press, 1946); P. Carlyle Buley, *The Equitable Life Assurance Society of the United States* (New York: Meredith, 1959); Wendell Buck, *The Old Reliable* (New York: Manhattan Life, 1950); *A Temple of Humanity* (New York: New York Life, 1909); *The Metropolitan Life Insurance Company* (New York: Metropolitan Life, 1908); James M. Hudnut, *Semi-Centennial History of the New York Life Insurance Company, 1845–1895* (New York: New York Life, 1906); Lawrence F. Abbott, *The Story of the New York Life Insurance Co.* (New York: New York Life, 1930); Frederick L. Hoffman, *History of the Prudential Insurance Company of America* (Newark, 1900); Earl C. May and Will Quisler, *The Prudential* (Garden City, N.Y.: Doubleday, 1950); and Louis I. Dublin, *A Family of Thirty Million* (New York: Metropolitan Life, 1943).

44. The insurance needs of immigrants were originally served by cooperative fraternal societies that provided insurance for burial fees. Private enterprise responded with what was called industrial insurance that required only a small, fixed premium with weekly payments. This type of insurance vied with fraternal societies, and was considered a step toward "Americanization." Morton Keller, *The Life Insurance Enterprise, 1885–1910* (Cambridge: Harvard University Press, 1963), 9.

45. Ibid., 26.

46. Ibid., 27–31, 39.

47. *King's Handbook of New York City, 1893* (1893; reprint, New York: Benjamin Blom, 1972), 674, 676, 682, 668.

48. Ibid.

49. Dublin, *A Family of Thirty Million*, 49.

50. James, *Metropolitan Life*, 112.

51. *King's Handbook*, 678.

52. James, *Metropolitan Life*, 174.

53. *The Metropolitan Life Building* (New York, n.d.), 1, 4.

54. The company published a series of these pamphlets on topics that ranged from first aid to healthy cooking techniques. These pamphlets can be found at the Warshaw Collection of Business Americana at the Smithsonian Institution.

55. Rubin, "Aesthetic Ideology," 342.

56. In 1896, eight of the twenty-four significantly tall buildings had names that were associated with neither a person nor an institution. In 1902 that ratio was fifteen out of twenty-one, and in 1908 the ratio was twenty-two out of thirty-five. The assumption here is that buildings named without apparent association were built as speculative office buildings.

57. David Hammack, *Power and Society: Greater New York at the Turn of the Century* (New York: Russell Sage Foundation, 1982), 46–47.

58. See *Digest of the Statues and of the Ordinances Relating to the Construction, Maintenance, and Inspection of Buildings in the City of Boston* (Boston: Rockwell and Churchill, 1893); *Pocket Manual of the Boston Building Laws* (Boston: Boston Building Laws, 1896); Samuel J. Elder, *Limitation of Heights of Buildings near Copley Square* (Boston: Samuel Usher, 1898); *Argument of J. H. Benton, Jr., for Legislation to Limit the Height of Buildings on and near Copley Square, in the city of Boston* (Boston, 1889).

59. Charles S. Damrell, *A Half Century of Boston's Buildings* (Boston: Louis P. Hager, 1895); Sydney A. Clark, *The First Hundred Years of the New England Mutual Life Insurance Company* (Boston, 1935); Jacob A. Barbey, *The Early History of the New England Mutual Life Insurance Company* (Boston, 1923).

60. *Illustrated Boston: The Metropolis of New England* (New York: American Publishing and Engraving, 1889), 67.

61. "Architectural Aberrations" first appeared in 1891. The term is generally credited to the architectural critic Montgomery Schuyler. "Architectural Aberrations," *Architectural Record* 7 (1897): 220.

62. For the best analysis of the "rational" attempts to control urban land use during this period, see M. Christine Boyer, *Dreaming the Rational City: The Myth of American City Planning* (Cambridge: MIT Press, 1990).

Chapter 4. Developing Boston's Back Bay

1. Bainbridge Bunting, *Houses of Boston's Back Bay* (Cambridge: Harvard University Press, 1967), 15.

2. Walter Firey, *Land Use in Central Boston* (Cambridge: Harvard University Press, 1968), chapter 3.

3. Walter Muir Whitehill, *Boston: A Topographical History* (Cambridge: Harvard University Press, 1959); Edward Stanwood, "Topography and Landmarks of the Last Hundred Years," in *The Memorial History of Boston*, ed. Justin Winsor (Boston: James R. Osgood, 1881), 25–63.

4. Harold Kirker and James Kirker, *Bulfinch's Boston, 1787–1817* (New York: Oxford University Press, 1964), 11–13 and chapter 7.

5. Bunting, *Houses of Back Bay*, 33.

6. Whitehill, *Topographical History*, 152.

7. Ibid, 154.

8. These efforts were undertaken for commercial gain, usually by private individuals. See ibid, chapter 4.

9. *Report of the Committee in Relation to Lands in the Back Bay, also, Fifth Annual Report of the Commissioners of the Back Bay* (Boston: William White, 1857), 4.

10. Bunting, *Houses of Back Bay*; Whitehill, *Topographical History*.

11. *Report of the Commissioners in Relation to the Flats in Boston Harbor* (Boston, 1850), 28.

12. *Remarks on the Project of Establishing a Line of Packets Between Boston and Liverpool* (Boston, 1825), 14. For an informative assessment of Boston's declining commercial position, see Hamilton Andrews Hill, *Boston's Trade and Commerce for Forty Years—1844–1881* (Boston: T. R. Marvin and Sons, 1884).

13. *Steam Connection between Boston and New Orleans, An Appeal of the Board of Trade to the Retired Capitalists and the owners of real estate* (Boston: James French, 1860), 4, 7.

14. Amos Lawrence, *Extracts from the Diary and Correspondence of the Late Amos Lawrence*, ed. William R. Lawrence (Boston, 1855), 80–81, quoted in Robert F. Dalzell, Jr., *Enterprising Elite: The Boston Associates and the World They Made* (Cambridge: Harvard University Press, 1987), 64.

15. Robert Varnum Spalding, "The Boston Mercantile Community and the Promotion of the Textile Industry in New England, 1813–1860," Ph.D. diss., Yale University, 1963.

16. Otis Clapp owned a bookstore on Beacon Street that was described as the "headquarters of advanced ideas in medicines, books and philosophy." He was active in local politics in the 1840s and 1850s, serving variously as ward inspector, member of the Board of Aldermen and the Board of Land Commissioners, and a state representative. His name was also associated with several charitable organizations in the city. *Boston Evening Transcript*, 18 September 1886, 12.

17. Abbott Lawrence the younger and Shaw had houses built for themselves in the Back Bay, on Commonwealth Avenue. See Bunting, *Houses of Back Bay*, 421–423.

18. Otis Clapp, *Letter to the Hon. Abbott Lawrence and the Hon. Robert G. Shaw on the Present Condition and Future Growth of Boston* (Boston: John Wilson and Son, 1853), 4. Clapp was not the only Boston merchant to express concern over the economic policies of the Boston Associates. Discussions, for example, concerning investments in newer railroad links to the west, suggest that many merchants in the city wanted better and more competitive railroad routes and rates. See *Record of Public Meeting held in Boston to Consult upon the Ways and Means of Securing an Uninterrupted Prosecution of the Work upon the Hoosac Tunnel* (Boston, 9 June 1857). The Boston Associates' interest in railroad construction did not extend beyond their own immediate need to transport their textiles to markets. They may not have openly opposed new railroad lines, but neither did they invest their money in such "risky" economic ventures.

19. Dalzell says that the Associates "also supported the policy of high freight rates and prompt payment by the railroads of all financial obligations, despite the adverse effect on the port of Boston." Dalzell, *Enterprising Elite*, 92.

20. Dalzell, *Enterprising Elite*; Frederick Cople Jaher, *The Urban Establishment: Upper Strata in Boston, New York, Charleston, Chicago and Los Angeles* (Urbana: University of Illinois Press, 1982).

21. A majority of the commissioners lived on Beacon Hill, where most of the Boston Associates also lived. Four commissioners' houses were clustered together on one side of Mount Vernon Street. Their occupations fell into three groups: law, engineering, or business. Franklin Haven was the president of Merchant Bank, Samuel Warren (part of the prestigious Warren family of Boston that helped establish Harvard Medical School and Massachusetts General Hospital), was a businessman who owned a textile mill, and Samuel Hooper, who had previously been a partner in the firm Bryant and Sturgis (one of the most prominent Boston trading companies), became a partner of William Appleton, who was the cousin of textile magnate Nathan Appleton. Hooper served three years in the Massachusetts House of Representatives, one term in the state senate, and fourteen years as a representative in the U.S. Congress. *Memorial address on the life and character of Samuel Hooper* (U.S. Congress, 1875); Martin Green, *The Mount Vernon Street Warrens: A Boston Story, 1860-1910* (New York: Charles Scribner's Sons, 1989); *The Boston Directory* (Boston, 1860); *The Boston Directory* (Boston: Adams, Sampson, 1865, 1870, 1875); Jaher, *Urban Establishment*.

22. In 1860, Abbott Lawrence and his family owned several valuable lots on Commonwealth Avenue, Marlborough Street, and Beacon Street. Samuel Hooper was the largest single land owner; he owned the two lots on the corner of Commonwealth Avenue and Berkeley Street and several other large parcels on Beacon and Newbury streets. *Catalogue of Fifty Lots of Land on the Back Bay To Be Sold Oct. 24, 1860* (Boston: Wright and Potter, 1860). Walter Firey has suggested that prominent Boston citizens offered to buy lands in the Back Bay at discount rates to compensate for the apparent risk they were taking as pioneers in the area. The commissioners agreed to this self-serving deal, of course, because it ensured that the inflated land values in the area would remain high. Firey, *Land Use*, chapter 7.

23. Spalding, "Boston Mercantile Community."

24. Ibid., 56-57, 59-60.

25. John Coolidge, *Mill and Mansion: A Study of Architecture and Society in Lowell, MA., 1820-1865* (New York: Russell and Russell, 1967), chapter 3.

26. Bunting has also pointed out the similarities between the design of the axial pattern in the Back Bay and Alexander Parris's design of the Quincy Market complex in 1824. The almost identical ratio of street widths in the two designs suggests that the similarity was not mere coincidence, but that Gilman directly followed some of Parris's design initiatives. See Bunting, *Houses of Back Bay*, 396.

27. Gilman was apparently given much attention by Sir Charles Cockerell, who was the president of the British Institute of Architects, and Sir Charles Barry, the architect of the Houses of Parliament. This trip was said to have "confirmed his faith in the principles and his love for the forms of the Anglo-Normans and German schools in architecture." *Boston Evening Transcript*, 17 July 1882, 8.

28. These new areas in London were laid out in the late 1840s and early 1850s. See Donald Olsen, *The City as a Work of Art* (New Haven: Yale University Press, 1986), and Donald Olsen, *The Growth of Victorian London* (New York: Holmes and Meier, 1976).

29. David H. Pinkney, *Napoleon III and the Rebuilding of Paris* (Princeton, N.J.: Princeton University Press, 1958), chapter 2.

30. Bunting, *Houses of Back Bay*, 289–291.

31. *Report of the Committee in Relation to Lands in the Back Bay, also, Fifth Annual Report of the Commissioners of the Back Bay* (Boston: William White, 1857), 13–15.

32. *Boston: Its Commerce, Finance and Literature* (New York: A. F. Parsons, 1892), 31.

33. Ibid., 31.

34. Raymond H. Robinson, "The Families of Commonwealth Avenue," *Proceedings of the Massachusetts Historical Society* 93 (1981): 80–94.

35. A significant proportion of the first people to own dwellings on Commonwealth Avenue in the Back Bay were from Boston's established elite class. For example, one half of the dwellings on the north side of the street between Arlington and Berkeley streets (the first block to be developed) were built for members of the Boston Associates or for people who were on the list of Boston's two hundred wealthiest in 1848. See Bunting, *Houses of Back Bay*, 421; Edward Pessen, *Riches, Class and Power before the Civil War* (Lexington, Mass.: D. C. Heath, 1973), 325.

36. *Thirteenth Annual Report of the Commissioners on Public Lands* (Boston, 1865), 3.

37. Control of speculative selling of Back Bay land was less successful in later periods, when many of the peripheral streets were sold off by blocks for speculation, particularly in the late 1870s and 1880s. See *Catalogue of Fifty Lots of Land on the Back Bay To Be Sold Oct. 24, 1860* (Boston: Wright and Potter, 1860); *Catalogue of Fifty Lots of Land on the Back Bay To Be Sold April 9, 1863* (Boston: Wright and Potter, 1863); *Catalogue of Fifty Lots of Land on the Back Bay To Be Sold* (Boston: Wright and Potter, 1867); *Catalogue of Fifty Lots of Land on the Back Bay To Be Sold Dec. 27, 1870* (Boston: Wright and Potter, 1870); *Catalogue of Fifty Lots of Land on the Back Bay To Be Sold March 2, 1872* (Boston: Wright and Potter, 1872).

38. Stanley Schultz, *Constructing Urban Culture: American Cities and City Planning, 1800–1920* (Philadelphia: Temple University Press, 1989).

39. Bunting, *Houses of Back Bay*, 391–392.

40. *Sixth Annual Report of the Commissioners on the Back Bay* (Boston, 1857).

41. David Schuyler, *The New Urban landscape: The Redefinition of City Form in Nineteenth Century America* (Baltimore: Johns Hopkins University Press, 1989).

42. Bunting, *Houses of Back Bay*, 391.

43. Christopher R. Elliot, "The Boston Public Garden, Horace Gray, Sr., Charles Francis Barnard," *Proceedings of the Bostonian Society* 12 (1939): 27–45.

44. Edwin M. Bacon, ed., *Boston of To-day; A Glance at its History and Circumstances* (Boston: Boston Post, 1892); M. D. Ross, *Estimate of the Financial Effect of the Proposed Reservation of Back-Bay Lands, prepared for the Committee of Associated Institutions of Science and Art* (Boston: John Wilson and Son, 1861), 17.

45. Bunting, *Houses of Back Bay*, 394.

46. Ibid., 19.

47. Gilman went on to a very successful architectural career, particularly after he moved from Boston to New York in 1865. *Boston Evening Transcript*, 17 July 1882, 8.

48. Michael and Susan Southworth, *The Boston Society of Architects' AIA Guide to Boston* (Chester, Conn.: Globe Pequot Press, 1991), 210.

49. Bunting, *Houses of Back Bay*, 303.

50. H. G. Wells, *The Future of America* (New York, 1906), 230, quoted in Bunting, *Houses of Back Bay*.

51. Bunting, *Houses of Back Bay*, chapter 3.

52. Hannah Josephson, *The Golden Threads: New England's Mill Girls and Magnates* (New York: Russell and Russell, 1967), 152.

53. Dalzell, *Enterprising Elite*, 94. The Massachusetts Hospital Life Insurance Company acted as a form of financial security for the Boston Associates. Because they controlled the company, they could direct the capital in whatever way benefited them. See Dalzell, *Enterprising Elite*, particularly 103–108.

54. Spalding, "Boston Mercantile Community." Dalzell shows that the ownership and sale of stocks was a highly controlled process, nothing like the modern public offering. See Dalzell, *Enterprising Elite*, 57–58.

55. Abbott Lawrence and Nathan Appleton were seen as the shapers of Whig political policies. See Dalzell, *Enterprising Elite*; Jaher, *Urban Establishment*; Josephson, *Golden Threads*.

56. For details of Lawrence's philanthropic activities, see Hamilton Andrews Hill, *Memoir of Abbott Lawrence* (Boston, 1883).

57. Josephson, *Golden Threads*, 164.

58. Abbott Lawrence to Amos Lawrence, 28 July 1824, Amos Lawrence Papers, Massachusetts Historical Society, Boston.

59. Abbott Lawrence to Amos Lawrence, 15 April 1831, Amos Lawrence Papers, Massachusetts Historical Society, Boston.

60. *Seven and Eight Park Street: A Brief History of the Home of the Union Club of Boston* (Boston: Thomas Todd, 1976).

61. Sarah Mytton Maury, *Statesmen of America in 1846* (Philadelphia, 1847), 56.

62. *Catalogue of Fifty Lots of Land on the Back Bay To Be Sold October 24, 1860* (Boston: Wright and Potter, 1860).

63. Jaher, *Urban Establishment*, 89.

64. The Boston elite's personal fortunes did not suffer serious decline, rather the relative economic power of this wealth in the city declined. See Jaher, *Urban Establishment*, 94–97; Ronald P. Formisano and Constance K. Burns, eds., *Boston 1700–1980: The Evolution of Urban Politics* (Westport, Conn.: Greenwood Press, 1984); Jaher, "The Politics of the Boston Brahmins: 1800–1860," in ibid.

65. Jaher, "Politics of the Boston Brahmins," 109.

66. Richard H. Edwards, Jr., *Tales of the Observer* (Boston: Jordan Marsh, 1950).

67. See *Memorial Tributes, Eben D. Jordan* (Boston: George H. Ellis, 1896); *Catalogue of Twenty-eight Lots of Land on the Back Bay to be Sold March 2, 1872* (Boston: Wright and Potter, 1872).

68. Martin Green, *The Problem of Boston* (New York: W. W. Norton, 1966), 103.

Chapter 5. Preserving Boston's Common and Planning Its Park System

1. *Boston Common* (Boston: William D. Ticknor and H. B. Williams, 1842), 9.

2. Walter Firey, *Land Use in Central Boston* (Cambridge: Harvard University Press, 1946), 142.

3. Ibid., 140.

4. Harold Kirker and James Kirker, *Bulfinch's Boston, 1787–1817* (New York: Oxford University Press, 1964), 175.

5. Walter Muir Whitehill, *Boston: A Topographical History* (Cambridge: Harvard University Press, 1968), 55.

6. According to Whitehill, this action was spearheaded by Harrison Gray Otis, who was able to wrangle an exceedingly good price for the land by offering to buy the property before Copley, living in England, heard about the new State House. See Whitehill, *Topographical History*.

7. Kirker and Kirker, *Bulfinch's Boston*, 177-178.

8. *Report of the Committee Chosen by the Inhabitants of the City of Boston, to take into Consideration the Expediency of Authorizing the City Council to make Sale of the Upland and Flats Lying West of Charles Street* (Boston, 1824), 19-20.

9. Nathaniel B. Shurtleff, *A Topographical and Historical Description of Boston* (Boston: Rockwell and Churchill, 1890), 357.

10. *Report of the Joint Committee on Public Lands in Relation to the Public Garden* (Boston, 1850), 18.

11. Marshall Pinckney Wilder, "The Horticulture of Boston and Vicinity," in *The Memorial History of Boston*, ed. Justin Winsor (Boston: James R. Osgood, 1881), 607-640; Cynthia Zaitzevsky, *Frederick Law Olmsted and the Boston Park System* (Cambridge: Harvard University Press, Belknap Press, 1982).

12. Christopher R. Eliot, "The Boston Public Garden, Horace Gray, Sr., Charles Francis Barnard," *Proceedings of the Bostonian Society* 12 (1939): 27-45.

13. City Document 18, 1850, quoted in ibid., 38-39.

14. Francis Tiffany, *Charles Francis Barnard* (Cambridge, Mass.: Riverside Press, 1895).

15. Warren Street Chapel publications, 1843-44, 16-17, quoted in ibid., 43.

16. Tiffany, *Charles Barnard*.

17. *Seventh Annual Report of the Commissioners on the Back Bay* (Boston, 1858), 4.

18. "Great Public Improvement," 22 April 1859.

19. Franklin Dexter, *Legal Opinion that Boston Common cannot Lawfully be sold by the City Council* (Boston: John H. Eastburn, 1843), 19.

20. *The Public Rights in Boston Common* (Boston: Rockwell and Churchill, 1877), ii.

21. Ibid., vi.

22. Ibid., viii, x.

23. Ibid., xiv.

24. *Argument of L. S. Dabney, Esq. for The Remonstrants Against the West End Railway Co.'s Bill, and for the Preservation of the Boston Common* (Boston: T. W. Ripley, 1887); Annie Brown, *The Integrity of Boston Common and the Rights of Citizens* (n.d.).

25. For example, in 1919, the Retail Trade Board (including Louis Kirsten of Filene's) asked for money to support the adoption of a referendum for widening Boylston and Tremont streets. See *Letter from Retail Trade Board of the Boston Chamber of Commerce*, 15 December 1919.

26. Firey, *Land Use*, 152.

27. Data of the location of Boston's main department stores were derived from city directories. See *The Boston Directory* (Boston: Adams, Sampson, 1865); *The Boston Directory* (Boston: Sampson, Davenport, 1875); *The Boston Directory* (Boston: Sampson, Murdock, 1885, 1895).

28. Firey, *Land Use*, 152.

29. *Appeal for the Preservation of the City Hall Park in New York City* (New York: American Scenic and Historic Preservation Society, 1910).

30. *Memorial of the Municipal Art Society Relative to Proposed Changes in and about City Hall Park, New York City* (New York, 1903).

31. The Boston elite were quite effective in early movements to preserve such historic landmarks as the Old South Meetinghouse and Park Street Church. See Firey, *Land Use*. Abbott Lawrence's home at 8 Park Street is preserved fairly intact, along with many of its neighbors, in its early nineteenth-century form. Since 1863 it has housed the Union Club, one of the most exclusive of Boston's private clubs.

32. Tamara Plakins Thornton, *Cultivating Gentlemen: The Meaning of Country Life among the Boston Elite, 1785-1860* (New Haven: Yale University Press, 1989), 145.

33. Tamara Plakins Thornton's *Cultivating Gentlemen* provides by far the best discussion of the relationship of the Boston elite to rural pursuits, and I have based much of my discussion on her analysis.

34. Thornton notes that horticulture was an exclusively male activity. Because horticulture was seen as counter to commercialism, it had no place for women, who were supposedly shielded from the marketplace. See ibid., 165–166.

35. Daniel Bluestone, *Constructing Chicago* (New Haven: Yale University Press, 1991).

36. Thornton, *Cultivating Gentlemen*, chapter 5.

37. *Transactions of the Massachusetts Horticultural Society for the Year 1842–43* (Boston: Dutton and Wentworth, 1843), quoted in ibid., 163.

38. Jaher, *Urban Establishment*, 28.

39. Thornton, *Cultivating Gentlemen*, 223.

40. George F. Hoar, "Memoir of Horace Gray, LLD," *Proceedings, Massachusetts Historical Society* 18 (1903–1904): 155–187.

41. *The Boston Common* (Boston: William D. Ticknor and H. B. Williams, 1842), 44–45.

42. David Schuyler, *The New Urban Landscape: The Redefinition of City Form in Nineteenth-Century America* (Baltimore: Johns Hopkins University Press, 1989), 66.

43. Nathaniel Shurtleff, *A Topographical and Historical Description of Boston* (Boston: Rockwell and Churchill, 1890), 348.

44. Edward Stanwood, "Topography and Landmarks of the Last Hundred Years," in *The Memorial History of Boston*, ed. Justin Winsor (Boston: James R. Osgood, 1881), 25–63.

45. Zaitzevsky, *Olmsted and Boston Park System*, 34.

46. Schuyler, *New Urban Landscape*, 138.

47. Roy Rosenzweig and Elizabeth Blackmar, *The Park and the People: A History of Central Park* (Ithaca, N.Y.: Cornell University Press, 1992), 7.

48. Many of these discussions were published in pamphlet form. See *Report of the Establishment of a Public Park* (Boston, 1874); *Report and Accompanying Statements and Communications Relating to a Public Park for the City of Boston* (Boston, 1869); *Parks for the People, Proceedings of a Public Meeting held at Faneuil Hall* (Boston: Franklin Press, 1876).

49. Schuyler, *New Urban Landscape*; Robert Morris Copeland, *Essay and Plan for the Improvement of the City of Boston* (Boston: Lee and Shepard, 1872); Zaitzevsky, *Olmsted and Boston Park System*.

50. For works that examine the career and impact of Olmsted on American cities, see Albert Fein, ed., *Landscape into Cityscape* (Ithaca, N.Y.: Cornell University Press, 1967); Laura Wood Roper, *FLO: A Biography of Frederick Law Olmsted* (Baltimore: Johns Hopkins University Press, 1973); Melvin Kalfus, *Frederick Law Olmsted: The Passion of a Public Artist* (New York: New York University Press, 1990).

51. Zaitzevsky, *Olmsted and Boston Park System*, chapter 3.

52. *Report on the Establishment of a Public Park* (Boston, 1874), 12. Boston was cited with only 115 acres of public land, while New York had 1,358, Philadelphia had 3,074, and Chicago had 1,892.

53. Schuyler, *New Urban Landscape*, 141.

54. For a description of Eliot's life and career, see Charles William Eliot, *Charles Eliot, Landscape Architect* (Boston, 1902), and Norman T. Newton, *Design on the Land: The Development of Landscape Architecture* (Cambridge: Harvard University Press, 1971), chapter 22.

55. Albert Fein, *Frederick Law Olmsted and the American Environmental Tradition* (New York: George Braziller, 1972), 41–42.

56. Zaitzevsky, *Olmsted and Boston Park System*, chapter 3.

57. Ronald Story, *The Forging of an Aristocracy* (Middletown, Conn.: Wesleyan University Press, 1980), 17, 15.

58. *Proceedings of a Public Meeting held at Faneuil Hall* (Boston: Franklin Press, 1876), 7.

59. For discussions of the ideology of the urban park movement and its relationship to sanitary reform, see Schuyler, *New Urban Landscape*; Fein, *Olmsted and Environmental Tradition*; Daniel Bluestone, *Constructing Chicago* (New Haven: Yale University Press, 1991).

60. "Of the twenty-three officers of the hospital from 1820–1850, the names of all but four appear on available lists of Boston's wealthiest 200 individuals." Story, *Forging of Aristocracy*, 11.

61. Jaher, *Urban Establishment*, 31.

62. Ibid.

63. Schuyler, *New Urban Landscape*, 144.

64. Ibid., p. 146.

Conclusion

1. David Harvey, *The Condition of Postmodernity* (Cambridge: Basil Blackwell, 1989), 91.

2. For a discussion of festival settings and other aspects of the new urban landscape, see Paul Knox, "The Restless Urban Landscape: Economic and Sociocultural Change and the Transformation of Metropolitan Washington, D.C.," *Annals of the Association of American Geographers* 81 (1991): 181–205.

3. Susan Buck-Morss, *The Dialectics of Seeing: Walter Benjamin and the Arcades Project* (Cambridge: MIT Press, 1991).

4. Like many critics of the postmodern city, Michael Sorkin contrasts recent urban transformations with what he suggests are more authentic cities of the past, cities that were based on "physical proximity" and that contained public spaces like streets and parks. I would argue that this is a case of misplaced nostalgia. Michael Sorkin, ed., *Variations on a Theme Park: The New American City and the End of Public Space* (New York: Hill and Wang, 1992), particularly the introduction.

Sources for Illustrations

Mary Farewell Ayer, *Early Days on Boston Common* (Boston: privately printed, 1910). Fig. 62.

Stella Blum, ed., *Victorian Fashions and Costumes from Harper's Bazar, 1867–1898* (New York: Dover, 1974), 98, 101. Figs. 18, 19.

Boston, Its Finance, Commerce, and Literature (New York: A. F. Parsons, 1892), 57. Fig. 64.

Margot Gayle and Edmund V. Gillon, Jr., *Cast-Iron Architecture in New York* (New York: Dover, 1974), 118, 163. Figs. 22, 23.

The History of Lord & Taylor, 1926, in Margaret Moore, *End of the Road for Ladies' Mile?* (New York, 1986), 15. Fig. 26.

Illustrated Boston: The Metropolis of New England (New York: American Publishing and Engraving, 1889), 49. Fig. 47.

King's Handbook of Boston (Cambridge, Mass., 1885). Fig. 54.

King's Handbook of Boston, in Douglas Shand-Tucci, *Built in Boston: City and Suburb, 1800-1950* (Amherst: University of Massachusetts Press, 1988), 7. Fig. 13.

King's Views of New York (New York: Moses King, 1906), 45, 16, 59. Figs. 42, 43, 44.

Frederick S. Lightfoot, ed., *Nineteenth-Century New York in Rare Photographic Views* (New York: Dover, 1981). Figs. 5, 20, 58.

James D. McCabe, Jr., *Lights and Shadows of New York Life; Or, The Sights and Sensations of the Great City* (1872; reprint, London: Andre Deutsch, 1971), 56, 382, 384, overleaf. Figs. 4, 21, 25, 31.

The Memorial History of Boston, ed. Justin Winsor (Boston: James R. Osgood, 1881), 363, 64, 60, 61, 617. Figs. 14, 60, 67, 69, 71.

Walter Muir Whitehill, *Boston: A Topographical History* (Cambridge: Harvard University Press, 1968), 56. Fig. 59.

Index

Abelson, Elaine S., 39

Albion, Robert G., 12

Alexander, James, 88

American Notes (Dickens), 8

American Revolution, 9

American Scene (James), 99

American Surety Building (New York), 75, 76

American Tract Society Building (New York), 78, *illus.* 79

Ames Building (Boston), 95

Amory, Jonathan, Jr., 124

Appleton, Nathan, 109, 122

Appleton, William, 123, 171*n21*

Architectural history, 6

Architectural Record, 96

Arnold Arboretum (Boston), 151

Arnold Constable and Company (New York), 44, 48

Arnold and Hearn store (New York), 44

Astor House (New York), 20-22

Bachman, John, 26

Back Bay (Boston): cultural symbolism of, 2, 99-100, 114-15, 119, 125-26; architecture of, 4, 112, 119, 120-22; as elite residential area, 30, 33, 34, 99, 115, 120, 122, 157; filling of, 101, 103, 104, 122; planning and design of, 101-05, 109, 110-14, 116; dispute between merchants and elites over, 105, 107-08; land values, 115-19, 120, 171*n22;* and Common and Public Garden, 135, 144

B. Altman Store (New York), 44
Bank of the Metropolis Building (New York), 80
Barnard, Charles Francis, 133, 134
Barth, Gunther, 36, 57-59
Beacon Hill (Boston), 30, 33, 100-01, *illus.* 102,
    109-10, *illus.* 132
Beacon Street (Boston), 100-01, *illus.* 118, 130,
    illus. 132
Beacon Street Mall (Boston), *illus.* 149
Bennett, James, 86
Bennett Building (New York), 86
Berlin, 156-57
Bigelow, Katherine, 123
Blackmar, Elizabeth, 148
Blackstone, William, 129
Bluestone, Daniel, 66, 143
Bon Marché (Paris), 53
Boston, *illus.* 26, *map* 28, *map* 131; cultural aspira-
    tions of, 1, 2, 8, 11, 114-15, 125-26, 128, 129,
    155; building height restrictions, 1, 95, 155;
    social and cultural determinants of landscape,
    1-2, 3-6, 8, 95, 100, 120, 129, 155, 157-58; elite
    classes, 1-2, 10-11, 15, 33, 95, 101, 107-08, 115,
    120, 126, 128-29, 143, 153-54, 156, 157-58; rela-
    tion of commerce and culture in, 2, 8, 11, 119,
    143, 156; retail districts, 5, 25-29, 34, 129, 138,
    140-41, 164*n25;* merchants, 8-9, 11, 14, 105-06,
    107, 108, 122; trade in, 9, 11-12, 13, 105-07,
    161*n14;* economic growth, 11, 12, 95, 107; poli-
    tics in, 11, 124, 136, 137; street patterns, 25, 110,
    illus. 111; residential districts, 29-30, 34, 101,
    157; immigration to, 30, 33, 34, 144, 145; fires,
    61, 129-30; corporate offices, 94; skyscrapers in,
    95; land expansion, 101, 103, 122, 129; residen-
    tial architecture, 119, 120; creation of park sys-
    tem, 148-54, 157; population growth, 162*n22.*
    See also Back Bay; Boston Common
Boston and Albany Railroad, 151
Boston Associates, 123; textile industry ownership,
    9-10, 101, 106, 108, 109; and economic develop-
    ment, 12, 106-07, 171*n18;* and development of
    Back Bay, 33, 101, 119, 124-25; and public parks,
    133, 137, 151
Boston Board of Aldermen, 136, 137
Boston Board of Trade, 106
Boston Common, 34, *illus.* 132, 157; prevention of
    commercial expansion, 1, 129, 138-41; residen-
    tial area around, 29, 33, 130-31, 147; as public
    space, 33, 127, 128, 144-48; disputed develop-

ment proposals, 127-29, 131-33, 135; historical
    symbolism, 128; preservation as open space,
    129, 133, 135-38, 140, 153; and creation of pub-
    lic parks, 148, 153-54
Boston Globe Building, 95
Boston Horticultural Society, 116
Boston Manufacturing Company, 108
Boston Museum of Natural History, *illus.* 118
Boston Natural History Society, 116
Boston Opera House, 125
Boston and Providence Railroad Company, 135
Boston Public Library, 125
Boston and Roxbury Mill Corporation, 33, 100,
    101-03, 104, 123
Boston Water-Power Company, 101, 103
Bowling Green Building (New York), 75
Boyer, M. Christine, 1, 36, 37, 46
Boylston Street (Boston), *illus.* 118
Broadway (New York), *illus.* 18; commercial expan-
    sion along, 16, 19-20, 22, 34, 36, 37, 44-46, 64,
    68-69, 141; architecture of, 24, 96; Stewart's
    department store and, 52; skyscraper construc-
    tion on, 72, 73, 75-76, 78, 80
Brooklyn Bridge, *illus.* 67, 72
Brooks, Peter C., 133
Bryant, W. C., 86
Bulfinch, Charles, 29-30, 31, 124, 130
Bunting, Bainbridge, 99-100, 110, 112, 116, 119,
    120

Cadness, John, 133
California, 15-16
Capitalism, 16
Carlyle, Thomas, 11
Cast-iron architecture, 59-60, 61
Central Park, 24, 34, 141, 148
Chambers, William, 29
Chandler, Alfred D., 13
Charles River, 100
Charles Street (Boston), 130
Chestnut Street (Boston), *illus.* 32
Chicago, 61, 66, 94, 143
Churches, 69
City Beautiful movement, 96-98, 141
City Hall Building (New York), 20, 55
City Hall Park (New York), *illus.* 20, *illus.* 142; as
    architectural display area, 24, 34, 72, 73, 141;
    commercial development at, 34, 52, 128-29, 141;

skyscraper construction at, 68, 72-73, 75, 76, 78, 87; land values, 166n3

City Investing Building (New York), 78, 80

Civil War, 39-40, 57

Clapp, Otis, 107, 170n16

Cleveland, H. W. S., 150

Cleveland, Robert Morris, 150

Cobb, Samuel, 150

Coleridge, Samuel Taylor, 11

Colonnade Row (Boston), 30, *illus.* 31

Columbia College, 19

Commerce: relation to culture in Boston, 2, 8, 11, 119, 143, 156; relation to culture in New York, 2, 59, 60-61, 66, 156; in New York economy, 8, 11-13, 14, 15-16, 37, 105-06, 161n14; in Boston economy, 9, 11-12, 13, 105-07, 161n14

Commissioners of the Back Bay, 101, 171n21; and Back Bay land use, 104-05, 107-8; and Commonwealth Avenue, 112-14; and land speculation, 115-16, 125; and Public Garden, 134

Committee on Commons and Squares (Boston), 136, 137

Commonwealth Avenue (Boston): in Back Bay design plan, 99-100, 110, 112-14; residential development, 112, *illus.* 113, *illus.* 114, 115, 172n35; Olmsted's westward extension of, 151

Consumerism, 42-44, 59, 64

Coolidge, T. Jefferson, 150, 151

Copley, John Singleton, 130

Copley Square (Boston), 116, *illus.* 117, 125-26

Corporate offices, 94-95

Cosgrove, Denis, 3

Cotton trade, 12

Cultural geography, 5

Culture: cultural aspirations of Boston, 1, 2, 8, 11, 114-15, 125-26, 128, 129, 155; relation to commerce in Boston, 2, 8, 11, 119, 143, 156; relation to commerce in New York, 2, 59, 60-61, 66, 156

Cunard Line, 13

Dalton, Charles H., 150, 151

Dalzell, Robert F., Jr., 12, 107

Daniels, Stephen, 3

Darnton, Robert, 4

Department stores, 36, 37, 38-39, 66; and women as consumers, 39, 42, 43, 44, 56, 57, 62-64; architecture of, 48, 52, 55, 158; and growth of retail districts, 164n25

Dexter, Franklin, 135

Dickens, Charles, 8

Dry goods trade: and New York retail development, 16, 35-36, 37-38, 48, 52, 53, 66; women shoppers and, 43

Eidlitz, Leopold, 61

Eliot, Charles, Jr., 150-51, 153, 154

Eliot, Charles W., 153

Erie Canal, 12

Erie Railroad, 12-13

Faneuil Hall (Boston), 25

Fashion, 40-42, 43, 62-63

Federal Revival style, 112, 113

Fein, Albert, 151

Fens (Boston), 151

Fifth Avenue (New York): residential district, 22, *illus.* 23, *illus.* 24, 99, 119, 120; skyscraper construction on, 78, 80

Firey, Walter, 128, 137-38, 141

First Presbyterian Church (New York), 19

Fiske, Haley, 89-90

Flatiron Building (New York), 80, *illus.* 81

Fort Hill (Boston), 29, 33, 101

Francis, Ebenezer, 133

Franklin Park (Boston), 150, 151

Gender ideology, 5, 42, 55, 57

Georgian style, 19

Giles, James, 48

Gilman, Arthur, 110, 120, 171n27

Godkin, E. L., 43

Grace Church (New York), 19, 62

Gray, Francis, 144

Gray, Horace, 133, 144

Gray, John Chipman, 144

Gray, William, 144

Gray, William, Jr., 150, 151

Great Britain, 9

Great Cat Massacre (Darnton), 4

Greek Revival style, 19, 24, 25, 55, 68

Green, Martin, 11, 126

Hales, J. G., 131

Hammack, David C., 15

Handlin, Oscar, 33

Harper's Bazar, 40

Harper's Weekly, 40, 73

Harvard Medical School, 153

Harvey, David, 156

Hatch, Stephen, 120

Haussmann, Baron Georges-Eugène, 110

Havemeyer Building (New York), 75

Haven, Franklin, 171*n21*

Hearn Brothers store (New York), 44

Hegeman, John, 89

Historical geography, 6

Hoff, Henry, 23

Home Life Insurance Company Building (New
York), *illus.* 74, 75, 88

Hone, Philip, 46, 53

Hooper, Samuel, 171*nn21, 22*

Horticulture, 143-44, 175*n34*

Houghton and Dutton store (Boston), 138

Hudson River Railroad, 12-13

Hunt, Richard Morris, 69, 82, 120

Immigration, 2, 4; to New York, 14, 24, 34, 96; to
Boston, 30, 33, 34, 144, 145; and life insurance
industry, 88, 169*n44*

Industrialization, 2, 4, 9, 34, 38, 39-40, 42

Insurance industry, 168-69*n42. See also* Life insurance industry

Irish immigrants, 33, 101, 126, 145, 154

Italianate style, 55, 61

Italian Renaissance style, 86

Jackson, Patrick Tracy, 108, 133

Jaher, Frederick Cople, 6, 11, 14, 15, 87, 124, 153,
168*n36*

James, Henry, 99, 126

James McCutcheon and Company (New York), 44

John Hancock Company Building (Boston), 95

Jordan, Eben D., 125

Jordan Marsh department store (Boston), 164*n25*

Josephson, Hannah, 123

Kellum, John, 48, 57

King's Handbook of New York, 73, 88, 89

Labor unions, 5

Ladies' Mile (New York), 36, 37, 61, 64

Land use regulations, 98, 116

Land values, 65-66, 68, 116-19, 166*n3*

Lawrence, Abbott: residence, 30, 124, 126, *illus.*
132; industrial development in Lowell, 106, 123;
and Back Bay development, 107, 131, 171*n22;*

acquisition of wealth, 122-24, 161-62*n21;* and
Boston Common and parks, 133, 137, 143-44

Lawrence, Abbott, Jr., 124, 126

Lawrence, Amos, 106, 122-23, 161-62*n21*

Lawrence, Mass., 108, 109

Leach, William R., 56, 62-63

Leaves of Grass (Whitman), 7

LeBrun, Napoleon, 88, 89

Life insurance industry, 82, 87-88, 94, 95, 168*n40,*
168-69*n42*

Liverpool, London, and Globe Insurance Building
(New York), 72

Lodge, Henry Cabot, 124

London, 110-12, 143

London Horticultural Society, 143

Long Wharf (Boston), 25

Lord and Taylor store (New York), 44, 48-51, *illus.*
50, *illus.* 51

Louisburg Square (Boston), 30, *illus.* 32

Lowell, Francis, 9, 10

Lowell, John, Jr., 152

Lowell, Mass., 9-10, 106, 108-09, 123

Lowell Institute, 151-52

Lower East Side (New York), 24-25

McCreery, James, 48

McCreery's department store (New York), 48, *illus.*
50

McKim, Mead, and White (architects), 120

Macy's department store (New York), 44, 48

Madison Square (New York), 19, 89

Mail and Express Building (New York), 72, 73

Manhattan Life Insurance Building (New York), 75,
88-89, *illus.* 91

Marble Palace. *See* Stewart's department store

Massachusetts Charitable Mechanics' Association,
136-37, 140

Massachusetts General Hospital, 152

Massachusetts Horticultural Society, 143

Massachusetts Hospital Life Insurance Company,
123, 173*n53*

Massachusetts Institute of Technology, 118

Massachusetts legislature: and Back Bay development, 101, 103, 116

Massachusetts Medical Society, 153

Massachusetts State House (Boston), *illus.* 29, 130

Meacham, George F., 148

Mechanics Bank Building (New York), 72

Medical profession, 152-53

Merchants: in Boston, 9, 11, 14, 122; in New York, 12, 13, 14; and Back Bay development, 105-06, 107, 108

Merchants' Exchange Building (New York), 55

Merrimack Company, 108

Metropolitan Life Insurance Company Building (New York), 78, 80, 89-94, *illus.* 92-93

Metropolitan Realty Building (New York), 75

Mill Dam (Boston), 33

Mill Pond (Boston), 33

Miller, Michael B., 53

Mills Building (New York), 72

Modernist architecture, 61, 96-98

Morse, R. C., 86

Morse, S. E., 86

Morse Building (New York), 86

Mortimer Office Building (New York), 72

Mount Vernon Proprietors, 30, 100, 130

Municipal Art Society of New York, 141

Mutual Life Insurance of New York Building (Boston), 95, *illus.* 96

Mutual Reserve Fund Life Association Building (New York), 88-89

National Shoe and Leather Bank Building (New York), 75

New England Conservatory of Music, 125

New England Mutual Life Insurance Company Building (Boston), 95

New Orleans, 12, 106-7

Newspaper industry, 20, 82, 86, 95, 167*n19*

Newspaper Row (Boston), *illus.* 97

Newspaper Row (New York), *illus.* 142

New York City, *illus.* 17, *map* 49, *illus.* 67; social and cultural determinants of landscape, 1, 2, 3-6, 7-8, 64, 68, 98, 120, 155, 157-58; skyscraper construction, 2, 4, 65-68, 69-80, *map* 70, *map* 77, 87, 95-96, 155; elite classes in, 2, 13-15, 19, 36-37, 59, 60, 87, 95-96, 120, 156, 157-58, 168*n36*; relation of commerce and culture in, 2, 59, 60-61, 66, 156; retail districts, 5, 16, 24, 34, 35-37, 44-46, 48, 51-52, 141, 157, 164*n25*; economic growth, 8, 11, 12, 14-16, 68, 158; trade in, 8, 11-13, 14, 15-16, 37, 105-06, 161*n14;* merchants, 12, 13, 14; immigration to, 14, 24, 34, 96; politics in, 15; residential districts, 16, 22, 24-25, 34, 36-37, 46, 119-20; commercial architecture,

19-20, 24, 56, 60, 61, 68-69, 86-87; newspaper industry, 20, 82; residential architecture, 22, 119, 120-22; public spaces, 24, 34, 141, 157; consumer culture in, 42, 64; land values, 65-66, 68, 75; spatial expansion, 68, 119; life insurance industry, 82, 87-88; corporate offices, 94-95; skyline, *illus.* 98; street grid pattern, 119

New York Evening Post, 53

New York Evening Post Building, 73, 86

New York Herald, 39, 43, 57, 86

New York Life Insurance Company Building, 88, *illus.* 90

New York Sun, 82

New York Times Building, *illus.* 21, 72, *illus.* 74, 80, *illus.* 81, 83

New York Tribune, 82

New York Tribune Building, 69, *illus.* 71, 82-83, *illus.* 84

New York World, 65, 86

New York World Building, 65-66, 72, 73, 76, 83-87, *illus.* 85

North American Review, 125

North End (Boston), 30, 33

Olmsted, Frederick Law, 150-51, 152, 154, 156

Olsen, Donald J., 3

O'Neill's department store (New York), 46, *illus.* 47

Otis, Harrison Gray, 30, 173*n6*

Palace (palazzo) style, 22, 68, 69

Panic of 1837, 12, 15

Pardee, Clara, 42, 64

Paris, 110, 112

Parker, Theodore, 10

Park Row (New York), 20, *illus.* 21, *illus.* 71, 82, 141

Park Row Building (New York), 78, *illus.* 79

Park Street (Boston), 130, 131, *illus.* 132

Park Street Church (Boston), *illus.* 146

Parks, urban, 147, 148-50, 152, 153, 156

Parris, Alexander, 25, 171*n26*

Peabody and Stearns (architects), 120

Pearl Street (New York), 19

Philadelphia, 12, 13, 87, 94

Pinckney Street (Boston), 163*n52*

Politics, 15, 124, 137

Post, George B., 65, 69, 75, 83, 86, 120

Postal Telegraph Building (New York), *illus.* 74, 75

Postmodernism, 156-57

Post Office Square (Boston), *illus.* 96

Potter Building (New York), 72

Proprietors of the Locks and Canals of the
    Merrimack River, 108-9

Public Garden (Boston), *illus.* 154; horticultural dis-
    plays, 116, 133, 143, 148, 153; as social area, 127,
    128; proposed development of, 133-35

Pulitzer, Joseph, 65, 66, 83-84, 86

Pulitzer Building. *See* New York World Building

Quincy, Josiah, 25, 27, 131

Quincy Market (Boston), 25, *illus.* 27, 125, 171*n26*

Railroads, 12-13, 171*n18*

Randall Plan (New York), 119

Religion, 62-63

Residential districts: New York, 16, 22, 24-25, 34,
    36-37, 46, 119-20; Boston, 29-30, 34, 101, 157

Resseguie, Harry E., 53

Retail (commercial) districts: New York, 5, 16, 24,
    34, 35-37, 44-46, 48, 51-52, 141, 157, 164*n25;*
    Boston, 5, 25-29, 34, 129, 138, 140-41, 164*n25*

Rogers Building (Boston), *illus.* 118

Rosenzweig, Roy, 148

Roxbury, Mass., 33

Rubin, Barbara, 86, 94

Ruskin, John, 11

St. Paul Building (New York), 78, *illus.* 79

Saint Paul's Church (New York), 69

Scherzer, Kenneth A., 22

Schuyler, David, 147, 148, 153

Schuyler, Montgomery, 83

Seamon and Muir store (New York), 44

Second Empire style, 112

Separate spheres, 42-43, 55, 63

Shand-Tucci, Douglass, 29

Shaw, Robert G., 107

Shurtleff, Nathaniel B., 147

Shuttleworth, Sally, 43

Singer Building (New York), 78, 80

Sixth Avenue (New York), 46, 48, 64

Skyscrapers: Boston height restrictions, 1, 95, 155;
    New York commercialism and, 2, 66, 87, 158;
    construction in New York, 4, 65-68, 69-80, *map*
    70, *map* 77, 155; New York elite and, 61, 86, 87,
    95-96; land values and, 65-66, 68; Wall Street

area, 68, 72, 73-75, 76, 78, 80; City Hall Park area,
    68, 72-73, 75, 76, 78, 87; Broadway area, 72, 73,
    75-76, 78, 80; newspaper buildings, 72, 82-87;
    Fifth Avenue area, 78, 80; life insurance build-
    ings, 82, 87-94; corporate office buildings,
    94-95; in Boston, 95; defining, 166*n1*

Snook, John, 120, 165*n40*

Social structures, 3, 4, 120

Somerset House (Boston), 29

South End (Boston), 30, 101, 109, 130

Spalding, Robert Varnum, 108, 109

Spann, Edward, 7, 14, 25

State House (Boston). *See* Massachusetts State
    House

State Street (Boston), 25, *illus.* 27

Stearn's store (Boston), 138

Steel-frame construction, 73

Stern Brothers department store (New York), *illus.*
    47

Stewart, Alexander T., 35, 44, 52-53, 55, 57, 60,
    165*n50*

Stewart's department store (New York), 68; Marble
    Palace, 22, 23, 39, 43, 44, *illus.* 45, 52-57, *illus.*
    54, 165*n40;* cast-iron palace, 35, 44, *illus.* 46, 48,
    57-62, *illus.* 58, 156-57

Story, Ronald, 152

Strong and Adriance store (New York), 44

Sturgis, John, 120

Suffolk Bank (Boston), 122-23

Taylor, William R., 37

Textile and garment industry, 8, 9-10, 11, 39, 40,
    124

Thornton, Tamara Plakins, 33, 143

Tiffany & Co., 48

Tontine Crescent (Boston), 29-30, *illus.* 31

Tower Building (New York), 73

Trade. *See* Commerce

Tremont Street (Boston), 30, 131, 135, 138, *illus.*
    139, 140

Tremont Street Mall (Boston), 130, 138, *illus.* 145,
    illus. 146

Trench, Joseph, 165*n40*

Trinity Church (New York), 16, 69

Union Club (New York), 19

Union Square (New York), *illus.* 18, 19, 76, 78-80

U.S. National Bank Building (New York), 72

Vance, James E., Jr., 16
Vanderbilt, Cornelius, 120
Vanderbilt, William H., 120
Vanderbilt, William K., 120
Vanderbilt mansions (New York), 120, *illus.* 121
Victorian era, 2; architecture, 60, 119, 120

Wall Street (New York): financial district, 16, 24; commercial development, 19-20; skyscrapers, 68, 72, 73-75, 76, 78, 80; land values, 75, 166*n3;* insurance companies, 87
Wall Street Exchange Building (New York), 78
Waltham, Mass., 108, 109
War of 1812, 12
Warren, Samuel, 171*n21*
Washington Building (New York), 72, 73
Washington Hotel (New York), 52
Washington Square (New York), 75, 76, 78
Washington Street (Boston), *illus.* 97, 138, 140
Weisman, Winston, 55
Welles Building (New York), 72, 73

Wells, H. G., 122
Western Electric Building (New York), 73
Western Railroad, 107
Western Union Telegraph Building (New York), 69, 73
Whig Party, 11
White and Company (Boston), 138
Whitehill, Walter Muir, 30
Whitman, Walt, 7-8
Wight, P. B., 59-60
Williams, Rosalind H., 39
Women, 5: textile industry workers, 10, 39; and department store consumerism, 37, 39, 42-44, 55-56, 59, 63, 64; and fashion industry, 40-42, *illus.* 41, 43
Women's associations, 5
Working classes, 5, 10; and Boston Common, 144-45, 147; and creation of Boston public parks, 148-50, 154
World Building. *See* New York World Building

Zoning ordinances, 98, 116